BLOODY
HILL

By the same author:

Glory at a Gallop: Tales of the Confederate Cavalry
(with David K. Snider)

BLOODY HILL

The Civil War Battle of Wilson's Creek

WILLIAM RILEY BROOKSHER

BRASSEY'S
Washington London

Library of Congress Cataloging-in-Publication Data
Brooksher, William R.
 Bloody hill: the Civil War battle of Wilson's Creek/William Riley Brooksher.
  p. cm.
 Includes bibliographical references and index.
 ISBN 1-57488-018-7
  1. Wilson's Creek, Battle of, 1861. 2. United States—History—Civil War, 1861–1865.
 3. United States of America. Army. 4. Confederate States of America. Army. I. Title.
E472.23.B76 1995
973.7'31—dc20 95-17040

10 9 8 7 6 5 4 3 2 1

Printed in the United States of America

To my children, William R., Jr., Stephanie, and Rebecca, and my son-in-law, Richard, with my deepest appreciation for their love and support.

Contents

Preface

Jesse James was the first movie shot in color that I ever saw. It was at the end of the Great Depression, and such pleasures were few and far between for a farm boy growing up in the midst of the Arkansas Ozarks. Because I knew little of the world beyond that around me, I was perfectly willing to accept as fact everything presented on the screen before me at the American Legion Hut where films were shown, as our town had no theater. After all, I lived in the same area where these marvelous adventures had supposedly taken place, and it seemed perfectly reasonable to me that they had occurred exactly as presented. The appearance of *The Return of Frank James* a year later simply confirmed my earlier conclusion that the James brothers, despite their faults, were actually heroes—not altogether unlike Robin Hood.

I left the showing of the films convinced that railroad officials, bankers, and Yankee soldiers were individually and collectively a sorry lot, devoted to separating hardworking, common folk from whatever meager assets they had been able to accumulate. Time has drastically mellowed that view; I have come to the conclusion that they were probably neither any worse, nor any better, than any other group of citizens randomly selected at that time. Frank and Jesse James and their ilk remained a reality, although my view of them was also greatly altered, and I acknowledged that they were simply murderous outlaws.

My youthful fascination with that period continued, however. Eventually, I became interested in the circumstances that created an environment in which the James brothers could not only flourish, but also be viewed as heroes by many. That environment, of course, was rooted in the bloody local struggle over the question of slavery in Kansas and the devastating Civil War that erupted as that question engulfed the nation. The depth of the emotions and the destructiveness of the actions that marked that struggle and its prelude were exemplified by what occurred along the Kansas-Missouri border and in the first major battle fought west of the Mississippi River.

There is comparatively little literature about Civil War activities in Missouri. Much of what happened immediately preceding and during the war profoundly affected the region and, indeed, the nation. Some of these early activities, culminating in the Battle of Wilson's Creek, undoubtedly saved Missouri, and perhaps other Border States, for the Union. They also created an environment, however, that enabled lawlessness throughout the region to rage virtually unabated for the duration of the war and only somewhat less so in the years following it. I believe that the era preceding this prolonged state of affairs offers a story worth telling and repeating.

In writing this book, it was not my goal to present a scholarly analysis of the events that occurred in this region just before and during the first few months of the Civil War. Neither was it my intent to focus on the outlaw personalities that were one of the legacies of that time. Instead, my goal was to tell a simple story of both the events that led up to one of the war's bloodiest battles and the valor of a group of largely untrained men who fought so fiercely and valiantly on the top and flanks of a small hill alongside Wilson's Creek, Missouri, on August 10, 1861, that forever afterward it has been called Bloody Hill.

I am deeply grateful to many people for the encouragement, assistance, and support they have given me while I have been writing this book. Scott Price went "way above and beyond" in his efforts to provide me with research material and all other help he possibly could. Robert L. Owens, Pierre Saget, Hans Vogel, Shirley Cash, and Pat Jackson provided difficult to find but important research material as well as encouragement. I am especially indebted to the staff of the Richland, Washington, Public Library, with special thanks to Judy McMakin, the librarian, Grace Crisp, the assistant librarian, and Susan Worgull, who accepted every challenge and worked wonders in finding research materials without which there could have been no book. I am very grateful for the assistance of the staffs of Wilson's Creek National Battlefield, the Carthage, Missouri, Chamber of Commerce, the Boonville, Missouri, Chamber of Commerce, and the

Cole Camp, Missouri, Chamber of Commerce for their courtesy and helpfulness. Thanks are also due to Don McKeon and Carsten Fries of Brassey's for their support. Carol D. Clark has my sincerest thanks. I am indebted to her for editing and improving the manuscript. I very much appreciate the U. S. Army Command and General Staff College permitting me to use their data for maps, chronologies, and orders of battle. Dave Snider, my coauthor in other endeavors, was, as always, quick to offer support. I am deeply grateful to him for "getting in the boat with me" in the beginning and for the encouragement he has given me these many years. I am also indebted to my friends George and Kari Paseur, Larry and June Runge, and Jerry and Lucille Bullock for their interest in, and support and encouragement of, my writing efforts. I owe a special debt of thanks to my son, Bill, for accompanying me on a survey of the Wilson's Creek and Carthage battlefields, his insightful comments, and suggesting the title for the book. As always, I owe a great deal to my wife, Avil, who willingly tolerates the inconveniences writing brings to our home and who is always ready with a word of encouragement. Finally, my thanks to all of those family members, friends, and associates who have encouraged and supported me over the years in all of my endeavors.

BLOODY
HILL

CHAPTER I

A Wolf by the Ears

A few miles south of Springfield, Missouri, Wilson's Creek rises from the ground and wanders in a southwesterly direction. Traveling along the northern slope of the Ozark Uplift where those mountains melt away to prairie, it meanders serenely through the hills, carving its bed in the brushy, blackjack-covered glades of the region. These woodlands that follow the creek's course sweep upward until they reach the shoulders of the hills that determine the creek's direction. Here and there along its route, brush-choked ravines, forming gashes in the hillsides, reach down toward the stream. Some of these also carry small streams that add their flow to the creek, substantially increasing its size until it reaches the James River and disappears. It is both unremarkable and indistinguishable from thousands of other such streams. In good geologic time, it probably would have eventually passed from existence without ever having been noticed—except by those that lived along it—had not circumstance made it the site of the first major Civil War battle fought west of the Mississippi River.

Along this little creek, the first "real" campaign of the Civil War ended—Nathaniel Lyon's all-out effort to keep Missouri in the Union. The end of that campaign witnessed a battle that, considering the number of troops involved, was one of the grimmest battles in a

1

war noted for grim battles. In many ways, it also was the culmination of ten years of bitter border strife between Kansas and Missouri that made the battle more than just war—it was also the high point of a murderous feud between neighbors.

The road that ended in the Battle of Wilson's Creek was a long one—thoroughly enmeshed in the history of the continent and the pressures that accompanied the development of a new nation. The area around Wilson's Creek had originally been Osage country, although the Indians had never settled it; instead, it was used as a tribal hunting and fishing area. Its usefulness to them was further enhanced because it provided the Osage easy access to major pathways leading to other parts of the continent, as it encompassed both the Osage Trace and Virginia's Warrior Trail.[1]

This beautiful country of sweeping prairies and clear, quietly running streams, buttressed on the south by the steep, rocky hills of the Ozarks, soon attracted the attention of new arrivals from across the sea who came to explore and exploit the continent. These white men, many of whom were avaricious and would eventually take the land from the Osage, initially appeared in 1785. The first to reach the area that would become Wilson's Creek were French explorers who came to the area in search of silver and gold. They did not find it, but the trails they marked pointed the way for a later influx of humanity that would eventually engulf the region.

In 1803, the United States acquired control of the region as part of the Louisiana Purchase. At the time of its acquisition, the area was still nominally Indian territory, which was perfectly acceptable to the young republic provided it had some control over which Native Americans "owned" it. At that moment it was inconvenient for that ownership to rest in the hands of the Osage. The burgeoning population of the new country was pushing westward and demanding that all of the land constituting the old Northwest Territory be made available to them. At the end of the War of 1812, this pressure could no longer be ignored.

To appease the demand of white settlers, a place had to be found for the Kickapoos and Delawares who claimed the Northwest Territory. Fortunately, in their view, the governing fathers found a ready solution for this problem. The Osage were really not using the territory that would become present-day southwestern Missouri because they had not settled it. Therefore, it could become a home for the Kickapoos and Delawares, putting idle territory to a useful purpose and solving the problem of opening the Northwest Territory to settlement. It, therefore, became a simple matter for the government to acquiesce to the demands of the proposed settlers and to order the Indians to move. Bowing to the inevitable, the Native Americans moved; the Kickapoos settled in the area of Wilson's Creek and established a village that would one day become Springfield.

When the Kickapoos came to the Wilson's Creek area, they brought with them a white man for whom it would eventually be named. This man, James Wilson, had lived among the Delawares for years before they were ordered to leave their home territory. He had completely integrated into the tribe and, at various times, had been married to three Native American women. In due time, each had been abandoned for one reason or another, but primarily for the convenience of James Wilson. These marriages had, however, isolated him from a white society that scorned him as a "squaw man."

When the Delawares, with whom he had lived so long, prepared to move, he found that he did not wish to accompany them. Essentially barred from white society and unwilling to accompany his adopted tribe, he used his long association with the Indians to find a suitable alternative. Capitalizing on his intimate association with the Delawares and his marriages to Native American women, he simply transferred his tribal association to the Kickapoos, who apparently accepted him willingly. When they moved, he accompanied them, and found himself a place along the banks of a clear, free-flowing stream in the foothills of the Ozark Mountains.

White men who had settled in the new Kickapoo homeland were in no hurry to leave. Not only did they stay, but others joined them. Before long, it became apparent to the Kickapoos that, unless they did something, it was only a matter of time before they would lose another "homeland." Their only hope of protection was the white man's government in Washington. Consequently, the Kickapoos complained to the federal government that white encroachment was forcing them from the land they had been given and requested its intervention. Surprisingly, the government, under no great pressure from its citizens to do otherwise, responded by ordering the white settlers to leave Kickapoo territory. Most of them went. James Wilson, however, claimed that his former marital and tribal relationships justified his remaining in the area. He was able to convince the government, and presumably the Kickapoos, to permit him to do so.

Once he had secured his status in the territory and was free of his Indian wives, Wilson found time to make an extended trip to St. Louis. When he returned, he brought with him a comely French lady who had become the fourth Mrs. Wilson, and they settled down alongside the clear, free-running stream that would henceforth bear his name—Wilson's Creek.[2]

Despite its being closed to settlement, the area continued to attract attention from would-be settlers who wished to emigrate to greener pastures. As ever-increasing numbers wanted to move there, the decision to close it to settlement steadily became more difficult to maintain. Before long, political inexpediency outweighed the government's commitment. Therefore, as had happened previously, the Native Americans were forced to leave, and the settlers moved in.

As that section of the country grew and prospered, it became an integral part of a larger area that soon petitioned for admission to the Union as a state. Now, however, the question of statehood had become inextricably bound, if it had ever been otherwise, to the issue of slavery. Whether, and if so how, this sad institution would be extended had become a critical issue in the political and social milieus of the nation.

When Missouri petitioned for admission to the Union as a state, there existed a "balance of power" between the slave and nonslave states. Before Missouri's request for statehood, the question of where slavery would be permitted had been decided by the provisions of the old Northwest Ordinance. These decreed that slavery would not be extended into the Northwest Territory; no restrictions were placed on it elsewhere, however. Thus, by observing the ordinance and by careful maneuvering in admitting states to the Union, it had been possible to maintain a shaky balance of power between slave and nonslave states, although not necessarily to the satisfaction of the citizens of either. There was, however, no such convenient arrangement to which the Congress could refer in the case of Missouri. As the matter stood, granting Missouri's request for statehood would upset the balance and, almost certainly, the stability of the Union, regardless of the status in which the new state was admitted. The result of this situation was that Missouri found itself thrust into a political and moral maelstrom in which she could not escape a central role until the pervasive issues stemming from slavery were resolved by a long and bloody civil war.

The progression toward war was not precipitous, but rather a long slow slide that suddenly plunged into the abyss. The year after Missouri's first request for statehood, an opportunity for compromise arose that would forestall the final resolution of the question. Maine also petitioned for statehood; thus, by admitting one as a free state and one as a slave state, a crisis could be averted.

Guided by men such as Henry Clay of Kentucky, one of the most powerful men in the United States who had been elected Speaker of the House five times, an agreement was finally hammered out that would not only resolve the question at hand but also enable legislating a "permanent" solution to this thorny problem. Under the provisions of this agreement, called the Missouri Compromise, slavery would not be permitted in new states located above 36°30" north latitude—the southern boundary of Missouri.[3]

Although the legislation may have solved one problem, as is often the case, it created another. It effectively made Missouri a peninsula of slavery jutting into a sea of freedom—a situation that would have profound implications as the nation continued to expand. An aging Thomas Jefferson, whose foresight as the third president of the young United States led to the acquisition of the territory that would be Missouri, recognized the compromise for what it was when he called it "a fire bell in the night."[4] But it would be almost forty more years before the flames began to flare out of control.

At midcentury, crisis again loomed on the horizon when California requested entry into the Union as a free state. Such a request was not compatible with the "rules" that had governed this question since 1820. Once again, Henry Clay led the search for compromise. He was supported now by Daniel Webster of Massachusetts, a spellbinding orator who, in addition to long service in the House and Senate, would serve three presidents as secretary of state. They were fiercely opposed by the redoubtable John C. Calhoun of South Carolina, a Senate power who had resigned the vice presidency in a dispute with President Andrew Jackson. Now seriously ill and near the end of his life, Calhoun was determined that there would be no more restrictions on extending slavery.

This time, the best the peacemakers could accomplish was to develop a rickety compromise consisting of a group of legislative measures, cobble them together, and offer them to the Congress. The proffered legislation was weak, fraught with the seeds of future trouble, and pleased no one, but it was the best that could be done. The

debate it engendered was as long and fierce as the animosities it pro-
voked.

As debate raged while Congress struggled with the problem, viabil-
ity of the Union itself came seriously into question. Although war was
not actively considered, it lurked in the wings as "peaceable secession" was earnestly examined. Farsighted men could easily perceive
the peril to the Union in such talk; it contained the seed of national
destruction. So, as the issue of compromise teetered in the balance,
Webster rose from his seat and spoke "for the preservation of the
Union." He eloquently urged approval of the legislation, not because
it was perfect, but because the alternative was unacceptable. He clearly and precisely delineated his case to his spellbound audience. He
then concluded with the prophetic words, "There can be no such
thing as peaceable secession. . . . I see that it must produce war."[5]

Clay and Webster carried the day, and the champions of slavery
again met defeat. The nation had endured, but no one believed that
the issue was resolved. It had simply been put on hold. The
Compromise of 1850, as it was called, was clearly a temporary expedient that pleased no one and guaranteed continued strife. Secession
and war still lingered prominently in the wings. People, regardless of
their persuasion, found at least some portions of it extremely
unpalatable. No group was more incensed than the abolitionists, who
were particularly unhappy with the provisions of its harsh fugitive
slave law. Speaking of them, Ralph Waldo Emerson called it a "filthy
enactment" adding, "I will not obey it, by God!"[6]

The struggle over slavery was continuous and steadily increased in
intensity, exacerbating the enmity between North and South, and
steadily reducing the possibility of a solution other than secession,
which would inevitably lead to war. In particular, the abolitionist
movement and antislave groups gave the issue no rest. And they
unquestionably had "moral right" on their side. No serious, thought-
ful person could fail to conclude that slavery was fundamentally
wrong. Certainly, it was seriously at odds with the precept upon
which the republic was founded—that of individual freedom. Even
most slaveholders acknowledged that the system was ultimately
doomed—they just did not intend for it to end on their watch.[7]

Already growing rapidly, the antislavery movement received a terrific boost in 1852 with the publication of Harriet Beecher Stowe's
Uncle Tom's Cabin. The book swept the land, and stage presentations
of varying quality, or lack thereof, appeared in every town, adding

dramatically to the antislave fervor sweeping much of the land. So great was the impact of Stowe's writing that Abraham Lincoln, when meeting her for the first time, is alleged to have greeted her, "So this is the little lady who made this big war."[8]

It was, in fact, a written document that finally pushed the nation over the edge. Despite the great impact of Stowe's book and Mr. Lincoln's alleged backhanded compliment, however, it was not her book that did so. Another less dramatic manuscript gave the added push—the Kansas-Nebraska Act of 1854. This was the brainchild of Sen. Stephen A. Douglas of Illinois, who defeated Lincoln for the Senate in 1858 and lost the presidency to him in 1860. This controversial legislation was hatched, as legislation often is, to satisfy the desires of a powerful legislator without sufficient regard for its potential impact.[9]

Douglas, chairman of the Senate Committee on Territories, wanted a transcontinental railroad that would run from Chicago to California. To get it, he had to have Southern support. The Southerners were prepared to give that support, but only for a price. That price was stiff: the law banning slavery north of the southern border of Missouri had to be changed. Otherwise, they would support a route through Texas and were prepared to filibuster either to make that happen or to kill Douglas's pet project.

Douglas, an astute politician who understood compromise and give and take, although perhaps shortsighted where a pet project of his was concerned, caved in to the pressure. In January 1854, he introduced the Kansas-Nebraska Bill, which, for the first time, incorporated the concept of popular sovereignty as a means of deciding the question of the extension of slavery.[10] This concept, developed by Sen. Lewis Cass of Michigan, was quite simple.[11] It would allow the citizens of a territory petitioning for statehood to decide whether or not slavery would be permitted in the new state.

The bill, with this provision, which clearly conflicted with the Missouri Compromise, not unexpectedly enraged those opposed to slavery. Its rhetoric had not been able to camouflage its ulterior motive. Now, those espousing slavery would be free, by whatever means they wished to employ, to attempt to extend slavery where it had already been barred by law.

To Douglas' surprise, the bill also proved unsuitable to the slave faction. It was not enough that a "loophole" be provided to permit escape from the strictures of the Missouri Compromise. Sen. David

R. Atchison of Missouri, an arrogant, rabid "slave man," wasted no time in informing Douglas that Southern support was contingent upon the repeal of the provisions of the Missouri Compromise.[12]

Douglas had anticipated the antislavery reaction and was prepared to deal with it. The Southern demand was not anticipated, however, as Atchison had been actively involved in preparing the bill. Douglas feverishly sought a way to escape the box constructed by the Southern demand, hoping to avoid the politically hazardous step of attempting to repeal the Missouri Compromise. It was not to be. Sen. Archibald Dixon of Kentucky, in a private discussion, finally convinced Douglas that his bill could be saved only by including in it provisions that specifically repealed the compromise.[13]

Giving in, Douglas said to him, "By God, Sir, you are right. I will incorporate it in my bill, though I know it will raise a hell of a storm."[14]

As predicted, the "hell of a storm" struck instantly. Opposition was fierce, immediate, and unrelenting, but Douglas was to be neither swayed nor denied. Bringing all of his considerable political skill to bear and calling in outstanding chits, he deftly maneuvered through the waves of dissent that threatened to swamp his bill. Finally, there remained only the need to nail down the administration. On the night of January 22, 1854, the taste of victory already in his mouth, he paid a call on Jefferson Davis of Mississippi, the secretary of war and future president of the Confederate States of America. Douglas wanted the backing of the future president of the Confederacy, which he received almost immediately. Then, together, the two marched to the back door of the White House and asked to see President Franklin Pierce. Convincing the president was not much of a challenge either. His only concern was maintaining party loyalty and extending his presidency another term. He listened as they placed the legislation before him and he promptly agreed to sign it.[15]

The bill's passage polarized the feuding factions beyond all previous boundaries, sounded the death knell for the Whig Party, and opened the door for the creation of the Republican Party. Furthermore, its adoption ended the last real chance for a North-South compromise. The path down which the nation was wandering toward civil war suddenly became much steeper and slicker.

The attention of both sides now locked onto Kansas. This territory, bordering on the slave state of Missouri, appeared to offer the best opportunity to the slave faction to extend their influence, and they were prepared to go to any length to do so. The antislave group was just as determined to block them. Hatreds that had been lurking, barely concealed, in the bushes for years now moved confidently into the open. Conflict soon passed the verbal, becoming physical and dangerous, as both sides saw opportunity and moved recklessly to grasp it, whatever the cost.

Thomas Jefferson had once said that slavery was like holding a wolf by the ears: You didn't like it, but you didn't dare let it go.[16] The wolf had now jerked loose. Soon the people of Missouri and Kansas would feel the sharp pain of its pup's first bites. For the pup that would be a ravening monster at Wilson's Creek had just been whelped along the Kansas-Missouri border.

CHAPTER II

A Lot Like War

The cauldron of witches' brew already boiling over slavery was filled to overflowing by the Kansas-Nebraska Act. Far from ameliorating the situation, it exacerbated it, resulting in strife and bloodshed that engulfed the Kansas-Missouri border. It was from this deadly, merciless, and often shadowy conflict that hatreds grew that would last a generation or more and that underlay the ferocity with which the two sides met at Wilson's Creek.

Proslavery forces by no means got all they wanted with the passage of the Kansas-Nebraska Act. What they did get, however, was very significant. The wall that had previously blocked them now had a crack in it. Their challenge was to capitalize on their opportunity. That they would tackle it was not in doubt. The year before, led by Senator Atchison, they committed themselves, resolving, ". . . if the Territory [Kansas] shall be opened for settlement, we pledge ourselves to each other to extend the institutions of Missouri [slavery] over the Territory at whatever sacrifice of blood and treasure."[1]

Antislave forces, dismayed by the passage of the Kansas-Nebraska Act, were equally determined that this breach not be successfully exploited. Horace Greeley, in his *New York Tribune*, had denounced the act as ". . . the first great effort by slavery to take American freedom directly by the throat."[2] Many who shared his views now raised the greatest ruckus over the bill's passage. They generated petitions, held mass meetings, prepared resolutions, and flooded with screams of outraged protest the office of any politician who would listen. More tangible actions were taken by others who founded societies, such as the Emigrant Society, to encourage and support those willing to risk their personal welfare to block the proslavers.

The proslavery Missourians moved first. They rushed into the territory, staked claims to the best land, and established the villages of Atchison and Leavenworth. By these actions, they had not only clearly stated their intent but also, in their minds at least, forestalled the abolitionists. This accomplished, most of them, in the fashion that had previously been accepted by the frontier, left their newly staked claims and returned to Missouri.

The abolitionists were in no frame of mind to accept what had been customary. Close on the heels of the proslave men, the first group of free-staters arrived to take Kansas, as they saw it, for freedom. They were led by Charles Robinson, a veteran of the frontier, who had returned East to practice medicine after participating in a squatter's revolt in California that brought him time in jail. The jail term had not quenched his willingness to confront controversy concerning fundamental rights, however. Therefore, it was easy for abolitionists to enlist him to lead the struggle for Kansas.

The early actions of the proslave Missourians, eventually known as Border Ruffians, did not intimidate Robinson or divert him from his course. Never mind what "customary" practice may have been, he was determined to have the land he wanted for the people who were there to live on it. Without notice, negotiation, or discussion, he instructed his people to pull the stakes on the unoccupied claims and stake out their own. Realizing that this challenge would bring trouble, he put the absentee claimants on notice that the new Kansans were prepared to defend their claims, and anyone interfering with them would do so at his peril. By his actions, he established a pattern for others that soon followed. In short order, Kansas had a substantial and growing population of free-staters.[3]

The federal government, fully cognizant that incipient civil war was brewing along the border, moved to establish control over the area and defuse the tension threatening its stability. Andrew Reeder, a believer in popular sovereignty who had been appointed governor, attempted to forestall trouble by holding an election that would permit residents to establish home rule. The effort proved to be a farce, however, when lack of residence requirements allowed the Border

Ruffians to flood the polls. More than a thousand Missourians, under the leadership of future governor Claiborne Fox Jackson, flooded the area and the ballot boxes. When the election was over, only one free-state man had been elected to a solidly packed proslavery legislature, and the new legislature refused to seat him when it convened.[4]

When Reeder refused to honor Robinson's request to void the obviously fraudulent election results, the latter concluded that there would not be a peaceful solution to Kansas' problems. Preparing for the worst, he wrote supporters back East asking for weapons, telling them, "It looks very much like war, and I am ready for it and so are our people."[5]

George W. Deitzler, who would command the 1st Kansas Volunteer Infantry Regiment at Wilson's Creek, was selected to carry the warning to eastern supporters and to bring back the requested weapons. He immediately departed on his mission, while those remaining set about fortifying Lawrence. They harbored no illusions about their opposition; trouble was certainly on the way. The only questions remaining were when it would come, and what form it would take.

Events had also convinced Governor Reeder that problems in Kansas could not be resolved by a territorial governor acting alone. He had to have support from the national level. To his dismay, when he called on President Pierce for support and understanding, he received neither. Pierce, who believed he had to have proslavery support both to win the second term he coveted and to maintain the solidarity of the Democratic Party, wasted no words in making it clear to Reeder that he expected the proslavery side to succeed. When Reeder displayed a reluctance to accept this approach, the president dismissed him. Wilson Shannon, who had been minister to Mexico and had frontier experience, was named as his replacement.[6]

At this juncture, Robinson, titular leader of the settlers, suddenly found himself challenged by a newcomer who threatened to wrest leadership from him. James H. Lane, power-hungry braggart, political opportunist, and former Indiana congressman whose vote for the Kansas-Nebraska Act had foreclosed opportunity in that state, had arrived in Kansas seeking a route to renewed political power. Originally a proslave Democrat who said he would "just as soon buy a nigger as a mule," he sniffed the wind, determined where opportunity existed, and promptly converted to a free-state man. A spellbinding demagogue, Lane rapidly built a large and active following, and Robinson soon found himself sharing the leadership role.[7]

Led by the uneasy partnership of Robinson and Lane, the Kansans increased their efforts to gain control of their destiny and have their territory declared a state, which they intended would be free. Ignoring the territorial, and proslave dominated, legislature, they met in Topeka and drafted a free-state constitution. The immediate result of this action was a confrontation with the newly appointed governor. Shannon, who believed in following normal legislative processes, regarded their action as defiance of constituted authority and refused them support.[8]

Real trouble now raised its head down along the Wakarusa River. There, a slavery man named Frank Coleman killed Charles Dow, a free-state man, in a dispute unrelated to politics. The opposing sides did not let that little nicety stand in their way, however. Trouble had been brewing for a long time, and now was as good a time as any to settle things. With that in mind, Dow's friends went for their guns. Coleman chose another alternative. He went for assistance to Shawnee Mission, where the proslavery legislature was in session. Coleman, claiming his life had been threatened by Jacob Branson, who had supported Dow in the dispute, was able to obtain an order for the latter's arrest. Samuel Jones, the proslavery sheriff, promptly took the order and a posse to the Wakarusa, arrested Branson, and started back with him. When they reached Blanton's Crossing, a group of free-state men relieved Jones of his prisoner.

Jones demanded help from Shannon. The governor, convinced that the peace of the territory was threatened, called up the militia. To his surprise, as most of the militia were free-state men, only a few individuals responded. He then asked the U.S. Army for help, but it declined. The governor suddenly found himself helpless to deal with the potentially explosive situation.[9]

At this point, the territorial secretary, Daniel Woodson, a proslavery man acting on his own, called on the Border Ruffians for help, cautioning them not to involve the governor. These worthies, untroubled by the restriction, were pleased to accept. Approximately fifteen hundred of them responded with leaders such as Hiram Bledsoe, who would command an artillery battery at Wilson's Creek, and Joseph O. (Jo) Shelby, a planter and manufacturer of rope, who would find a niche in the Confederate cavalry.[10]

While the governor had been thrashing about, the free-state men had not been idle. Gathered in Lawrence, they wasted no time in preparing for an attack. Robinson was elected "major general" with Lane as his deputy and action was taken to form up a fighting force, lay in supplies, and strengthen fortifications. As these preparations proceeded, the force on hand was continually augmented by men from outlying areas. Notable among this group was a gaunt old man from down about Osawatomie with a smoldering fury shining in his eyes. John Brown, who had committed his life to the destruction of the slavery he called a ". . . rotten whore of an institution," was joining the fray.[11]

Shortly, the two forces were confronting each other. Despite all of the bluster and belligerent display, however, they did not appear overly eager to engage. After a bit of posturing, as if preparing for combat, they found salvation. Winter struck, hard and unrelenting. Now, surviving the winter was of more urgent concern than the opposing force. Huddled against nature's fury, each side waited for the other to make a move.

Taking advantage of the enforced inactivity and hoping to avert what might be an all-out war, a small group of free-staters from Lawrence went to Shannon seeking his intervention. After listening to their side of the story—he had already heard the proslavery side—he was no longer so certain that he fully understood and appreciated the facts. Not wanting to act further without a complete understanding of the situation, he decided to visit Lawrence.[12]

When Shannon reached Lawrence, the leaders of the free-state men pleaded their case earnestly and persuasively before him. When they finished, he was unable to conclude that the actions they had taken in relieving the sheriff of his prisoner were intended to flout the law, or even unjustified. He had no trouble, however, in concluding that they intended to fight, if it came to that.

Anxious to avoid conflict, the governor asked Robinson and Lane to accompany him under a flag of truce and repeat their story to the leaders of the Border Ruffians. They did so and, after some intense discussions, their opponents agreed to return to Missouri. The Lawrence leaders, for their part, agreed to sign a treaty with Shannon stipulating that they would obey legal processes and that he would not call upon outsiders. This seemed to satisfy everyone but John Brown. Calling maledictions down on the treaty and its signers, he slunk off toward Osawatomie with fury in his heart. Notwithstanding Old Brown's displeasure, however, the Wakarusa War was over. With peace at least temporarily restored, the citizens of Kansas, to the disgust of the Missourians, who had found no way to intervene, voted by a very comfortable margin to accept the Topeka Constitution.[13]

Continuing the pressure for recognition, in January 1856 the free-state forces, still vainly attempting to wrest control of the territorial government, held an election to elect legislators to the "Topeka government" which, of course, had no legal standing. Not surprisingly, free-state men swept the balloting, while the slave faction and the Missourians fulminated against the election. In another unsurprising event, Robinson was elected governor.

In Washington, the president, still fearful for his chances to win a second term and to maintain party solidarity, agonized over the Kansas situation. Determined to do whatever was necessary to calm the troubled waters of the territory, he tendered Shannon the services of the U.S. Army. In the president's mind, peace was the solution to the Kansas problem, and peace he would have, even if by force.

In March, Robinson and Lane journeyed to Washington to petition Congress for the admission of Kansas to the Union as a free state. Their effort began auspiciously. The bill for admission sailed through the antislavery House of Representatives without delay; any objections that were raised were summarily rejected. Matters appeared just as rosy in the Senate. Lewis Cass of Michigan introduced the legislation, and William Seward of New York moved its acceptance. Then, the stalwart Douglas rose in opposition. Believing approval of the legislation would wreck his party, and thus his chances for the presidency, he presented a long list of reasons that the request for admission should be denied, including an allegation that a large portion of the signatures on the petition were either fraudulent or forgeries. With solid Southern support, Douglas carried the day. Admission was refused.[14]

Now it was time for the army's baptism into Kansas strife. So far, it had remained on the periphery, interested and fully informed, but uninvolved. Pierce's determination to pacify the territory changed that. The president's action in offering army support to Shannon would result in its assuming an active role and earning a share of the hatred that inflamed the border. The experience of some of the army Regulars stationed there would greatly influence the actions that led to Wilson's Creek.

Command in Kansas rested on the shoulder of Col. Edwin V. Sumner, a veteran of thirty-seven years of service, during the temporary absence of Brig. Gen. William S. Harney. Sumner, known as "Bull Head" for the "devil take the hindmost" manner in which he tackled problems, was backed by a thoroughly professional corps of officers. Two of these men would eventually end up on opposite sides and play major roles at Wilson's Creek.

One of them was Lt. James M. McIntosh, a Floridian who had finished last in his class at West Point. A veteran of the frontier, he had begun his career in the infantry and later had transferred to the cavalry. He had reached the rank of captain before resigning to join the Confederacy. A close confidant of Brig. Gen. Ben McCulloch, he commanded the 2nd Arkansas Mounted Rifles at Wilson's Creek.

The other was redheaded Capt. Nathaniel Lyon, a New Englander and former ardent Democrat turned rabid abolitionist. Dr. William A. Hammond, the surgeon at Fort Riley, said of him that had he lived four centuries ago ". . . he would have been burned at the stake as a pestilent and altogether incorrigible person, whose removal was demanded in the interests of the peace of society."[15] This veteran of the Seminole and Mexican wars, who had been brevetted for bravery and wounded at Chapultepec, would command all Union forces at Wilson's Creek.

Kansas would not be pacified by either "treaties" with a territorial governor or presidential decisions to use the army, however. Trouble promptly arose again when proslavery forces prevailed on a judge to issue subpoenas for leaders of the "Topeka Movement," charging them with treason. Lane, absent in Washington, escaped capture, but Robinson was taken at Lexington, Missouri, and returned to Kansas as a prisoner. A few others, such as George Deitzler, joined him, but others evaded the dragnet. Despite their best efforts, that was all Sheriff Jones and some deputy U.S. marshals could accomplish. The remainder of the free-state leadership dropped completely from sight, eluding all efforts at capture. Frustrated, the "law" invoked the presidential offer and asked the army for help.

In response, Sumner sent McIntosh with a detail of dragoons to Lawrence. The army searched, but they had no better luck than the sheriff. McIntosh's presence, however, offered the much disliked sheriff protection, which he used to further exacerbate his relations with the citizens of Lawrence. The depth of their feelings became evident late one afternoon as a group of them milled about near the military encampment where Jones sat outside a tent.

Just as the last light of day was fading, from somewhere in the group, a shot rang out. The sheriff screamed that he had been shot, and the soldiers tumbled out to catch the miscreant. Their efforts were futile; the intended assassin, if indeed there was one, had disappeared into the night.

Jones stoutly maintained that the shot had wounded him, but, strangely enough, there was never any reliable confirmation of it. In any event, his life had, from the available evidence, been endangered. And, whether or not it had, the unfortunate circumstances had certainly played into the hands of the proslavery people. Using the "wounding" of the sheriff as an excuse, they demanded "justice," and some even suggested leveling the town of Lawrence.[16]

Not unexpectedly, the Border Ruffians perceived the ensuing uproar as a cry for help. They were only too willing to provide it. On May 21, 1856, the people of Lawrence arose to find an "army" standing before the town. While they waited in anticipation, the "army" slowly sized up the situation, evaluating the response an incursion might bring. Satisfied with their initial observations, the leaders sent scouts forward. When they met no resistance, a marshal followed them and made some arrests. Still, the locals did not protest. Sheriff Jones, who had been watching from a safe position, now entered the town and demanded that Samuel C. Pomeroy, as agent of the Emigrant Society that represented free-state interests, surrender the town's cannon and all other weapons. Pomeroy agreed to give up the cannon, but said other arms were private and beyond his control. The answer was not satisfactory.

The "army" now moved into town in strength, halting in front of the hotel, which was reputed to be opposition headquarters. The owners of the hotel pleaded with Jones to let them save their property. He gave them two hours to move as much as they could. Meanwhile, he sent men to destroy the town's two newspapers. When the two hours had expired, the "army" destroyed the hotel building. Watching it go up in flames, Jones shouted to the crowd, "Gentlemen, this is the happiest day of my life. I determined to make the fanatics bow before me in the dust and kiss the territorial laws. I have done it, by God. You are now dismissed." The "army" promptly looted the town before moving off under cover of darkness.[17]

The raid on Lawrence was too much for John Brown. His seething rage erupted. On his way to Lawrence, when he received news of what had happened, he halted to devise a plan of retaliatory action. Before he could decide upon a course of action, word arrived that proslave men were making trouble near Dutch Henry's Crossing on Pottawatomie Creek. Brown needed to plan no longer; he now had the answer. Taking six men armed with cutlasses, he moved out for Dutch Henry's. Using the cover of darkness, Brown's group called five proslavery individuals, two of them merely boys, from their homes and hacked them to death.[18]

Brown's murderous actions only further incited the proslavery faction. Henry Clay Pate, a rabid proslavery activist, considered Brown's action an opportunity for him to advance his interests. Grabbing for headlines, he announced that he would take his Westport Sharpshooters and bring Old Brown to justice.

Brown was disinclined to go to "justice" peaceably; he received word of Pate's coming and set out to meet him. He found him camped along the Santa Fe Road near Black Jack, not expecting to be attacked. Taking advantage of a brushy gully running behind Pate's camp, Brown dispersed his men along it and opened fire. Pate's men hurriedly scrambled for cover and were soon steadily returning the fire. A brisk exchange continued for some time before Pate, who was getting the worst of it and hoped to disengage, sent an emissary under a flag of truce to his foe. He explained that he was only acting as a deputy seeking men who were wanted and otherwise had no quarrel with them. Brown responded with a demand that Pate surrender. Pate asked for fifteen minutes to think it over. Brown refused. Pate threw in the towel, later saying ruefully, "I went to take Old Brown, and Old Brown took me."[19]

Upon receiving news of Pate's capture, the governor again called in the troops. Sumner came down on Brown immediately, demanding that he release his prisoners. Not eager to take on the army, Brown asked for a parley. Sumner refused, bluntly telling him that he would make no agreement "with lawless and armed men." Brown knew that he was beaten and immediately released the prisoners. Sumner then told both sides to disperse to their homes.[20]

The detested "civilian" squabble settled, Sumner prepared to depart the area, when Brown pointed out that he was being left to the mercy of rapidly advancing Border Ruffians. Sumner realized that Brown was correct, and that, regardless of his personal feelings, he could not abandon him to the Missourians. Determined to stop this nonsense once and for all, he immediately set out for the Missourian's camp. On arrival, without ceremony, he rode through their perimeter and ordered them out of the state. They had no choice but to obey. Jo Shelby later reported that Sumner brought plenty of men and "drove me clear out of the territory." The Missourians would not forget. To their hatred of free-state men, they now added the U.S. Army.[21]

The destruction in Lawrence, Brown's butchery at Dutch Henry's Crossing, and the Brown-Pate conflict had national repercussions as the political parties assembled to nominate candidates for the presidency. On the one hand, the turmoil in Kansas had strengthened the new Republican Party, offering it a real opportunity to have a major impact on the national electorate. To carry its banner, its leaders chose John C. Frémont, the famed Pathfinder, who would also play a major role in the conflict at Wilson's Creek. On the other hand, it made the horrified Democrats realize that major changes had to be made if the party were to both survive and win the election. In an effort to put this horror behind them, or at least to divert attention from it, they jettisoned Pierce and nominated James Buchanan, an unencumbered northerner who was "sensible about slavery." Nevertheless, they still had Pierce for seven more months. He used that time to continue the already failed policies regarding the Kansas-Missouri conflict.[22]

Lane, who had been in the East on a speaking tour when the subpoenas for treason had been issued in Kansas, made the most of this fortuitous circumstance, using his "narrow" escape to draw crowds to hear his tirades against the government and proslave activity in Kansas. In response to the excitement that he and others generated, a number of state societies joined to form the National Kansas Committee. This joint venture committed itself to the free-state element in every respect, until it could support itself against all comers in realizing the destiny of the territory to become a free state. One of the ways the committee intended to help was by supporting further settlement of the state by those of the correct "persuasion."

Soon the committee had a large party of emigrants headed toward the territory by way of a northern route to avoid the blockade Missouri had instituted to screen out free-state emigrants headed to Kansas. Lane smelled opportunity and, without benefit of either invitation or sanction, joined them. Suddenly, the group found itself designated Lane's Army of the North.

Lane proved to be a problem for the committee. The army had begun patrolling the northern border of Kansas in an attempt to prevent more weapons from being introduced into the territory. Concerned that Lane's presence would result in conflict with this force, the National Committee made an effort to stop him. They chose a fanatic antislavery man, Samuel Walker, who was a friend of Lane, for the mission. Instead of stopping Lane, Walker joined him. Lane left the emigrants anyway, however, and was soon back in Lawrence.

There, Lane learned that the opposition had fortified three build-ings along routes leading into town and were preventing supply deliv-eries. Facing starvation, the locals were responding in an attempt to eliminate the blockade. Lane promptly rode off to take charge. While his actual role in the activity that followed is very much in question, the "forts" did fall. In true Lane fashion, he took credit for it for his Army of the North, even though its participation had been a mixed bag and his contribution suspect in the extreme.

Once again, the beleaguered Shannon was forced to scramble to make peace. Working with the opposing sides, he succeeded in reduc-ing armed conflict to slightly below the boiling point. That done, he notified the army commander, now Brig. Gen. Pulsifer Smith, of the seriousness of the situation and submitted his resignation. It crossed in the mail a letter from Pierce dismissing him.[23]

John W. Geary was selected to be the new Kansas territorial gover-nor. Once again, a man had been selected who possessed all the cre-dentials for success. Geary had won fame during the Mexican War by leading the charge on Chapultepec, which proved his courage. He had also won respect by dealing effectively with vigilantes as mayor of San Francisco, which proved his executive ability.

The new governor did not have long to wait to demonstrate both. Aroused by the fall of the "forts" at Lawrence, the Border Ruffians had formed again and were on their way to Kansas. Woodson, again taking advantage of an opportunity to act as governor pending Geary's arrival and eager to strike a blow against the free-staters, called up the militia and accepted the proffered services of the Border Ruffians. Labeling the entire group "Kansas Volunteers," he gave them their orders relative to the free-staters: "Let the watchword be extermination total and complete."[24]

The Border Ruffians advanced in three columns for an invasion that would be short-lived. Two columns, one led by Atchison and the other by John W. Reid, a Missouri legislator, headed for Lawrence. The third, led by George W. Clarke, a former Indian Agent of doubt-ful character, struck into southeastern Kansas.

Clarke, who had moved out ahead of the other columns, ran head-on into a tough little preacher named James Montgomery, who hated slavery. Montgomery, called one of God's angry men, pounced on Clarke without warning at Middle Creek, pummeled him a bit, and sent him and his men skedaddling back to Missouri.

The second column under Reid fared only slightly better. They ran into Old Brown and his men along Marais des Cygnes Creek.

Barricaded behind a stone fence, the old zealot gave them what for until the Ruffians finally produced a cannon. A few rounds from the late-arriving field piece was sufficient to cause Brown and his group to beat a hasty retreat. Reid then contented himself with burning a few houses and returning home.

The last column under Atchison headed straight for Lawrence, and Lane rallied to meet him. Their forces clashed near Osawatomie along Bull Creek. After a sharp exchange of gunfire without much damage, Lane went back to Lawrence and Atchison returned to Missouri. The North loudly proclaimed victory.[25]

Lane, flushed with "his victory," decided that it was time to take the territorial capital, Lecompton, and release the free-state men held as prisoners there. Forming his force into two columns, one led by him, the other by "Colonel" J. A. Harvey, a former Chicago saloon owner, Lane set in motion a plan to strike the town simultaneously from the north and south. Harvey arrived on time; Lane did not. After waiting an hour or so, the "Colonel" returned to Lawrence, disgusted with the entire affair.

After Harvey's departure, the tardy Lane finally arrived at Lecompton and deployed his force. Before they could attack, however, they were confronted by Lt. Col. Philip St. George Cooke and a detail of U.S. dragoons. Cooke informed Walker, whom Lane had discreetly placed in command of the attackers while he hid in the ranks, that the only fight he could have was with the army. Walker was unimpressed and let Cooke know that they intended to free the prisoners. If that entailed a fight with the army, so be it. Cooke knew a fight when he saw one and was determined to avoid it, while maintaining the prestige of the army. To accomplish this, he first assured Walker that the prisoners would be released and then, in no uncertain terms, made sure Acting Governor Woodson understood the necessity for doing so. Walker accepted Cooke's assurance and disbanded his force. Woodson released the prisoners. Once again, widespread open war in Kansas had been narrowly averted.[26]

John Geary arrived in Kansas to find signs everywhere of the lawlessness that had kept the area in turmoil. Dismayed by what he saw, the new governor issued a proclamation ordering all sides to lay down their arms. Then he traveled to Lawrence to meet with Robinson, who presented the free-state settlers' position to him and told the governor that they intended to defend themselves and their property. Geary listened and acknowledged their right to protect themselves in the absence of other help. Now he told them he would provide the help they needed to protect their property and they, in turn, must conform to the law. On this basis, they agreed.[27]

Almost before the agreement had cooled, it was endangered. Atchison was back in Kansas, looking for trouble. The governor, determined to protect the progress he had made, hastened to head him off. Traveling alone to Atchison's camp, the spunky governor met with him and convinced him to take his men back to Missouri.[28]

With peace superficially restored, Geary had time to investigate thoroughly his new area of responsibility. The more he looked, the more he found to support the contentions of the free-state men, although they were not entirely blameless. With this new understanding, he searched for solutions to the maze of problems besetting him. Before he could move, however, the proslave legislature dropped a bombshell by calling a convention to frame a constitution that would not be submitted to a vote of the people for approval.

Realizing that such a constitution would permit slavery, Geary vetoed the legislature's action. They promptly passed the measure over his veto. When the delegates met, to no one's surprise, they were all proslave. Enraged, Geary turned to Washington for support. He need not have bothered, for his protestations fell on deaf ears.[29]

Following Buchanan's inauguration, Geary resigned. Robert J. Walker, a former senator from Tennessee, was selected to replace him. The new nominee accepted but only after demanding and obtaining a presidential commitment to support the will of the majority of the citizens of the territory in regard to their government.

The new governor energetically threw himself into his job. He quickly scheduled an election designed to determine majority wishes and urged the free-state men to vote. He assured them that they would get a fair shake, promising to throw out fraudulent votes and to use the army to keep the Missourians out. When election day arrived, the Border Ruffians, afraid to challenge the army, stayed home. Even so, election fraud was widespread, and ballot boxes were freely stuffed. True to his word, Walker tossed out the fraudulent vote, and Kansas appeared at last to have a "free-state" legislature.[30]

Those hopes went "a glimmering," however, when the sitting legislature ignored both the governor and the election results. They simply pushed the constitutional convention to complete its work. Walker retaliated by calling a special session of the new legislature to force a vote on the issue. This was too much for Buchanan, who recalled Walker. The convention calmly produced a proslavery constitution that was accepted by the legislature.[31]

Acting Governor Frederick P. Stanton was desperate to avoid new violence. He ignored what had just happened to the governor and called the new "free-state" legislature into session. This group, which finally had the opportunity to govern, convened with much hoopla. George Deitzler, who had gone East for the first weapons, was elected Speaker of the House, and Jim Lane was made major general. The euphoria was short-lived. Almost before the lawmakers could settle in, a call for help came from southeastern Kansas.

This thinly populated region of the state, in which the majority of citizens were proslave, had largely been bypassed by the prosperity that had come to the rest of the territory. There was constant trouble between supporters of Montgomery and those of Clarke. Now it had flared up again in a dispute over land. Montgomery's people had decided they would not accept the decision of a local judge in the matter and resisted a marshal who came after them. Threatened by Clarke's forces, they called on the legislature to help. Lane promptly dispatched his "command." To the surprise of those who expected him to sweep all before him, he soon had his back to the wall. All the major troubles of old seemed ready again to plunge Kansas into bloodshed.[32]

Buchanan, anxious to prevent a recurrence of Kansas violence, appointed James W. Denver, a Californian already familiar with the frontier and Kansas, as governor. Denver wasted no time in coming down hard on the problem. He ordered the army to disperse the contending forces and announced that Walker's policies would be continued.

Most citizens were supportive of the governor's actions because they had other things on their minds. Kansas was booming as settlers continued to pour in, which generated a wave of prosperity. The economic machine had also received a tremendous boost from the money that had gushed in to outfit military expeditions against the Plains Indians and the Mormons. Soon, the exciting word would flood the area that gold had been discovered in the Rocky Mountains in the far western reaches of the territory. Collectively, these events worked to reduce conflict, except in southeastern Kansas, where the pot of trouble continued to bubble away.

In addition, the contest over the constitution was unresolved. In an effort to slide it by, and as a sop to the free-state faction, the populace was permitted to vote—not on the constitution, but on whether to accept it with or without slavery. Typically, through massive fraud, the "with" slavery position was accepted by a landslide. With this vote to support it, the Lecompton, proslave constitution was taken to Washington. President Buchanan found it acceptable and urged the admission of Kansas to the Union as a slave state.[33]

This time Douglas rose in opposition to the president. The administration, torn by dissension within its own ranks, could not bring the necessary force to bear to overcome the resistance and gain acceptance of Kansas as a state with the Lecompton Constitution. With neither the Topeka nor Lecompton constitutions able to pass muster, Kansas statehood remained elusive.[34]

Trouble in the area was anything but elusive. It flared again in southeastern Kansas when Charles A. Hambleton, a transplanted Georgian with a penchant for violence, led a raid into the area in retaliation for having been driven out by Montgomery. At the head of a small group, he rounded up eleven citizens of Blooming Grove and marched them down on the Marais des Cygnes. There, in a gully leading to the stream, the raiders shot them down, took what possessions the victims had, and disappeared into the woods. Five of the victims died, five were severely wounded, and one, unhurt, escaped by pretending to be dead.[35]

Outrage was loud and immediate. Montgomery formed his men and rode north, taking vengeance on proslave settlers along his route. Lane called up his forces and went to help him. Others crossed the border into Missouri in an effort to find the culprits, but without success. In doing so, however, it became clear that in the future, Missourians could expect retaliation on their home ground for depredations in Kansas.

Denver hustled south hoping to defuse the situation. He met Montgomery but accomplished little besides learning that the residents fully supported the little preacher's activity. He also got the disturbing news that John Brown had entered the area accompanied by several hard-core, abolitionist fanatics. Trouble was sure to follow them.[36]

Trouble came when a free-state man was sentenced to jail at Fort Scott. Montgomery had formed a group to liberate him when Brown suddenly appeared. Montgomery retained overall command of the expedition but invited Brown to join them. Old Brown was tired of waiting for meaningful action. He wanted a full-scale assault and Fort Scott left in ashes. The group listened to him but preferred Montgomery's approach to release the prisoner without the ashes. Brown, in a huff, went along but had a very small part to play in liberating the prisoner.[37]

Unwilling to either wait longer or submit to another's leadership, Brown decided to administer to Missouri citizens the same medicine that Border Ruffians had dispensed in Kansas. He gathered a small force, divided it into two groups, and led them into Missouri on December 20, 1858. Moving swiftly through the countryside, they raided two plantations. They stole eleven slaves and a number of horses, and either destroyed or stole other property. One slave owner was killed during the raid, and two whites were taken prisoner. Their mission completed, they crossed the border into Kansas, and by mid January Brown had disappeared. In the ensuing uproar, the Missouri General Assembly fulminated against the action and threatened violence in response. Even President Buchanan got into the act, offering a two-hundred-fifty-dollar reward for Old Brown's head. The folks in Kansas proved to have little interest in Brown's capture. He remained on the loose, and the reward went uncollected.[38]

Missourians, however, were not at all reluctant to search for the reward. Several groups charged into Kansas, sweeping the country, but Brown did not appear. One group did stumble onto an Underground Railroad operation conducted by John Doy, who had come to Kansas with Robinson in the first group of emigrants. Without benefit of legal action, the Border Ruffians took everyone involved back to Missouri. The blacks were sold back into slavery, and the whites were jailed to stand trial. Again, conflict between Missouri and Kansas was in danger of blooming into open warfare.

In Missouri, the courts took up the matter of Doy and his accomplices. There could be little doubt that they were guilty under Missouri law. Considering the circumstances surrounding their appearance, however, there was plenty of doubt about the jurisdiction of the court and the legality of the proceedings. Without worrying about the niceties of law and jurisdiction, the court found them guilty and sentenced them to prison. Kansans immediately rose to the challenge, rode into Missouri, and spirited the prisoners away to freedom across the border.[39]

As the "liberators" of Doy and company rode back to Kansas, Old Brown was far away preparing for other things. In October 1859, he rocketed back onto the national scene when he and a small group of supporters captured the arsenal at Harper's Ferry, Virginia. His success gave him instant, but short-lived, fame. A detachment of U.S. Marines, under the command of Col. Robert E. Lee, quickly captured the insurrectionists. The South howled for Brown's blood. He was promptly brought to trial, found guilty, and sentenced to be executed. On December 2, 1859, he swung from the gallows at Charles Town.[40]

As the troubled decade staggered to a close, and "Old Osawatomie" John Brown metamorphosed into a martyr, there was reason to think about a note he left behind. It said: "I, John Brown, am now quite certain the crimes of this guilty land will never be purged away but with blood." His words would prove prophetic.[41]

CHAPTER III

"A Hell of a Fix"

As the new decade dawned, there was a continuation of the guerrilla warfare—perhaps outlawry would be a more accurate term—that had become endemic to Kansas. Groups under men such as Montgomery formed throughout much of the territory to keep pressure on the proslave settlers. These groups also increased their raids into Missouri in retaliation for those by Missourians into Kansas. The raiding, killing, theft, and destruction that were commonplace throughout the long-suffering borderland formed a pattern of violence that would plague the area during the coming war and for years afterward. This strife would fill to overflowing, and keep replenished, the reservoirs of hatred on both sides. In it was the fuel that fired the ferocity they would bring to "formal" combat.

Politically, Missouri was sharply divided, as was the nation. Strong antislavery sentiment centered in the German population of St. Louis. Another slice of the population, concentrated along the rivers, was just as strongly proslavery. The majority of its citizens, however, despite what had gone on with Kansas, were moderate in their views. Most of them had come from either the South or the Border States and did not believe that slavery in and of itself was necessarily wrong. They believed that it was an economic problem. Most Missourians supported the concept of relocating the slaves outside the country, as opposed to their being made citizens and posing competition to other cheap labor sources. They were not, however, inclined to support coercion in the matter—whether relocation or emancipation—and certainly were opposed to either the North or the South telling them what to think and do. Missourians were interested in maintaining their cultural and kinship ties with the South and their economic ties with the North and West. They saw themselves ideally positioned to profit from the latter because of the Missouri River and, potentially, because of a transcontinental railroad that would eventually pass through the state. Thus, a choice between the two would be extremely painful. The status quo suited them, and they wanted it maintained.[1]

As the nation prepared for a presidential election in 1860, the Democratic Party, held tenuously together for years, began to unravel. Unable to agree upon a common platform, the party split. Those supporting the concept of popular sovereignty nominated Stephen A. Douglas. Those who espoused slavery nominated John C. Breckenridge, who had been Buchanan's vice president. The antislave Republicans nominated Abraham Lincoln. Those who could find solace in none of these camps joined together in the Constitutional Union Party and nominated John Bell, an advocate of leaving the resolution of the slavery issue to those states that had slaves.

Missouri's Democrats, caught up in the national divisiveness, nominated Claiborne F. Jackson for governor. Jackson, a tall angular man with a full head of hair that started well back of his forehead, had little formal education and less than outstanding ability. Much married, he had wed three sisters in succession, causing their father to comment after the third wedding, "Reckon Claib'll come back next for the old woman."[2]

Jackson had long been heavily enmeshed in Missouri politics, including activities involving Kansas, and was strongly proslavery. He had once written Atchison concerning Kansas that, if slaves were not allowed in the territory, the Indians might as well keep it. He said, "They are better neighbors than the abolitionists, *by a damn sight*."[3] To those who knew him, there was no doubt that, should the country break up, he would opt for the South.

With the Whigs moribund and the Republicans just forming in the state, Jackson had reason to expect an easy run to the statehouse on a platform that supported the extension of slavery. It was not to be. From down in Green County, a farmer with the unlikely name of

Sample Orr challenged the ticket as an independent. Orr advocated compromise, as did the Douglas wing of the party. Because Jackson was desperately anxious not to get involved in a contest that would make him show his true colors, he decided to kill Orr's candidacy by ignoring him. The tactic failed. The gray-bearded, somewhat beetle-browed farmer would not be ignored. He proved to be a tenacious campaigner who tirelessly trailed his opposition with a message advocating maintaining the status quo that fell on receptive ears. Soon, Orr, who had now also been adopted by the Constitutional Union Party as its candidate, became a serious challenge to Jackson.

Jackson was also under constant pressure by both wings of the national party to endorse them. He had been content to remain silent on the subject, hoping to garner the support of both. Orr's rapid growth in popularity forced him to reconsider. After agonizing over the choices, Jackson decided that endorsing Douglas was the only way to assure his own election. His announcement of that support enraged the Democratic State Central Committee.

The committee promptly repudiated Fox Jackson and selected another candidate. Fortunately for Jackson, a significant number of pro-Breckenridge supporters, led by James Green, fearing that Orr would win the election, did not defect. This action, and the fact that the state election was held in August, which was well ahead of the national election in November, saved the day. When the votes were counted, Jackson was governor; but he had defeated Orr by only about eight thousand votes.[4]

In the national election, in which Abraham Lincoln won the presidency, the results in Missouri reflected those of the gubernatorial race. Douglas and Bell split 70 percent of the vote; Douglas won by fewer than five hundred votes. Breckenridge ran third and Lincoln was a distant fourth. Missourians had sent a clear message. They wanted a middle course.[5]

The president-elect and other powerful Republicans took seriously the threats of secession from the Southern states. Because secession would mean an internecine war, they were determined to do all they could within reason to prevent it. In an attempt to allay Southern concerns and, failing that, to minimize defections, they were careful to reassure the slaveholding states that they had no intention of disturbing their peculiar institution. Sen. John Sherman reflected the party line when he wrote that the new administration was unlikely to interfere either directly or indirectly with slavery in the states that had it.[6]

The South did not believe it, and their skepticism was reinforced by a very large and vocal faction of the Republican Party that would not cater to Southern needs or desires. These ardent partisans were not going to compromise away their victory, and many of them welcomed a breakup of the Union. Horace Greeley advised, "Let the erring sisters go in peace."[7] The South was not long in going. On December 20, 1860, hotheads took South Carolina out of the Union, and six other states followed shortly thereafter.

The long-feared secession caused dismay in the Border States. Feelings ran high as they condemned Northern abolitionists for having driven the states apart and castigated South Carolina and the others for seceding. The Border States, who had a strong desire to save the Union, found themselves torn between their cultural and familial ties to the South and their economic ties to the North. These states were critically important to both sides. If they went with the North, they denied the South vital resources and manpower and became a knife pointed at her vitals. If they went with the South, they gave the Confederacy a strong line along the Ohio, threatening what had been the old Northwest Territory. If this occurred, the Union's capital would be virtually surrounded by the new Confederacy. Armed neutrality, which many hoped would prevent war by keeping the belligerents separated, was simply infeasible. The North would not have honored such a policy because doing so would have guaranteed the South's independence. Furthermore, the adoption of such a policy by the Border States would not have prevented war, even if the North had honored it. The North could have prosecuted the war simply by invading the South by sea or, should Virginia secede, through that state without violating any state's neutrality.[8]

Missouri was of vital importance to both sides. Poised strategically relative to the Missouri, Mississippi, and Ohio rivers, it possessed considerable manpower and abundant natural resources. The state virtually sat astride major routes to the West which, in Southern hands, would have isolated the Union from this region. Missouri's eastern border along the Mississippi gave it major importance in regard to, and perhaps control of, river traffic. It also had St. Louis—the largest and wealthiest city west of the Mississippi. Acquisition of these resources by the South would be a major factor in reducing the imbalance that existed between it and the North. Loss of Missouri would also have a major psychological effect upon the Union. Located north of the old Missouri Compromise line of demarcation for slavery, the state's loss to the Union would certainly have a major impact on Kentucky and, perhaps, southern Illinois and Indiana. Should Missouri go South and they follow, the loss would be devastating to the Union.[9]

In the midst of this political uncertainty and turmoil, Jackson took office, hiding behind a rather thin screen of moderation but secretly determined to take Missouri out of the Union. In his inaugural address, he said, "As matters are at present, Missouri will stand by her lot, and hold to the Union as long as it is worth an effort to preserve it." In this regard, he warned both sides that the state could not be frightened by "unfriendly legislation of the North" or be "dragooned into secession" by the South. "She will rather take the high position of armed neutrality," he said.[10] But, he reminded his listeners, "Common origin, pursuits, tastes, manners, and customs. . . . bind together in one brotherhood the states of the South." Then he declared, "[Missouri should make] a timely declaration of her determination to stand by her sister slave-holding states."[11]

Jackson was confident that he could lead his state out of the Union, but believed he had to move quickly. Among his first acts was an attempt to obtain a grant of extraordinary powers from the legislature to enable him to marshal the resources of the state. This "military bill," if approved, would give him virtually dictatorial power in utilizing the state militia. He also asked the legislators to call a convention to determine Missouri's status relative to the Union. Although the legislature agonized over the first part of the governor's request, it authorized a convention as requested but specified, should it decide for secession, that the decision had to be submitted to a vote of the people for ratification.[12]

Necessarily, Jackson also had a hidden agenda; gaining control of the St. Louis Arsenal was the most urgent item on it. Should the state go in the direction he wanted, the weapons it contained would be of incalculable value as the only sure source of the arms the state would need in the war that would certainly follow. Any thrust to move forward decisively in this regard was defused, however, by the commander of the state militia, Brig. Gen. Daniel M. Frost. The general assured his commander in chief that there was no cause for alarm or hurry—the arsenal would be theirs in due time.

Frost, a native of New York and a West Point graduate, was an ardent secessionist despite his origin. He had fought bravely in the Mexican War, had earned a brevet at Cerro Gordo, and had served effectively on the frontier until he resigned from the army in 1853.

After settling in Missouri, he became a successful businessman, served in the state legislature, and headed the militia.

Eager to determine the status of the arsenal, Frost had already met with its commander, Maj. William H. Bell. He found Bell, a forty-year veteran from North Carolina who had become quite wealthy from his investments in St. Louis, completely sympathetic toward the South and disinclined to disturb his interests in Missouri. In short, he was willing to "listen to reason" concerning the arsenal's future. During the meeting, Bell had also assured Frost that he would allow nothing to leave the facility without informing the militia commander. Furthermore, he told Frost, should the state demand the arsenal, he would regard it as the property of the state and turn it over. Bell had made it clear, however, that he would be forced to defend the arsenal against mob action. In light of this, Frost felt completely comfortable in counseling his chief to wait patiently until they were ready and, meanwhile, to do nothing to call the government's attention to the facility.[13]

Although the arsenal might have been a less urgent matter than Jackson had originally thought, other things were not. His hope of having all federal resources fall into his hands when needed was dashed as the governor was forced to watch helplessly while the funds in the St. Louis Sub-Treasury slipped out of his reach. Isaac H. Sturgeon, Assistant U.S. Treasurer in St. Louis and supposedly of Southern leanings, was the source of this disappointment. Reacting to the political situation as he saw it, Sturgeon had taken it upon himself to notify President Buchanan that he believed there was cause for concern for the safety of four hundred thousand dollars in gold stored in the vault of the subtreasury. The president gave credence to this warning and referred the matter to the head of the army, Maj. Gen. Winfield Scott, for resolution. Scott promptly ordered Jefferson Barracks to see to the matter. Hard on the heels of Scott's order, Lt. William Robinson showed up with forty troops from Newport Barracks, Kentucky, and took the funds to safety. This resulted in a great outcry in St. Louis, whose leaders regarded it an arbitrary and unnecessary action that unfairly cast doubt upon their loyalty. Unrest over the matter continued to grow, and the peace of the city was threatened. General Harney, who had been promoted from Kansas to command of the Department of the West headquartered in St. Louis, was forced to send troops to quiet things down. A chagrined governor called the operation an ". . . act insulting to the dignity and patriotism of the people."[14]

In St. Louis, there was a strong Republican constituency that had no doubt about Fox Jackson's ulterior motives and was determined to block him at all costs. The leader of this group was Francis Preston Blair, Jr., youngest son of the politically powerful Blair family. His father, "Old Man" Blair, had been a member of Andrew Jackson's kitchen cabinet and was currently an adviser of the new president-elect. His brother, Montgomery, would be appointed postmaster general by Lincoln in payment for the role the Blair family had played in his winning the Republican presidential nomination.[15] The Blairs were former slave owners who had become free-state men as early as the late 1840s. Frank Blair had served in the ranks during the war with Mexico and had spent time on the Pacific Coast before returning to St. Louis to practice law. He had become active in state politics and had served in the state legislature before being elected in 1856 to the seat he still held in the U.S. House of Representatives. The clean-shaven, except for a somewhat droopy mustache, slender, blue-eyed lawyer was an intense, hard-driving man, determined to keep Missouri in the Union.

Under his leadership, the Union men of St. Louis wasted no time in organizing themselves to protect their interests. Oversight of their efforts was provided by a Committee of Public Safety whose membership consisted of O. D. Filley, John How, Samuel T. Glover, James O. Broadhead, and J. J. Witzig—all leading men of the community. Available to them, should use of force become necessary, was a large number of organized and disciplined men who belonged to Blair's Wide Awakes organization. This group had originally been formed to march at political functions and to maintain order. With the Republican victory and war in the offing, Blair found a better use for them. He converted the group, consisting primarily of German-Americans who had supported Lincoln, into a paramilitary organization pending the opportunity to place them in federal service. They were now drilling secretly in breweries, warehouses, and sports arenas, under the tutelage of officers who had fought in the German Revolution of 1848. These mostly new citizens were absolutely loyal to the Union and prepared to fight to maintain it.[16]

Opposed to them were the secessionist Minute Men—a group formed before South Carolina seceded. It was led by men such as Basil W. Duke, a lawyer who would gain fame with Morgan's Cavalry, and Colton Greene, a successful local merchant. The group they led was composed of Southerners who had come to St. Louis in search of opportunity, and Irish immigrants who feared the cheap labor that would be available if slavery were abolished. The Minute Men were open in their activities and had established their headquarters in the Berthold Mansion over which they flew a secessionist flag. This group had as one of its objectives seizure of the arsenal but actually lacked the strength to do it. Nevertheless, its presence not only demanded attention but also contributed significantly to the unrest prevalent in the city.

Blair was apprehensive about what the governor and secessionists might do and, in addition, had no confidence in the loyalty of either Bell or his senior, General Harney. His need for concern was confirmed when he obtained a copy of a memorandum Frost had sent to his militia subordinates on January 8, 1861. This memorandum warned them to be alert for an alarm that would be given at some future unspecified time by a continuous ringing of church bells. Upon hearing the alarm, they were to assemble their troops at their armories and await orders. Blair recognized this as an ill-concealed threat to the arsenal and moved quickly to block it. A hurried investigation of the plan revealed that the church bells to which Frost referred were those in Catholic places of worship and that the alarm would be executed by the Irish element of the Minute Men. A quick visit by Blair to the archbishop of St. Louis scotched the plan.

Blair, convinced that the arsenal commander was disloyal, moved to eliminate him. Utilizing the support of Montgomery Blair, Gov. Richard Yates of Illinois, and the president-elect, he contacted General Scott and asked that Bell be relieved. Blair's request was honored, and Bell received orders relieving and reassigning him within a few days. Unwilling to leave his lucrative investments, the major resigned. Maj. Peter V. Hagner, a Southern sympathizer willing to do anything he could to support the secessionist cause short of endangering his own commission, was appointed to replace Bell.

Concurrently, with the action against Bell, Lt. Thomas Sweeney, a native of Ireland who had left an arm at Churubusco during the Mexican War, was assigned to Jefferson Barracks in the hope that he could offset the influence the Minute Men had with his countrymen. His command consisted of a squad detached to him from Newport Barracks.[17]

In response to Blair's continued urging for the assignment of an officer of unquestioned loyalty to command the troops at the arsenal, on January 31, the army ordered Capt. Nathaniel Lyon from Fort Riley, Kansas, to St. Louis. In Lyon, Blair got all the loyalty anyone could have desired and then some. A fanatic abolitionist who would literally foam at the mouth when discussing the subject, Lyon had a violent temper and an unwavering conviction that he was right about all things. His friend, Dr. Hammond, summed him up as ". . . intolerant of opposition, prone to inject the most unpopular opinions at times and places where he knew they would be unwelcome; easily aroused to a degree of anger that was almost insane in its manifestations; narrow-minded, mentally unbalanced, and yet with all this, honest to the core, truthful, intelligent, generous to a fault with those he liked, absolutely moral, attentive to duties, a strict disciplinarian, and . . . was one to trust in emergencies with absolute confidence that he would do what he said he would do, even though he gave up his life for his constancy."[18] Lyon had won a brevet for his actions at Contreras and Churubusco, was mentioned for bravery at Belen Gate where he was wounded, and was a part of Harney's command that stormed Cerro Gordo. This rather odd little man with the dour personality, scraggly red beard, thin unsmiling mouth, and chilling blue eyes would have an explosive impact on not only St. Louis but also the entire state.

An indication of what could be expected from Lyon was contained in a letter he wrote to a friend just before departing from Fort Riley. In it he said, "It is no longer useful to appeal to reason but to the sword, and trifle no longer with senseless wrangling."[19] By this letter, he gave ample warning that he was coming to St. Louis ready to use the sword. Anyone doubting his willingness to do so needed only to look at his record—particularly at his annihilation of the Indians at Clear Lake, California—to have his doubts put to rest.[20]

The arsenal Lyon was to protect covered an area of about fifty-six acres adjacent to the Mississippi River. Its boundaries, except for the riverside, were protected by high stone walls surrounding the six major buildings that constituted the arsenal proper. Stored at the arsenal were sixty thousand muskets, one and a half million cartridges, ninety thousand pounds of powder, forty pieces of field artillery, some siege guns, and machinery for the manufacture and repair of all types of weapons.[21] At the time of Lyon's arrival, its cadre consisted of fewer than two hundred men, including his Company B, 2nd U.S. Infantry that he brought with him. It was the largest arsenal in the South, and its retention by the North was imperative. To the South, it represented a potential windfall of almost unimaginable magnitude.

Shortly after the bedraggled little captain at the head of his company of seasoned Regulars debarked at St. Louis, he hustled off to meet his sponsor, Blair. In him, to his great satisfaction, Lyon found a kindred spirit, at least concerning the danger and the actions needed. The opinionated Lyon found little else that suited him. He regarded the cadre assigned to the arsenal, even with the addition of his men, woefully inadequate for what he saw to be the task at hand. Neither did he consider the addition of four officers and three hundred and one men, who arrived shortly, to be an adequate remedy. In Lyon's view, the actions Hagner had taken to fortify his position were far less than needed, and he did not approve of the lack of military presence outside the arsenal. He also disagreed completely with Harney regarding the magnitude and seriousness of the threat, which the senior officer believed to be both minimal and unlikely. Finally, to his chagrin, he discovered that he had command only of the troops designated for defense with no authority over the arsenal nor the personnel assigned for its operation. Lyon was especially incensed at this, as Hagner's majority was brevet, and he outranked him in "the line."

In an effort to force some action to correct this state of affairs, Lyon wrote to Blair and outlined the actions he believed necessary to fortify and defend the arsenal adequately. Regarding the actions Hagner had taken, Lyon wrote, "This is either imbecility or damned villainy, and in contemplating the risks we run and the sacrifices we must make in case of an attack in contrast to the vigorous and effective defense we are capable of. . . . I get myself into a most unhappy state of solicitude and irritability." There was no shortage of either of the latter whenever Nathaniel Lyon was around.

In the same letter, he also complained that Hagner, who was an ordnance officer, was in command. In language that in other times would have resulted in his relief, if not court-martial, he stated his case. "As I have said," he wrote, "Maj. Hagner has no right to the command, and, under the 62nd Article of War, can only have it by a special assignment of the President, which I do not believe has been made; but that the announcement of Gen. Scott that the command belongs to Maj. Hagner is his own decision, and done in his usual sordid spirit of partisanship and favoritism to pets and personal associates and toadies; nor can he, even in the present straits of the country, rise above this, in earnest devotion to justice and the wants of his country."[22]

In fairness, there was more involved in Lyon's complaints about Hagner than professional jealously. He was genuinely concerned about the situation and absolutely believed that only he could meet the challenge. So strong was this belief that he went outside normal channels and appealed directly to President Buchanan to resolve the question of command. The president referred the matter to Scott. The general-in-chief naturally sustained his original decision. This left Lyon no alternative but to stew in his own juice—at least until the new administration entered office.

On February 28, the convention to consider whether Missouri should secede met as required by the action of the legislature. The electorate had not seen fit to elect a single secessionist to the convention. Except for the St. Louis delegation, which consisted of dyed-in-the-wool Unionists, the remainder of the delegates were Conditional Unionists who believed that the Union should be maintained unless, and until, there were compelling reasons to dissolve it. They assembled for one day in Jefferson City, and then adjourned to reconvene in more comfortable quarters in the Mercantile Library Hall in St. Louis. They reconvened there on March 4 and on March 9 dealt Jackson a blow by deciding ". . . at the present time there was no adequate cause to impel Missouri to dissolve her connection with the Federal Union." The convention left him some hope, however, by voting to reconvene in July to reconsider the question in view of currently prevailing conditions.[23]

Lincoln was sworn in on March 4, 1861. The new president made it clear that he intended to discharge his duty—one facet of which was to enforce the law. That, of course, set him on a collision course with those that had flouted it by taking public property, which included all of the states that had seceded. Lincoln, however, made a major conciliatory effort to prevent further secession by saying, "I have no purpose, directly or indirectly, to interfere with the institution of slavery in the states where it exists. I believe I have no lawful right to do so, and I have no inclination to do so." This assurance did not placate the Southern states that had not seceded and probably had not been expected to do so. It did have an effect in another area that Mr. Lincoln was ever mindful of—the Border States. With them in mind, he refused to retract the statement, despite pressure from his supporters, saying, "We should lose more than we should gain."[24]

Lincoln's assumption of office had an immediate impact in St. Louis. One week after the inaugural, Frank Blair wrote Simon Cameron, the new secretary of war, asking that Lyon be given command at the arsenal and Hagner relegated to Ordnance Department duties. He used as justification the same "rank" argument that Lyon had advanced. Cameron took the matter to Lincoln, who overruled Scott's decision. On March 13, 1861, the War Department issued an order giving Lyon command of the troops and defenses of the arsenal.[25]

A thoroughly irritated Harney implemented the order but informed the captain that he had no authority over ordnance personnel nor the operation of the arsenal. Further, in an attempt to control the firebrand, he instructed Lyon that the existing "accommodation of the troops . . . and for the defense of the place will not be disturbed without the sanction of the commanding general. . . ."[26]

Lyon received these instructions with mixed emotions. He was pleased that Hagner had essentially been removed from the arena but was frustrated at the restrictions Harney had placed on him. Lyon, in typical fashion, decided to do what he thought was proper—orders be damned. He was determined to·implement his own plans for defense of the arsenal with or without sanction and so informed Blair.

Blair knew the army and realized that there would be a flashback if Lyon did what he had promised to do. Not really convinced that Lyon would not succumb to "the Old Army" pressure when it was applied, as it surely would be, Blair asked him, "What'll you do if Major Hagner kicks up a row?"

"I'll pitch him in the river," the feisty little captain replied.[27]

Fortune saved Hagner from an untimely bath. On April 6, Harney sent him instructions to transfer to Lyon all the mounted artillery in the arsenal with fifty rounds of ammunition for each weapon. He also authorized Lyon to make major upgrades in the arsenal's fortifications and to occupy outbuildings with a night force as, in the captain's judgment, was necessary.[28]

Lyon moved immediately, initiating action to place artillery at strategic locations, cut portholes in the walls, build positions that would allow defenders to fire over the walls, and reinforce positions with sandbags. He also mined the walls of the interior buildings at key points with the intent of blowing them up should the Minute Men mount a raid and successfully occupy them. Finally, a comprehensive sentry system was devised and implemented.

Harney's relaxation of his control over Lyon reflected his increasing concern about the state of affairs in Missouri and especially in St. Louis. As early as February 13, Scott had expressed fears for the safety of the arsenal and warned the department commander that it was "better to move in advance of excitement" in protecting it.[29] Now Harney, apparently deciding that Lyon was at least partially correct in this assessment, gave him virtually full authority by ordering Hagner to support him and authorizing him to throw up earthen defenses and occupy buildings as he deemed necessary. Harney also gave orders to Capt. James Totten. This profane but expert artilleryman, with an abiding fondness for brandy, had been forced to give up his battery at Little Rock to the secessionists. Now he and his company of the 2nd U.S. Artillery were told to move from Jefferson Barracks to the arsenal.[30]

Meanwhile, the state legislature labored in Jefferson City. The object of their labors was the governor's request for the sweeping powers he alleged were necessary for him to govern the state properly in a crisis. The request had proved to be a bone of contention that was too big to swallow. In the end, the legislature declined his request other than to authorize him to appoint a board of police commissioners in St. Louis. This act effectively removed home rule from the city by giving the governor control over "all . . . conservators of the peace." He immediately appointed a board consisting of Charles McLaren, John A. Brownlee, James W. Carlisle, and Basil W. Duke—all Southern sympathizers. St. Louis mayor Daniel Taylor, who was a Republican and Conditional Unionist, was also appointed as an ex-officio member.[31]

The situation in which St. Louis, and indeed the nation, found itself in by mid April is well summed up by an experience of William T. Sherman. In anticipation of the coming war, Sherman had given up his position as superintendent of the Military Academy of Louisiana and had offered his services to the nation. To his surprise, he found no demand for them in what he believed to be a suitable military position. With military service apparently not in the offing, he had decided to accept the offer of the presidency of a streetcar company in St. Louis. But before he could formally do so, his brother, Sen. John Sherman, asked him to come to Washington in the hope that he could obtain a position for him. Sherman agreed and, shortly after his arrival, found himself meeting the new president.

"Mr. President, this is my brother, Colonel Sherman, who is just up from Louisiana; he may give you some information you want," the senator said by way of introduction.

"Ah! how are they getting along down there?" the president asked.

Surprised at the question, Sherman responded, "They think they are getting along swimmingly—they are preparing for war."

To Sherman's astonishment, Lincoln's response was a casual, "Oh, well! I guess we'll manage to keep house."

Thunderstruck at the presidential comment, Sherman said no more until he and his brother had left Lincoln's presence. Then, he turned to the senator and warned him in no uncertain terms that the nation was "sleeping on a volcano." Disgusted, he concluded by saying, "You have got things in a hell of a fix, and you may get them out the best you can." With that, he returned to St. Louis.[32]

On April 12, 1861, the Confederate Army opened fire on Fort Sumter. Things were indeed "in a hell of a fix."

CHAPTER IV

"The Secessionists Are Euchred"

The Confederate attack on Fort Sumter changed the game. It was no longer political maneuvering and legal wrangling. It was now clearly and irrevocably war. Lincoln acknowledged the new game by issuing a call to the states for seventy-five thousand troops to enforce the law in secessionist territories. In his call for support, the president justified his action by acknowledging the nation was dealing with ". . . combinations too powerful to be suppressed by the ordinary course of judicial proceedings. . . ."[1]

The response of both Southern states that had not seceded and the Border States to the call for troops was predictable. All declined the president's request. Their responses ran the gamut. Delaware said it could furnish no troops because it had no militia. Maryland would send troops—but with the proviso that they could be used only to defend Washington, D.C. The remainder of the states flatly refused—usually in fiery language. Governor Jackson was second to none in this regard. In his response, which met with wide approval throughout the state, the governor told Lincoln, "Your requisition in my judgment, is illegal, unconstitutional and revolutionary in its object, inhuman and diabolical, and cannot be complied with. Not one man will the state of Missouri furnish to carry on such an unholy crusade."[2]

If all attention in Missouri had not been focused on the arsenal previously, it now was. Jackson wanted it desperately. But, inhibited both by his desire to conceal his secessionist intentions and a lack of courage, he was not able to act decisively. Frost, who had counseled patience, now recognized the need for expeditious movement. Further delay might be fatal. The general, reversing his previous advice, now urged his governor to act before opportunity was lost.

On April 15, Frost, without directly mentioning capture of the arsenal, provided a plan of action to Jackson. In it, he pointed out the growing strength of Lyon's position and the threat he represented to the city. To counter this, he recommended, among other things, that the governor call the legislature into special session for the purpose of preparing the state to suppress insurrection or invasion. He also suggested that Confederate authorities be requested to provide weaponry, to include mortars and siege guns, from those they had seized at the Baton Rouge Arsenal. Finally, he recommended the militia be called into encampment at St. Louis for the purpose of training, mustering troops into state service, and erecting batteries as necessary.[3]

Jackson accepted this plan and took the required steps to call the legislature into session and the militia into an encampment at St. Louis. He also dispatched Basil Duke and Colton Greene to see Jefferson Davis, the Confederate president. With them went a letter requesting muskets, artillery, siege guns, and a supply of appropriate ammunition. In it, Jackson also assured Davis that, with the arsenal captured, he could lead the state out of the Union and into the Confederacy.[4]

On the Union side, Harney was rapidly losing his conviction that the arsenal faced no significant threat. He now informed his superiors that he had reliable information that the state intended to place batteries on the heights overlooking the arsenal and on nearby islands. He told them that this action would bring all the arsenal's facilities within easy range of hostile cannon, and although the facility could probably be defended against an assault, it could not withstand fire from batteries so positioned. He added that his information also included intelligence that, should Missouri secede, the surrender of the arsenal would be demanded. He concluded by asking for guidance.[5]

Lyon also got busy. Never one to let channels stand in his way, he wrote a memorandum to F. J. Dean for his use during a forthcoming visit to Springfield, Illinois. In it, he pointed out for the benefit of Illinois governor Richard Yates that several facilities in St. Louis, including the arsenal, were in imminent danger of attack. He suggested that the governor arrange with Washington to hold six of his regiments in readiness to defend the arsenal, and that he request that a large supply of arms be shipped from St. Louis to Springfield to assure their safety. The memorandum reached Yates as intended and was also forwarded to the president. Concurrently, in a further step to secure his position, Lyon began sending patrols outside the arsenal, both as a show of strength and to preempt any surprise move on the part of the secessionists.[6]

Back in Washington, Frank Blair had been active. Still convinced that Harney's loyalty could not be trusted, he had been working to have him replaced and was actively seeking a way to arm and muster his Wide Awakes. With progress now being made in that arena under the watchful eye of Montgomery, Frank returned to St. Louis to be on the scene where he felt he could better influence the action.

First on his agenda, when he returned to St. Louis, was a meeting with Lyon to assure that the two were working in concert. He found them in agreement on all points. Particularly irritating to them was Harney's cautious approach and reluctance to take what they perceived to be essential actions. To counteract this, Blair believed he had brought some authority from Washington that would allow Lyon to move forward meaningfully. With a flourish, he presented Lyon a War Department authorization for five thousand stand of arms to be issued to Home Guards that the captain considered loyal.

In contrast to his normal behavior, Lyon greeted this development with a decided lack of enthusiasm. He had strict orders from Harney requiring him to obtain the latter's approval before changing the status quo. To proceed without his permission was to invite court-martial. Furthermore, if Harney gave permission, which Lyon thought extremely unlikely, there still remained a problem. Lyon believed, if he proceeded, ". . . the news would leak out before it became public. As a result, the arsenal would be surrounded by a wall of secessionists so thick that few Union men would dare to try to push through." Under these conditions, he saw no way to use the authorization.[7]

Undaunted, Blair composed a message to Washington asking that Lyon be given permission to muster in the troops that the president had requested and that the governor had refused. He assured the War Department that the required troops could be mustered within two days. He also wrote to his brother, Montgomery, urging the relief of

General Harney and his replacement with someone "who is not to be doubted."[8]

Harney, beset by aggravation on all sides, seemed unable to please anyone, no matter how he tried. His latest trouble stemmed from Lyon's sending armed patrols outside the arsenal. Many influential citizens of St. Louis were displeased and wanted the practice stopped. In response to their complaints, the Board of Police Commissioners asked Lyon to halt the patrols and to keep the men inside the arsenal. Lyon, who was disinclined to take direction with which he disagreed in any event, absolutely would not acquiese to such a request from a group he considered to be disloyal. Not only did he refuse to eliminate the patrols, he actually increased them, telling the board, "If the City Police interfered with them, they would do so at their peril."[9]

The board, insulted by Lyon's response, appealed to Harney, calling Lyon's actions an "affront to the peaceful citizens of St. Louis." Lyon's reaction to the board's request was too much for the long-suffering Harney, who was valiantly attempting to avoid trouble. He ordered Lyon to get the guard back inside and to keep it there. Moreover, he was not to execute the authority he had received that permitted him to issue five thousand weapons without Harney's sanction.[10]

At approximately this time, Blair sent a secret note to William T. Sherman requesting a private meeting at Blair's home. When Sherman arrived, Blair told him of his distrust of Harney and of the need for the department commander to be replaced. He told Sherman that he had asked for the meeting because he thought that he was the man for the job. He assured Sherman that he had the power to make a brigadier general and offered the post and rank to him. Sherman refused, saying that he had already offered his services and they had been declined. He had now made commitments in St. Louis that precluded his accepting the offer. Blair "reasoned" with him, but Sherman could not be moved. Blair told him, ". . . in that event, he would appoint Lyon."[11]

As time passed, Governor Jackson's attempt to conceal his true colors was coming unraveled. In a letter dated April 18, 1861, to David Walker, chairman of an Arkansas convention considering secession, he wrote, "From the beginning, my own conviction has been that the interest, duty, and honor of every slave holding State demand their separation from the non-slave holding States. I have been, from the beginning, in favor of decided and prompt action on the part of the Southern States, but the majority of the people of Missouri, up to the present time, have differed with me. What their future action may be, no man with certainty can predict or foretell; but my impression is, judging from the indications hourly occurring, that Missouri will be ready for secession in less than thirty days, and will secede if Arkansas will only get out of the way and give her free passage."[12]

Jackson's nerve was also beginning to improve as his charade became more obvious. One of Frost's recommendations to him had been to take over the small arsenal at Liberty, Missouri. On April 20, a group of armed militiamen from Clay and Johnson counties implemented this suggestion. They entered the facility unannounced at about ten o'clock one morning and captured the man in charge of the depot—Nathaniel Gant. He was informed by the group that they were taking all of his military stores. Gant, who had no means of resistance, submitted and watched the stores, including thirteen hundred muskets, depart.[13]

The day the arsenal fell at Liberty, Secretary of War Simon Cameron moved to provide additional protection to the arsenal in St. Louis. Cameron asked Governor Yates to send two or three regiments of the Illinois men, which the president had solicited from the states in his call for troops, to its defense. A concurrent message was sent to Lyon directing him to arm these troops and to issue the governor or his agent an additional ten thousand weapons over and above those required to equip the troops.[14]

In St. Louis, Lt. John M. Schofield, on leave from the army to teach physics at Washington University, wanted to get back into the army mainstream. He saw an opportunity when he heard of Lincoln's call for troops. In anticipation of the state's compliance, he wired Governor Jackson and offered his services as mustering officer. He received no acknowledgment of his offer, and understood the reason when he read Jackson's response to the president in the newspaper.[15]

Determined to become involved, the lieutenant now went to see Harney with the same offer. He fared little better. Harney informed him that he had no authority to muster troops. Astonished at this response, Schofield pointed out that it was common knowledge that the state intended to use militia to take the arsenal. In a comment that revealed how completely naïve the harassed general was, Harney responded, "Why, the State has not as yet passed an ordinance of secession; she has not gone out of the Union." The flabbergasted lieutenant gave up and returned temporarily to his classroom.

As Harney fussed and did nothing, the deteriorating situation in the city was causing Lyon great anxiety. Clearly, there was a plan afoot to take the arsenal, and he was by no means certain that he could thwart it. Having already failed to gain Harney's permission to enlist volunteers, he decided to try once again, but he failed. The general would not be moved. After Lyon had sent him two strong letters recommending this action, Harney informed him that he deemed it "inexpedient" to approve the recommendation.[16]

On top of the outside threat they faced, both Blair and Lyon were fearful that the "troops" Blair had in training would take their services elsewhere. Their fears were well-founded. On April 21, a group of about three hundred gathered in one of the city's beer gardens to discuss this option. As the discussion wore on, it became clear that most of the younger men were for leaving now for Illinois, while the older members counseled patience. Neither side could carry the day, and the danger that the group would fragment grew likelier by the minute. But before a decision was reached, Frank Blair rushed in and called for silence. He informed the group, "I have just received a telegram from the War Department. It is authority to enlist four volunteer regiments at the arsenal in St. Louis."

The troops cheered the news and prepared to march immediately to the arsenal. Blair quickly stopped them, explaining to the group that, should the secessionists find out what was going on, there was a danger of riots, and they might lose control of the city. Caution had to be the watchword. After further discussion, it was decided that the men would slip into the arsenal, one by one, beginning at midnight. Each would carry an identity card that would permit entry. Committee for Public Safety members Filley and How, who were in attendance, set out to find Schofield. The lieutenant was about to get the mustering duty he had so earnestly sought.[17]

As soon as he was contacted, Schofield hurried to the arsenal and presented himself to Lyon. He found the captain caught in a perplexing situation. Calmly smoking a cigar, Lyon pointed out to him that Blair's order authorizing the formation of the volunteer regiments did not contain the authority for Schofield to muster them. Furthermore, there was a specific order from the commanding general forbidding the proposed action. The order could be ignored, of course, but only at great peril to the careers of the officers doing so. There was, however, a pressing reason to proceed at once to muster in the volunteers. The Minute Men had met earlier that evening, according to Lyon's information, and had insisted on action against the arsenal. In fact, they had been prevented from marching that very night only by the intercession of Mayor Taylor. To further complicate matters, the arsenal was in a virtual state of siege, surrounded by a mob of secessionists. This group would undoubtedly cause trouble if it became aware of any action to muster volunteers. Lyon, having thoroughly reviewed the situation, threw down his cigar and suggested that Schofield and Blair approach Harney in a final attempt to get him to see the situation as it was and authorize mustering the troops.

With no apparent alternative, the two accepted Lyon's suggestion, but they wasted their time, for Harney flatly refused. When they returned with this message, Lyon told them that he was prepared to proceed without regard for the personal hazard such action would create and ordered them to proceed.[18] With that, the mustering of troops got under way. As Lyon watched it, no doubt anticipating his arrest and court-martial, he was handed a message dated April 21, 1861. He opened it quickly and read, "General Harney has this day been relieved of his command. The Secretary of War directs that you immediately execute the order previously given to arm the loyal citizens, to protect the public property, and execute the laws. Muster four regiments into the service." Montgomery Blair had done his job.[19]

Harney had also received a message informing him of his relief and ordering him to report to the general-in-chief in Washington. His relief was a terrible shock to him. Only three days earlier, he had recommended Lyon's relief in a letter to Lt. Col. E. D. Townsend, assistant adjutant general. "I deem it of the highest importance to the public interest," he had written, "that an officer of rank should be forthwith assigned to the command of the troops at the St. Louis Arsenal and to the charge of the defenses of that place." He then commended Lyon's "courage and fidelity" but concluded, "There are reasons however which in my judgment render it expedient that the change in the command I have suggested should be made without delay."[20]

Now it was the general who had been relieved. Harney had not been unaware that Blair and Lyon were dissatisfied with his actions. He had hardly expected, however, that they would be able to engineer his relief. He had been in the army for forty-three years with his loyalty and integrity unquestioned. And while his career had had some rough spots, such as his being removed from the Department of Oregon as a result of conflicts with the British, it had many more bright spots. He had won brevets in both the Seminole and Mexican wars and performed with distinction across the frontier. A brash, tough, stiff-backed cavalryman, he had brooked no nonsense, and had once hanged sixty men at one time for desertion. This brashness had caused him problems occasionally, but none that were significant. Even that had changed. He had moved away from the storminess that had marked much of his career and was now inclined to deal patiently and diplomatically with problems. He believed his actions in the current matter had been proper and had, in fact, prevented violence. And despite Blair's concern, his Virginia origins, and close friendship with many of the "secessionist" element in St. Louis, he was loyal to the core. Still, he was relieved and, ever the good soldier, he quietly accepted his orders and left for Washington on April 23.

News of Harney's relief could not have pleased Jackson. With the general's departure, he lost the only hope he really had of maintaining the status quo until he was ready to make his move. The governor knew that Lyon's animosity toward the state government was unequivocal, and he had no reason to believe that the captain lacked the courage to back up his opinions.

Still, the news was not all bad. On the day of Harney's departure, Jefferson Davis responded favorably to Jackson's request for assistance, although the response was far short of what he had requested. Davis told him that his resources for providing assistance were limited, but agreed to give him two twelve-pound howitzers and two thirty-two-pound guns and adequate ammunition for both. The rebel president took advantage of his military experience to point out the obvious to the governor whose military experience had been limited to a bit of service as a captain in the Blackhawk War. The guns would, Davis told him, be very effective against both garrison and walls when utilized from the surrounding heights. He also assured Jackson that he concurred with him about the importance of capturing the arsenal. Davis closed by saying, "We look anxiously and hopefully for the day when the star of Missouri shall be added to the constellation of the Confederate States of America."[21]

While the governor was waiting for Confederate support, Lyon's efforts to protect the arsenal and its contents began to bear fruit. Dressed in mufti, Capt. James H. Stokes, Governor Yates' emissary, pushed his way through the secessionist crowd surrounding the arsenal on April 24 and presented Lyon a requisition for ten thousand muskets. He also told the captain he had heard rumors that Jackson was moving two thousand troops to St. Louis and placing batteries on the levee and at Powder Point. Therefore, if this were true, they had but little time.

Lyon was more than ready to fill the requisition but was concerned about his ability to do so with the arsenal surrounded by Southern sympathizers. Somehow, the mob's attention must be diverted. Lyon had thought the problem through, however, and had devised a trick that he believed would do it. The next evening he put out a rumor that a substantial number of weapons would be transferred to the Tenth Ward Union Guards. It traveled with the speed of light to the Minute Men, who took the bait and prepared to capture the shipment. Concurrently, Lyon had Stokes wire for the steamboat *City of Alton* to proceed to the arsenal's landing next evening under cover of darkness.

The arsenal contained a large number of dusty old flintlock muskets that had been in storage for years awaiting possible modification. Lyon had these weapons packed in strong, heavily banded wooden boxes marked "Department of the Ohio USA—Springfield Rifled Muskets, 1860." At nine o'clock the next evening, four streetcars loaded with the bogus weapons moved slowly out of the arsenal. The alert Minute Men spotted the movement and sounded the alarm. A short while later, a mob descended on the shipment and carried it away. The "capture" of these weapons created a great commotion, distracting virtually all unwanted attention away from the arsenal, as the secessionists celebrated their "victory" over the Yankee captain.

At eleven o'clock, the *City of Alton*, running unseen in the smothering darkness, quietly slid into the arsenal landing. Capt. Harry Stone and his detachment of arsenal personnel were waiting to load her cargo. The weapons for the governor's regiments, plus the additional ten thousand were rapidly put on board. When the loading party had completed its work, Lyon decided that his best course of action would be to empty the arsenal except for ten thousand weapons he thought he might be able to use. The loading began again and continued until another 10,000 muskets, 5,000 carbines, 500 revolvers, 100,000 rounds of ammunition, and other miscellaneous arms and equipment had been loaded. At two o'clock in the morning the work was complete.

With steam up, the order to cast off was given. The paddle wheel thrashed the water as the boat strained to leave the landing, but she would not move. The heavy cargo of weapons had put her hard aground on some rocks. Frantic to get away, her captain rocked the vessel in an attempt to break free but only succeeded in damaging the boat. Fearful that further attempts would breach the steamer's hull, the loading party was once again called aboard. Urged on by their

officers, the party worked feverishly to shift the cargo and were finally rewarded by the steamer's floating free.

Stokes had watched anxiously as the detail worked, expecting
momentarily to see a group of the Minute Men bearing down on the
pier. He breathed a sigh of relief when she broke free, and ordered
her captain to make for Alton, Illinois, up the main channel at top
speed. The captain was only too glad to oblige. As they tore away, the
furiously churning paddle wheel leaving a frothy wake behind them,
it occurred to the steamer captain they might be pursued and
attacked on the river. He mentioned this to Stokes and asked what he
should do if that happened. Stokes told him to take the boat to the
deepest part of the channel and sink her. The captain nodded acceptance and turned his attention to the river.

At five o'clock in the morning, the steamboat docked at Alton.
Stokes ran to the nearest fire bell and rang it. Soon, the area was
filled with the city's citizens, some of whom were still dressed in their
bedclothes. Stokes told them that he needed their help to transfer the
weapons to a waiting train. Men, women, and children fell to work
with a will. Only two hours later, at seven o'clock, the train chugged
out of Alton on its way to Springfield, Illinois, and safety. A Union
man who heard of the exploit proclaimed loudly, "The secessionists
are euchred."[22]

Back in St. Louis, about twenty-five hundred volunteers had been
mustered into service. One regiment, the 1st Missouri Volunteer
Infantry, had filled its rolls and had elected Blair its colonel. The
other regiments were filling up rapidly. Clearly, Lyon would have no
problem recruiting the number authorized. Without waiting for the
remaining regiments to be formed, the troops already mustered by
consensus elected Lyon their brigadier general. Blair had done what
he had told Sherman he would do.

On April 30, Lyon fired off a wire to Washington outlining his
situation. He had approximately three thousand troops under arms,
he told army headquarters, and could acquire another ten thousand
if given the authority. Furthermore, he did not intend to wait for a
response. Instead, he was going to accept all the volunteers he
could get until ordered otherwise. His justification for pressing
ahead pending authorization was that his action would keep them
from the secessionists. Anyway, he reasoned, they would be needed
sooner or later. The newly elected "general" also emphasized his
urgent need for support, noting that he suffered from lack of facilities, properly trained personnel, camp equipage, and horses. He

made it clear that he expected to be attacked and was prepared to defend his position.[23]

In response, Secretary of War Simon Cameron authorized him to enlist an additional ten thousand men and, in cooperation with the Committee for Public Safety, to place St. Louis under martial law, if deemed appropriate. So extraordinary was this action on the part of the secretary that it was sent to the general-in-chief for his endorsement. He gave it, saying, "It is revolutionary times, and therefore I do not object to the irregularity of this."[24]

Additional news of the rapidly developing storm came on May 4. Capt. Langdon C. Easton, assistant quartermaster at Kansas City, notified department headquarters that the ordnance stores at that location consisting of 102 carbines, 37 muskets, 9 pistols, 86 sabers, and 34,000 cartridges had been forcibly taken the previous evening.[25]

That same day, Frank Blair wired Cameron complaining of lack of equipment and supplies in almost every conceivable category. He urged the secretary to issue orders to quartermasters wherever the necessary resources were available to fill their needs. He concluded by urging that the local quartermaster, Maj. Justus McKinstry, be authorized one hundred thousand dollars to be used in meeting their needs. In doing so, he defended the major, who had been accused of wrongdoing, by saying, ". . . there is no ground for the nonsense that has been put afloat by those who want his position here."[26] Blair would regret this later, when it was proven that McKinstry was up to his armpits in fraud and graft, and he was dismissed from the service.

As for Jackson, although he had taken some severe blows, contrary to what the Union gentleman had said, he was far from "euchred." Instead, he was pushing steadily forward toward his objective—taking Missouri out of the Union. Furthermore, he remained convinced that, given time, he could work his will. He had to have time, however, as he made clear in his response to a request from L. P. Walker, Confederate secretary of war, for a regiment of troops to serve in Virginia. He flatly told the secretary that he had no legal authority to provide them and added that the state was "woefully deficient in arms." There was a way out, however. The legislature, he informed the secretary, had just been called into special session, and he had no doubt that they would give him all necessary authority over the matter. Then it would be a different story. As for men, he said, ". . . we have plenty of them, ready, willing, and able to march at any moment to the defense of the South. . . . Missouri can and will," he promised, "put one hundred thousand men in the field, if necessary."[27]

Despite his forthright secessionist stance toward Confederate officials, Jackson was not ready to reveal his intentions publicly to his own citizens. In a letter to his friend David Walker, Jackson wrote, "I do not think Missouri should secede today or tomorrow, but I do not think I should *publicly so declare*, I want a little time to arm the state, and I am assuming every responsibility to do it with all possible dispatch." He also acknowledged lost opportunity when he added, "She [Missouri] ought to have gone out last winter when she could have seized the public arms and public property and defended herself. This she had failed to do, and now must wait a little while."[28]

In an attempt to perpetuate the sham that he wanted only neutrality, he told the legislature that, although the state's interests and sympathies matched those of the South, the state ". . . at this time has no war to prosecute." Instead, he told them that he had called them into special session ". . . for the purpose of enacting such laws and adopting such measures as may be necessary and proper for the more thorough organization and equipment of the militia of the State, and to raise money and such other means as may be required to place the State in a proper attitude of defense." While he was telling the lawmakers this, he was ordering the militia into encampment at St. Louis. The arsenal still dangled tantalizingly in front of him and, although he had lost his opportunity to capture its weapons, he meant to have it.[29]

Once in session, the legislature issued the "requisite" Border State resolution. It said, "So abhorrent is the doctrine of coercion that any attempt at such would result in the people of Missouri rallying on the side of their brethren to resist to the last extremity." This done, they began to haggle over the governor's legislative package, and indicated little interest in speedily passing it. As to secession, they refused even to discuss it.

This rebuff caused the state treasurer to say to an undoubtedly chagrined governor, "The long and the short of it in my estimation is that a very decided majority of the governing influences are in favor of Missouri remaining with the old U. S."[30]

CHAPTER V

"Sweeney, They Surrender"

Governor Jackson, in conformance with state law, called the militia into encampment the first week in May. The ostensible purpose of the encampment was training. In compliance with these orders, Frost assembled almost nine hundred troops at Lindell's Grove, located on the western edge of St. Louis. Here, they laid out a typical military camp in company streets, which they christened Camp Jackson. Passersby were quick to note that signs containing the names of the camp's streets had been carefully posted. The most prominent of those were on the two main streets: Davis, for the Confederate president, and Beauregard, for Rebel Gen. P.T.G. Beauregard, who had commanded Confederate forces at Fort Sumter. Neither did visitors to the camp miss the point that the troops were dressed in gray. Still, the U.S. flag flew over the brigade commander's headquarters, although flags of less certain origin and allegiance flew at other places.

Lyon, who earlier had moved to occupy the heights commanding the arsenal, viewed the encampment with undisguised suspicion. Granted, the attractiveness of the arsenal had diminished significantly. Still, its importance to maintaining a Union presence and to the control of the city left no doubt in his mind that the ulterior purpose of the encampment was seizure of his facility. Determined to neutralize this threat, he began planning the actions he might take to counter any threatening move of theirs.

The state's first move was not long in coming. Directly after the militia entered its encampment, Lt. William D. Wood, aide-de-camp to Frost, called at Lyon's headquarters. Ushered in, the lieutenant delivered Lyon a message from Frost that removed any doubt regarding the real motive for the encampment that may have been lingering in the Union officer's mind. According to the militia commander, he had an urgent need to provide training for his pioneers, which would require use of the heights surrounding the arsenal. Therefore, Frost told Lyon, he intended to send Lt. William H. Finney and forty men to occupy and train on the bluff south of the arsenal. Further, he added, in order to complete their extensive training schedule, it would be necessary for them to remain in this location throughout the period of the encampment.

Lyon was not buying it. Never doubting that the real intent behind this move was to emplace artillery, Lyon put a stop to the plan in a stiffly worded reply. He reportedly told the militia commander, "If anyone not authorized by [Lyon] stuck a pick or a spade into the top of that bluff, or any other spot within shelling range of the Arsenal, [Lyon would] turn [his] guns on him and salute the enterprise with the music of whistling shells." There was no more talk of training pioneers on the heights.[1]

Now Lyon received more news that disturbed him. One of his spies in the city had picked up information concerning Jackson's request for weapons. According to this man, a fast steamboat, the *J. C. Swan*, was en route from Baton Rouge, Louisiana, and had just stopped at Cairo, Illinois, to refuel. Aboard the vessel were boxes and barrels containing artillery and ammunition destined for Frost's militia. Furthermore, according to the spy, with the addition of this armament, the militia intended to seize the arsenal.[2]

This intelligence again confirmed Lyon's suspicions regarding the true mission of the militia camped at Lindell's Grove. Based on this information, Lyon called a meeting of the Committee for Public Safety and his officers. When they arrived, they found him pacing the floor, obviously agitated. As soon as they had all assembled, he closed the door so that he could speak in confidence and turned to them. He quickly outlined the latest developments, and carefully explained the seriousness of the situation as he saw it. What he did not tell them, but what was of equal concern to him, was that Harney was on his way back. Undoubtedly, once he returned, any action against the state troops would be forbidden. Determined not to be thwarted by Harney, Lyon insisted to the group that action had to be taken and that time was of the essence. He concluded the meeting by saying, "We must take Camp Jackson and we must take it at once."[3]

Despite his exhortation to the members of the meeting and his own anxiety, he could, in fact, not move immediately. Essentially, Lyon simply had no basis, other than his opinion, for taking action. Intelligence reports from a couple of spies were far from sufficient justification for direct action against a legally formed state militia that until now had engaged only in authorized activity. He need not have fretted, however, for that lack of justification was about to be removed.

The *J. C. Swan* arrived in St. Louis under cover of darkness shortly after midnight on the morning of May 9. A militia detail led by Capt. John Tobin was standing by to unload her. The detail worked rapidly to get some extremely heavy boxes marked "Tamora, care of Greely & Gale, Saint Louis" and a number of heavy, unmarked barrels off the steamer and onto waiting wagons.[4] Apparently, the boxes had been marked for Greely & Gale because they were known as strong Union men, and it was unlikely that a shipment to them would be carefully inspected. In any event, the cargo was soon loaded on the wagons and taken through the dark city streets to Camp Jackson, where it was unloaded and concealed.[5]

Lyon was duly informed of this activity by members of the steamboat's crew who were loyal Unionists. This was the confirmation he needed. He had already decided to attack the "traitorous" camp, but was moving carefully to assure the long-term success of his actions. As far as he was concerned, this news set him free to proceed at will. In his view, the acceptance of the weapons by the militia provided ample proof that they intended to seize the arsenal. To Lyon's way of thinking, that justified attacking them.

He continued to play his hand cautiously, however. He wanted more proof than the word of a spy, although he believed implicitly what he had been told. To get what he wanted, he summoned U.S. Marshal Daniel A. Rawlings and requested that he confirm the information concerning the *J. C. Swan*'s cargo. To Lyon's disgust, Rawlings was unable to do so. Irritated by the marshal's failure, Lyon looked for another way to obtain the necessary information. He finally concluded that there was no way to obtain it quickly other than by direct reconnaissance. Therefore, Lyon decided that he would personally visit Camp Jackson to witness personally the disloyal conduct of the militia.[6]

Because he obviously could not openly visit the encampment, Lyon sent for Franklin Dick, Blair's brother-in-law, and sought his help in formulating a scheme that would permit him to survey the camp.[7] As the two discussed the problem, Dick proposed an audacious plan that promised to meet the need. Frank Blair's blind mother-in-law, Mrs. Mira Alexander, was accustomed to taking coach rides through the city. Unable to see, she customarily went heavily veiled and relied on her black driver, Old Peter, to describe to her the activity and sights he observed. A well-known figure, Mrs. Alexander was frequently greeted by those they passed while driving through the city. She never spoke in response, but merely lifted her hand. Given these circumstances, it would be a simple matter, in Dick's opinion, to disguise the slightly built Lyon as Mrs. Alexander. He could then survey Camp Jackson by touring it during the afternoon when it was open to visitors. In Dick's view, there was only the remotest of chances that the ruse would be discovered. Lyon agreed, and the plan was presented to Frank Blair, who approved it.

The chosen day had dawned overcast and a bit threatening but, by afternoon, had cleared into a sunny, pleasant, late spring day. As usual, that afternoon Camp Jackson swarmed with civilians as family, friends, and the curious flocked to the camp to visit with friends or relatives or just to gawk. Shortly after three o'clock that afternoon, a handsome, ornate barouche, pulled by a high-stepping team of horses, rolled into the camp. Sentries noted it but paid little attention, recognizing the familiar black-draped figure of Mrs. Alexander sitting in the back listening as Peter animatedly described the sights. They found nothing unusual in Frank Blair's mother-in-law joining the throng spending a quiet afternoon sightseeing.

In the back of the barouche, Lyon sat garbed in one of Mrs. Alexander's black bombazine dresses with a shawl thrown over his shoulders. A large bonnet was pulled low over his heavily veiled face to hide his red hair and scruffy whiskers of the same hue. In his lap, he held a basket containing two revolvers—just in case. Lyon peered intently through the veil as the barouche rolled along, observing every visible detail of the camp while Peter, sitting high up on the box, chattered away. In less than an hour, Lyon had seen what he came for, except for the newly delivered cannon, and returned to his headquarters. As soon as he arrived, he sent a message to members of the Committee for Public Safety to meet with him at seven o'clock that evening.[8]

Once the committee had convened, Lyon reported the results of his reconnaissance. After reporting the details of his observations, he informed the committee that he intended to attack Camp Jackson, enumerated his reasons for doing so, and requested their support. Four members of the committee voted in favor of his decision. Samuel Glover and John How disagreed with the proposal. They pointed out that the encampment had been legally called, the militia had made no move against the arsenal, and there was no evidence that it would not disband as scheduled. They also noted that the U.S. flag flew over the camp, which placed its activities in accordance with federal requirements. They agreed that, if the munitions from Baton Rouge were actually stored there, they should be seized. The proper way to do that, however, they pointed out, was by writ of replevin served by a U.S. marshal, not capture by the U.S. Army. If the marshal deemed it necessary, they told Lyon, the army could back him when he served the writ. In short, they considered Lyon's proposal illegal.

Because Lyon had completed legal training, he understood them as well as the possible ramifications of his proposal. It made no difference, however, as Lyon had not the slightest intention of working through the judicial process. He sarcastically told the committee that he did not have time for "Mr. Blackstone." Furthermore, he told them, it was not a question of law, it was a question of the supremacy of the U.S. government. "The United States flag did not shield loyal Union troops at Ft. Sumter," he reminded the committee. "Why," he asked, "should the name of the State shield disloyal militia in St. Louis?"

Glover would not agree and refused to be part of an illegal action. Lyon, his mind made up, really did not care what Glover thought; neither, in his opinion, did he need his concurrence. Still, to keep peace with the committee, he told Glover to go ahead and draw up the papers. He also made clear however, that he would not wait. Turning to a subordinate, he said, "I have something better than writs; I have powder and ball."[9]

When business was relatively completed, the meeting started to break up. At that point, Lyon dropped the bombshell he had been withholding. He told the group that he had been informed that Scott had reinstated Harney and that the latter would return on May 11 to reassume the command. He need not remind them, he pointed out, that Harney would certainly never approve the action he had planned. It was now or never. This additional information caused a reevaluation and won him the reluctant agreement of all the committee members.[10]

Although he had assented, Glover was still not truly convinced of the wisdom of the proposal. In a final effort to rectify the situation, he returned home, prepared a writ of replevin, and gave it to the marshal to serve. His efforts were futile. The next morning, when the officer appeared with the writ, Lyon would neither see him nor allow him to become involved.[11]

May 10 dawned cloudy and threatening. Lyon was active early, assembling troops and issuing arms and ammunition. The location of the camp and the necessity of approaching it through the streets of the city made any surprise attack completely impossible. Without the element of surprise, Lyon had decided that his best course of action would be to wait until the militia had completed its morning training. Following that, they would stand down as usual and open the camp to civilian visitors. In that configuration, the militia would have the most difficulty getting into position to oppose him effectively. And, perhaps by that time, the weather would clear. With these considerations in mind, he set two-thirty in the afternoon as the hour to strike the militia camp.

The gathering of the Union troops and their movement to an assembly point did not long go unnoticed. Rumors of impending federal action had been rife in the city for some time. In response to them, Police Chief James McDonough had posted men to watch for unusual activity. As reports poured in of the troop assembly and preparation at the arsenal, McDonough informed the Board of Police Commissioners. Basil Duke instantly realized what was happening and sent Frost word of what he believed to be an impending attack. Initially, the militia commander, who had known Lyon at West Point, was skeptical that he would do anything so rash and out of character for a Regular Army officer. Continued reports of Union activity finally began to erase the skepticism, however, and to replace it with concern.[12]

In an effort to determine federal intentions, Frost dispatched his chief of staff, Col. John S. Bowen, to the arsenal with a message for Lyon. In it, Frost informed his counterpart that he had received intelligence that it was Lyon's intention to attack him. Expressing his astonishment that an attack would be considered on troops lawfully going about their business, he stated that he doubted that such an attack was contemplated. Furthermore, he assured Lyon, lying through his teeth, insofar as hostilities of any sort being contemplated by state forces, he could ". . . say positively that the idea has never been entertained." In reference to the information he had concerning Lyon's intention of attacking him, he said, "I would be glad to know from you personally whether there is any truth in the statements that are constantly being poured into my ears."[13]

Lyon not only ignored the message that arrived about one o'clock that afternoon, he also refused to see Bowen. He had his troops formed and was preparing to move. The proximity to possible combat, the complexity of his plan, and the enormity of this officially unsanctioned step all bore down on him with unrelenting pressure. He would not permit another pressure to be added, nor would anything nor anyone divert him from his elected course. Sherman's description of him earlier in the week as "running about with his hair in the wind, his pockets full of papers, wild and irregular" fit exactly, as he prepared to give the order to advance.[14]

Lyon had planned an extremely complicated attack on the camp. He had formed his troops into seven units that were to march in three columns by different routes and converge simultaneously on the enemy. Such a maneuver would have been a daunting task for seasoned troops. Most of these troops were green volunteers, although many, including some of the senior officers, were veterans of the German Revolution of 1848. Nevertheless, that was the plan; at the appointed time, Lyon set it in motion. At his command, more than six thousand troops stepped off under now sunny skies to march the six miles to Lindell's Grove. Not surprisingly, the movement of such a large body of troops through the city caused a great deal of excitement and confusion. Despite the confusion and muddy roads, however, at three-fifteen that afternoon, almost miraculously, all arrived as planned.[15]

Lyon deployed his troops and positioned his artillery to cover the camp. During these movements, a substantial number of the militia, to the jeers of their comrades, took to their heels to avoid combat or capture. Others stood fast and some made some slightly threatening movements. Noticing activity near a four-gun battery commanded by Lt. Henry Guibor, Lyon told Sweeney, "Watch those men. If they take steps to serve their pieces, deploy your leading company as skirmishers. Charge the battery and take it."[16]

In response, the one-armed captain, a hardened veteran of Indian fighting, turned to the two companies nearest the militia artillery. He quietly ordered them to place their cartridge boxes toward the front.

He watched as his order was executed and, as ready as possible, turned back to watch developments.

With Sweeney positioned, Lyon handed Maj. Benjamin Farrar, one of his aides, a letter to deliver to Frost. Without preamble, Lyon's letter informed the militia leader that his command was regarded as hostile and cited the reasons. "In view of these considerations," he wrote, ". . . it is my duty to demand, and I do hereby demand, of you an immediate surrender of your command, with no other conditions than that all persons surrendering under this demand shall be humanely and kindly treated." Lyon gave Frost thirty minutes to decide on his course of action.[17]

Frost regarded Lyon's demand as an outrage and extremely insulting to a sovereign state. Nevertheless, he realized that he was in no position to force the issue. Summoning his officers, Frost briefed them on the letter's contents. After some discussion, they decided to see whether there were other options. In the hope of avoiding a total and humiliating surrender, Frost asked Farrar to take a message to Lyon requesting a meeting between the two commanders.

Lyon quickly read the message, turned it over, and scribbled a note on the back telling Frost that he now had ten minutes. If he did not surrender unconditionally within that time, Lyon wrote him, he would order his men to open fire.[18]

Frost was appalled and infuriated at Lyon's response. He was also unable to do anything about it. Boiling with anger, he sent Lyon a note saying, "Sir, I never for a moment conceived the idea that illegal and unconstitutional demands as I have just received from you, would be made by an officer of the United States Army." Then, he continued, bowing to the inevitable, "I am wholly unprepared to defend my command from this unwarranted attack, and shall, therefore, be forced to comply with your demand."[19]

Farrar hurried back to his commander with Frost's response. The tough little Yankee read it. With the shadow of a grin tugging at the corner of his lips and a glint in his eye, he announced in a casual tone of voice, "Sweeney, they surrender."[20]

Lyon, eager to finalize the surrender, started rushing around to attend to all the details. In his haste, and distracted by all that needed to be done, he made the mistake of passing too close to the rear of Maj. Horace Conant's horse. Without warning, the animal kicked Lyon squarely in the stomach, dropping him to the ground unconscious and barely able to breathe. As their commander writhed on the ground and struggled for breath, his officers rushed to render any help they could. While they crowded around the fallen captain, Sweeney spotted Frost's aide, Lt. Wood, heading toward them.

Determined not to let Wood see the injured Lyon, Sweeney intercepted him. When Wood told him he had a message for Lyon, Sweeney informed the lieutenant that his commander was occupied and asked for the message. Accepting Sweeney's word, the lieutenant said, "General Frost sends his compliments to Captain Lyon and wishes to know if the officers will be allowed to retain their side arms. Also, what disposition shall be made of government property, and if a guard will be sent to relieve his men now and take possession of everything when the camp shall be evacuated?"

After a brief conference with Schofield, Sweeney informed Wood that the officers could retain their side arms, public property would be confiscated, private property collected, and guards provided as necessary. As a courtesy, Schofield was sent with Wood to deliver the terms to Frost.[21]

The crowd attracted by the federal troops as they marched to Lindell's Grove had continued to swell. The festive air with which the crowd had initially gathered rapidly evaporated as they watched "their" militia taken prisoner. As what was happening slowly permeated the crowd, emotions reached a fever pitch. Animosity toward the Union troops, particularly those of German extraction, increased by the minute. As this mob, which had now become unruly and boisterous, pushed and surged around the activity, Lyon, who had recovered after about thirty minutes, prepared to deal with the prisoners.[22]

Immediate parole would have been the reasonable and common-sense thing to have done. Lyon was not a reasonable type nor did he unfailingly use common sense, however. He wanted to send a message to the secessionists and chose this time to do it. By marching the militia through the crowd as prisoners, he would serve notice loud and clear that the U.S. government was not to be challenged nor trifled with. That decided, Lyon began making preparations to march the prisoners under armed escort through the city streets to the arsenal. To accomplish this, he had Blair's regiment form a line down either side of the street and made the prisoners form a single file between them. The remainder of the force, except for Sweeney's troops who remained to secure the camp, fell in behind to complete the column. As the formation prepared to move out, on either side of the street, in open lots, and in any other available space, the crowd continued to grow and mill about restlessly.

Finally, the troops and prisoners moved off at about five o'clock that afternoon. Movement was excruciatingly slow, as the column moved forward in accordion fashion, unable to strike a smooth pace. The crowd surged alongside the slowly moving formation, steadily becoming more unruly. Soon, shouts of "Damn the Dutch" and "Hurrah for Jeff Davis" were heard, sprinkled with colorful expletives. As the verbal harassment intensified, profanity and obscenity, as well as physical abuse in the form of clods, rocks, spittle, and bricks were added to the barrage.[23]

Sherman reported what he saw when, in an apparent lapse of judgment, he brought his son, Willie, to view the excitement. Accompanied by Charles Ewing and John Hunter, they had established themselves in a favorable viewing position along the route, close by the column. Shortly, after the troops had made a couple of false starts, Sherman found Lt. Rufus Saxton, an acquaintance from his army days, halted in front of him. They exchanged a few words, and Sherman handed Saxton a newspaper to read.

About this time, a drunk attempted to pass through the line near where Sherman stood. A Regular Army sergeant blocked him with his weapon at port arms. In a serious error in judgment, the drunk grabbed the sergeant's musket. With a quick movement, the sergeant knocked him down. As the drunk fell, he skidded down a bank about eight feet high that was alongside the street.

It took the drunk a few seconds to regain his footing and reorient himself. While he was doing so, the Regulars moved forward to be replaced by the green troops of Maj. Peter Osterhaus, a native of Koblenz and veteran of the 1848 Revolution who had fled to America. Back somewhat unsteadily on his feet, the affronted drunk pulled a concealed pistol and fired at those who he believed had toppled him down the bank. Fortunately, his aim was not the best, and he succeeded only in hitting a soldier in the leg. Unfortunately, his ill-advised response triggered action on the part of others.[24]

More shots quickly followed. As the green troops started to panic in the face of hostile fire, one of the company commanders, Capt. Constantine Blandowski, struggled to control them. Now a round came out of the crowd, and Blandowski fell mortally wounded. With random shots continuing to whistle through the ranks, Col. Henry Borenstein, bespectacled commander of the 2nd Missouri Volunteer Infantry Regiment, ordered his men to return fire. At this, the troops began to fire at will. When the troops began to return the fire directed at them, total panic seized the crowd. The scene quickly degenerated into a screaming, swearing, crying, pushing, shoving, and running mêlée. Men, women, and children ran frantically about as they desperately sought safety. Sherman, terrified for Willie's safety, fell on top of the boy, while Ewing and Hunter huddled close to provide additional protection to the youth. In this position, they hugged the earth and listened to the bullets whiz through the leaves over their heads.

While the crowd sought a safe haven, Lyon and his officers rushed to gain control of their forces. It took effort to calm the shaken troops, but they soon succeeded. With the crowd scattered and the troops under control, things slowly quieted down, but not without a price. In the short time that had expired since the drunk's shot, twenty-eight civilians, one a babe in arms, three of the prisoners, and two of the soldiers had been killed. An unknown number on both sides had suffered injuries to some extent.[25]

The column finally got under way again and, shortly after dark, reached the arsenal. The prisoners were shoved into crowded quarters, with assurances that they would be released the next day. For the most part they were, but, with Lyon, nothing was easy. To the surprise of his prisoners, he established a requirement that, as a condition of their release, each must not only give his parole, but also take an oath pledging allegiance and promising not to take up arms against the United States. This caused an immediate outcry. Accepting the parole and taking the oath required by it was tantamount to an admission of treason. Their objections fell on very deaf ears. Lyon in his usual fashion was unyielding and, eventually, all but one prisoner gave his parole as the Union commander demanded. The lone holdout, Capt. Emmett McDonald, bested the stubborn New Englander by obtaining his release on a writ of habeas corpus.[26]

The morning after the capture of Camp Jackson, Frost addressed a letter to the restored Harney. In it, he reviewed the entire episode, lodging a protest against all actions taken and the terms for releasing the prisoners. In closing, he appealed to Harney ". . . as the chief representative of the United States . . . for justice on behalf of these loyal citizens who are now held as prisoners of war. . . ." He also pleaded for relief from the "indignity" of having to give parole. Harney forwarded it to army headquarters with a request for instructions.[27]

During the late afternoon and evening following the capture of Camp Jackson, reports and rumors about the events of the day swept the city. Businesses and homes were locked and barred against the possibility that riots would develop or, as rumor had it, the

"Germans" would take to the streets in reprisal for the day's events. Those who favored secession, many of whom were newly converted as a result of the day's events, mounted any available stump to harangue anyone who would listen, and many did. The largest of these crowds gathered at the Planter's House Hotel where secessionists castigated any and all forms of Unionism. Even Uriel Wright, a delegate to the convention to consider Missouri's relations with the Union, who had doggedly opposed secession, announced, "If Unionism means such atrocious deeds as have been witnessed in St. Louis, I am no longer a Union man."[28]

Relatively little violence actually occurred, although during the night at least three people of German extraction were killed. The low level of violence was certainly not because none was wanted by certain elements of the populace. Mobs of "wannabe" rioters formed at key locations such as the Planter's House Hotel and secessionist headquarters at Berthold Mansion. In addition, unruly groups marched on the voice of the Union Committee, *The Missouri Democrat*, and the leading German-language newspaper, *Anzeiger des Westens*. In virtually every instance, mobs found themselves facing policeman who made it clear, sometimes over gunsights and bayonets, that peace would be maintained. Chief McDonough, regardless of his or anyone else's political leanings, was grimly determined to protect "his city." Because of him and the dedication of his force, misbehavior on this potentially explosive night was reduced principally to "noise, empty threats, and fervid oratory." Nature also lent a helping hand late that night by dousing the city with a heavy rainstorm, further cooling the ardor of the demonstrators. Lyon, who had authority to impose martial law, had the good sense, or good fortune, to stay out of it.[29]

Initial news that "something" was up in St. Louis reached the capital at Jefferson City about three o'clock in the afternoon. The intelligence was supplied by J. W. "Deacon" Turner, editor of the *Saint Louis State Journal*, who wired the governor, "Lyon taking Frost." This was followed by additional reports, carefully presented in a light to satisfy Turner's secessionist views. By six o'clock that evening, the capital had details, including a report of the shooting of citizens by the Union troops.[30]

This last bit of news hit the capital like a thunderbolt. The legislature was enraged and very nearly in chaos. Jackson wasted little time in taking advantage of the opportunity that Lyon had unexpectedly thrust upon him. The governor immediately hustled to the legislative chambers where, as soon as some order had been restored, he made an impassioned speech concerning the recent events and sought passage of his requested legislation. The legislature, which had been called into special session for this very purpose, had been squabbling over it with little progress. Now, both houses passed the "military bill" in less than twenty minutes and sent it to Jackson for signature. The "military bill," and other acts that would be passed in support of it, gave the governor virtually dictatorial power over the militia and, because it made every able-bodied man a member of the militia, the state as well. Measures were also passed to provide the necessary funding and borrowing authority to support the new legislation. Harney later described the act ". . . as an indirect secession ordinance, ignoring even the forms resorted to by other states." Lyon had unintentionally given Claiborne Fox Jackson what he had long wanted and schemed to obtain. Missouri appeared to be on its way into the Confederacy.

At midnight, just as a violent thunderstorm struck the capital, the governor received fresh news confirming the casualties among civilians in St. Louis and word that approximately two thousand federal troops were on their way to Jefferson City. At his order, church bells began to sound the alarm, while the storm lashed the unhappy city. Citizens were again roused in fear and uncertainty as the thoroughly panicked members of the legislature, armed with weapons of every description, made their way through brilliant lightning, booming thunder, and slashing rain to reassemble in secret session. By the time the legislators adjourned at three o'clock that morning, they had given the governor full control over St. Louis and dictatorial power to deal with Union activity elsewhere in Missouri.

In other actions, men were dispatched by rail to determine whether or not the rumored troops were indeed en route. They had orders to burn the bridges over the Gasconade and Osage rivers if that were found to be true. It was not, but a span of the Osage bridge was destroyed nonetheless. Action was also taken to safeguard funds in the state treasury and to transfer a substantial amount of powder located at the capital to the interior of the state.[31]

Reaction in cities across the state mirrored that in the capital. Citizens were alarmed and wanted something done about the crisis. The actions of their elected leadership did not, of course, meet with universal approval. Some denounced the actions taken as creating a "military tyranny," while others wanted direct action against the "invaders." One of the latter was M. Jeff Thompson, former mayor of St. Joseph.

Thompson got busy and rapidly assembled a group of men who were prepared to fight and asked the governor for authority to supply and equip them. Such authority was not granted, so the group was forced to break up and members returned to their homes. This was more than the irate Thompson could abide. Determined to set things right, he boarded a steamboat and headed for Jefferson City to confront Jackson. Immediately upon his arrival, the bellicose former mayor was ushered into the governor's presence. Jackson listened to his highly agitated guest but showed little interest in forcing a fight with Lyon at that time. Unable to convert the governor to his point of view, Thompson stalked out in high dudgeon. Before he left, however, he took one last shot. Turning to Jackson, he said, "Governor, before I leave, I wish to tell you the two qualities of a soldier; one he must have, but he needs both: one of them is Common Sense and the other is Courage—and By God! You have neither."[32]

Saturday dawned over a troubled St. Louis. Although the unrest of the previous evening had abated during the wee hours, it now resurfaced. Trouble erupted sporadically in various places, resulting in the death or injury of a few of the citizens unwise enough to leave themselves unprotected. City authorities continued to do their best to defuse and control the situation. The police were everywhere, breaking up gatherings, removing rowdies from the street, arresting lawbreakers, and protecting property. As a part of the overall effort to maintain peace, the mayor established a curfew requiring that minors remain indoors for the next three days and that others be off the streets by nightfall. The effectiveness of these generally successful efforts was somewhat minimized as rumor fed on rumor, and the wildest tales were circulated and believed. Many residents, especially those with known Southern sympathies, feared for their safety and began to leave the city. This exodus continued over the next several days until several thousand people had departed.

The most serious incident of the day involved a group of Home Guards. Lyon had mustered and armed a significant number of these "loyal citizens" as had been authorized by the president at the end of April. During the course of the day of May 11, Capt. F. D. Callender swore in an additional twelve hundred Home Guards. This group, designated 5th Regiment, U.S. Reserves, was marched across the city en route to its station late in the evening. As the guards entered north

St. Louis, they were surrounded by a mob that began to harass them. As the shouting and threats increased, shots were fired at Callender's men. This was too much for the green troops, who turned and fired into the mob. When the smoke cleared, two soldiers and four civilians lay dead. Again, the army took no action, leaving the matter in the hands of the civil authorities.[33]

On May 12, Lyon reported the incident to Washington, noting in his report that General Harney had returned and assumed command. Making the most of the opportunity to communicate directly with headquarters, he used this report as a vehicle for expressing his displeasure at the general's restoration. In the report, he stated his view that his actions of May 10 had been necessary and argued that it was necessary to "persevere" in this manner against anticipated "combinations and measures of hostility against the General Government." He concluded by saying, ". . . the authority of General Harney under these circumstances embarrasses, in the most painful manner, the execution of the plans I had contemplated, and upon which the safety and welfare of the Government . . . so much depend, and which must be decided in a very short period." Clearly, Lyon was not going to accept quietly the change in his fortunes and, given his political backing, this boded ill for his commander.[34]

Late in the day on May 11, Harney, presumably fully restored to grace, had returned to St. Louis and had resumed command of the Department of the West. The next morning, he moved to restore order in the city. Believing the use of the "German" militia had been the principal cause of the problem, he assured the city fathers that he would have them removed or disbanded. He found out shortly that he could not fulfill his promise.

When Harney summoned Frank Blair and informed him of his intentions, Blair reminded him that the volunteers were in the federal service and that the department commander had no authority to either move or disband them. To reinforce his words, he showed Harney the order from the president authorizing the formation and use of "loyal citizens" to protect the city. Harney did not give up easily, but after a long and heated discussion with Blair, he finally acknowledged that his hands were tied. He could not override a presidential directive.

He could use the Regulars, however, and he moved them nearer his headquarters where they were poised to respond to any unrest. As he was doing this, word was spread that Harney "had no control" over the volunteers. This rumor, coupled with the movement of the

Regulars, caused increased apprehension in the city. Before events could get out of hand again, however, Harney moved to allay the citizens' fears. He did this by issuing a statement conceding that he had no authority to move the Home Guards, but he promised that martial law would be imposed only if necessary and, if it should be, that only Regulars would be used to enforce it. Finally, he made it clear that if he took action, it would be to assist local authorities in preserving the peace, not to usurp their police powers.

This statement motivated Mayor Taylor to make an announcement of his own. Speaking from the steps of the Planter's House, he told the populace, "There's no insubordination among the armed men known as the Home Guards. They are entirely under the command of their officers and there is no reason whatever to believe that there will be riots and bloodshed." He then asked that the crowds disperse and that people go home. Slowly, quiet and order returned to the streets of St. Louis.[35]

CHAPTER VI

"This Means War"

Jackson wasted little time in taking advantage of the expanded gubernatorial power that the legislature had conferred on him. The militia, now called the Missouri State Guard (MSG), was divided into eight districts with a brigadier general appointed by the governor over each. To tie this structure together, the governor was authorized to appoint a major general. A willing candidate was available. Former governor Sterling Price, who had until now assumed a stance of moderation, was so incensed by the actions of Lyon and Blair that he offered his services. Jackson had some misgivings about Price because of his past moderation, but he was finally persuaded by his advisers that Price was the right man. He offered the post, and Price accepted.[1]

Virginia-born Sterling Price was a successful farmer and slaveholder to whom freeing the slaves was anathema. He held this position not so much because he believed in slavery, but because he believed that freeing them would be degrading to society. In his view, it would mean destruction of a society he held as ideal, and that he could not accept. Even so, he was a believer in the Union and had been opposed to any action that might destroy it.

The portly, silver-haired Price had long been active in politics. He had served as a state legislator, as a U.S. congressman, and as governor of the state. During the Mexican War, he had achieved the rank of brigadier general of volunteers and had served as military governor of New Mexico and Chihuahua. He had no formal military education, however, and held West Pointers in such disdain that he once bought newspaper space to deny that he had such training. A genial, dignified leader, his men loved him, and nicknamed him "Old Pap." Missourians, in general, felt much the same. He also had opponents, however, some of whom were supposedly on his side. These men, at best, considered him vain and pompous; even Jefferson Davis called him the "vainest man he ever met." Included among the list of men who hated Price was Frank Blair, whose animosity dated from Mexican War days. In this case, Price reciprocated the feelings.[2]

The new major general immediately ordered the district brigadiers to organize their districts and prepare to defend against hostile action from the federal government. His new position had not diminished his desire for neutrality, however, and he cautioned these subordinates to use every lawful means to protect the populace and to keep the peace. They were also warned to avoid conflict with other armed forces except in emergencies. And only the state flag was to be flown.[3]

While the state was moving to strengthen its position, opposition to Lyon's actions appeared from another quarter. The influential moderate element in St. Louis concluded that he was too radical and took steps that they hoped would result in his replacement. Discussions concerning the best action they could take led to a decision to send representatives to Washington to petition directly senior government officials. As their representatives, the group chose James E. Yeatman, a banker, and Hamilton R. Gamble, the future provisional governor.

Word of their plan leaked out, however, and Blair moved promptly to defuse the threat. He dispatched Franklin Dick to Washington to assemble the necessary forces to blunt the effort of the moderates and, specifically, to enlist brother Montgomery's support. Blair was very much aware that although there were reservations about Lyon, he was also regarded very favorably by a majority of those who would influence any decision concerning his removal. Dick and Montgomery were to capitalize on those feelings. In addition, they were to press for the alternative of relieving Harney, promoting Lyon to brigadier general, and giving him command of the department.[4]

Lyon, who was a bit concerned that he had overplayed his hand, also got into the act. Aching to regain command of the department, and determined to get rid of McKinstry, whom he distrusted, along with Harney, he asked Dr. Charles Bernays, editor of the *Anzeiger des Westens* and friend of Lincoln, to intervene personally on his behalf with the president. Specifically, he wanted the editor to tell Lincoln, ". . . they [Harney and McKinstry] are against us and will throw all kinds of difficulties in my way." He also told him, "Tell the President to get my hands untied and I will warrant to keep this State in the Union."[5]

When Yeatman and Gamble arrived in Washington, they found themselves already behind the power curve—facing a determined attack from Lyon's supporters. The greatest part of their strategy involved winning the support of Attorney General Edward Bates, a St. Louis man and the first cabinet member appointed from west of the Mississippi. This hope, which was a key element in securing the success of their plan, vanished like a mirage when Bates refused to push for Lyon's removal. This left the two without support inside the administration and with virtually no hope of succeeding. Nevertheless, they pressed on and forcefully presented their case for the removal of the crusty little captain.[6]

As for Dr. Bernays, the president received him graciously and listened carefully to his arguments. Lincoln agreed with some of the proposal but was not ready to do all that was asked. He informed the editor that he was not prepared to relieve Harney but did promise that McKinstry would go. Unfortunately, it was weeks before that promise was fulfilled. During that time, Lyon had fully committed himself to a course of action in Missouri, and McKinstry had jeopardized him by denying him critical transportation.[7]

The Blair camp, which had the ear of the president, was too much for Yeatman and Gamble. The moderate emissaries were forced to return to St. Louis virtually empty-handed, although they had succeeded in convincing Bates of the usefulness of Harney in his current position. This gave them some small comfort and the general, who had no part in this, a renewed lease on life. Ominously, however, the Blairs had succeeded not only in protecting their protégé, Lyon, but also had made major progress toward obtaining his promotion to brigadier general. Worse yet for the department commander, they had also been able to instill more doubt in senior administration minds about the advisability of leaving Harney in that position.

Harney had returned to his assignment with a considerably altered view of the situation in Missouri, and quickly informed Washington that he fully approved of the action Lyon had taken. He followed this with a proclamation to the people of Missouri in which he referred to the "military bill" as an "indirect secession ordinance" and urged them to consider carefully their "obligations and duties," which were paramount under the constitution, before they permitted the state to leave the Union. In it, he reviewed the reasons for the action at Camp Jackson, and affirmed his approval of the actions that had been taken against it. He justified his position by saying, "No Government in the world would be entitled to respect that would tolerate for a moment such openly treasonable preparations." Then, in an attempt to set the minds of the state's citizens at ease, Harney ended his message by assuring them that he would uphold the law and suppress any group who defied it.[8]

Harney did not discount the possibility of hostile action directed against himself, either. If such action materialized, it would, he believed, be because of the composition of the force he commanded. In an effort to minimize that possibility, he asked for authority to muster a regiment of Irishmen into service immediately. He believed that such action would counter the prejudice currently exhibited toward the troops because of the heavy German element in the force. Blair, who understood the need to calm public animosity against "the Dutch," concurred. In addition, to reinforce further his ability to deal from a position of strength and to provide adequate resources should military action become necessary, Harney requested ten thousand muskets for issue to reliable Union men in the state. Supplementing that, Harney wanted Iowa and Minnesota to be directed to place at his disposal six thousand and three thousand men, respectively. The War Department, which had other plans for Harney, did not respond—nor did these actions in any way mollify Blair and Lyon, who were steadfast in their determination that Harney be removed.[9]

As Harney struggled to bring order to the state, Lyon continued to take actions that generated resentment among its citizens. In response to the outraged reaction to his troops killing civilians in the Camp Jackson episode, he showed no remorse. Instead, he gave the newspapers a statement that said, "If innocent men, women, and children whose curiosity placed them in a position, suffered with the guilty, it is no fault of the troops." This was undoubtedly a correct, albeit undiplomatic, assessment. Certainly it won him no friends. He also dispatched troops to Potosi, Hillsboro, and Ironton to quell secessionist disturbances. This they accomplished easily and, in the process, confiscated a substantial amount of lead, which they brought to the arsenal. These actions did nothing to inspire confidence in his commander's statements and actually created additional tension throughout the state.[10]

The conduct of his subordinate and his own dissatisfaction with the actions of the state government notwithstanding, Harney still earnestly but naïvely believed that well-intentioned men could bring peace to Missouri and retain its place in the Union. He enlisted no less than Sterling Price in this effort. The move to involve the state actively in maintaining order seemed to achieve the desired results on May 21 when the two reached an agreement. Under its provisions, Price undertook to assure that the people of the state and their property would be protected regardless of individual political loyalties. Harney, for his part, agreed to refrain from using federal troops or moving them about the state unless necessary to support Price. Delighted by the results of his efforts, the department commander hastened to inform Washington by wire and the citizens of Missouri by proclamation of the agreement. With the conclusion of this "pacific manifesto," Harney felt that he had found the solution to the problem of unrest in the state.[11]

The Blair camp received the news with a decided lack of enthusiasm. While writing to Montgomery Blair on behalf of the Union Committee for Public Safety, Broadhead told him, "We fear no good will come of this arrangement but that it will only result in putting off the evil day until such time as the enemy will be better prepared to make resistance."[12]

Frank Blair reflected the same pessimistic outlook when he wrote to Secretary Cameron, saying, "The agreement between Harney and Price gives me great disgust and dissatisfaction to the Union men; but I am in hopes we can get along with it, and think that Harney will insist on its execution to the fullest extent, in which case it will be satisfactory." Actually, he had no intention of getting along with it. He wanted Harney out and would not rest until that happened.[13]

More trouble for Harney was not long in coming. Complaints that citizens loyal to the Union were being harassed, were suffering violent attacks, were having their property stolen, and were being driven from their homes began to trickle in to Harney from various points. The trickle soon became a flood, and the complaints were sent to Washington as well as to Harney. Harney responded to them by keeping Price informed and by asking that he take appropriate action. In response, Price assured the harried general that matters were under control, that reports were exaggerated, and that stability would rapidly come to all parts of the state.

The response in Washington was one of deep concern. Foremost among those concerned was Abraham Lincoln. He wanted to be certain that the situation was controlled and that his field commander was alert to possible chicanery; therefore, on May 27, he had Brig. Gen. Lorenzo Thomas, the adjutant general, contact him. After informing him of the president's concern, Thomas told Harney, "It is immaterial whether these outrages continue from inability or indisposition on the part of the State authorities to prevent them. It is enough," Thomas continued, "that they continue to devolve on you the duty of putting a stop to them summarily by the force under your command, to be aided by such troops as you may require from Kansas, Iowa, and Illinois."

Having spelled out the general's duty, the adjutant general then lectured him regarding the state authorities. "The professions of loyalty to the Union by the State authorities of Missouri are not to be relied upon," he said. "They have already falsified their professions too often, and are too far committed to Secession to be entitled to your confidence, and you can only be sure of their desisting from their wicked purposes when it is out of their power to prosecute them." He ended by reemphasizing to the general what his government expected of him. "The authority of the United States is paramount," he was told, "and whenever it is apparent that a movement, whether by color of State authority or not, is hostile, you will not hesitate to put it down."[14]

Harney was fully aware of the information being given to Washington and felt that it did not represent the true situation. He was convinced that the action he had taken was working and so informed headquarters on May 29. In his message to headquarters, Harney told them that Missouri was "rapidly becoming tranquilized. . . . I am convinced that by pursuing the course I have thus far," he wrote, ". . . peace and confidence in the ability of the Government . . . will be fully and permanently restored." Furthermore, he assured Washington, he had means to determine what was happening and that he would promptly punish any violation of the agreement with Price or any attempt at rebellion. His assurances did not relieve the unease in Washington.[15]

Undoubtedly, plunder and violence were common occurrences in many areas of the state. Missouri had long been subjected to such, particularly along the Kansas border, and it was unrealistic to expect it to stop abruptly. Furthermore, all the illegal acts that occurred were not politically motivated. There were plenty of freelancers who were quick to use politics to shield actions designed to line their own pockets or to settle personal scores.

Moreover, unquestionably, there were many fraudulent reports that Union men were being persecuted. In one instance, Harney received a letter from St. Joseph, Missouri, telling him that former governor Stewart and other prominent Union men in that city had been driven from their homes. In an attempt to determine the credibility of the writer, Harney showed the letter to Frank Blair and asked whether he knew the author.

With barely a glance at the letter, Blair said, "Oh, yes, he is perfectly reliable. You can believe anything he says."

"Then I will write immediately to General Price and ask him to attend to it," Harney told him.

"Are you going to wait to hear from Price?" an astonished Blair asked.

"Certainly," the general told him.

Harney did not have long to wait. Within three days, he received a clipping from *The St. Joseph News* containing a letter written by former governor Stewart. It said, "Neither I nor any other Union man has been driven out of St. Joe."[16]

This case and others as well clearly indicate that the situation was less serious than the flood of complaints suggested. It left no doubt about a substantial lack of either spontaneity or truth in many of the reports. The general appears not to have gotten the message that there was mischief afoot, however. It is difficult to believe that he could have missed the obvious after his conversation with Blair, but there is no evidence of such awareness. The actual situation in Missouri may, or may not, have been improving. Harney's certainly was not.

The support Harney was receiving from his subordinate, Lyon, also left much to be desired. The general moved to correct this part of his troubles by giving Lyon orders that severely circumscribed his freedom to act. No longer was he permitted to search citizens and river traffic, the Home Guard was effectively placed on standby, Regular officers were not permitted to lead volunteer units, and Lyon was ordered to make all purchases through the quartermaster, Justus McKinstry, whom he justifiably distrusted. Chafing under these restrictions, the irascible little captain did not hesitate, in any forum, to express his displeasure with the general. His dealing with a group of would-be volunteers illustrates his proclivity for outspokenness and open nonsupport of his commander.

A group of St. Louis men had formed themselves into an organization called the American Zouaves and presented themselves to Harney for induction into service. Rather undiplomatically, the crusty old soldier told them they were not needed and to go home. Insulted, they promptly marched to the arsenal and told Lyon what had happened. His reaction was vintage Lyon. Instead of supporting his superior and soothing troubled waters, Lyon said, "You are a fine-looking body of men and no doubt ought to be accepted. But General Harney has the power, I have not. Had I the mustering authority, I would take you and all others presenting themselves." Then, indicative of what was to come, he added, "I'd finish this business up at once by putting the traitors in such a position that they could not organize. You had better keep up your spirits and organization. The present state of affairs cannot last very long."[17]

In fact, the game had been up since May 16, although Harney had no inkling of it. At the insistent urging of the Blair faction, an order relieving the department commander had finally been issued on that date. It had been delivered to Frank Blair instead of Harney, however, with instructions that it was to be held pending the outcome of Harney's attempt to restore and maintain the peace through his agreement with Price.

The action to relieve the general had been taken neither lightly nor without reservations. Following issuance of the order relieving Harney, the president began to have doubts. In a letter to Frank Blair he said, "I understand an order has gone from the War Department to you, to be delivered or withheld at your discretion, relieving General Harney from his command. I was not quite satisfied with the order when it was made," the letter said, "though on the whole I thought it best to make it; but since then I have become more doubtful of its propriety. I do not write now to countermand it, but to say I wish you would withhold it, unless in your judgment the necessity to the contrary is very urgent."

Going on to say that relief of a military man by a politician might not be particularly wise, the president added, "We had better have him a friend than an enemy." Then, noting Harney had already been relieved and reinstated, he expressed concern about public reaction. "Now," Lincoln said, "if we relieve him again the public will ask, 'Why all this vacillation?' Still," he said, "if in your judgment it is indispensable, let it be so."[18]

As the month ended, so did Blair's willingness to wait. Apparently considering it indispensable, he had Maj. Benjamin Farrar deliver to the general the order relieving him and placing him on indefinite leave.

The old man was thunderstruck. Although he knew that Blair opposed him and even doubted his loyalty, it had never occurred to him, despite his previous relief, that his country would so reward him for a lifetime of service. He was loyal to the core, as he felt he had amply demonstrated, and, further, he believed his actions to pacify the state were working. Again, he gave up the command, but not so quietly this time. He fired off a communication to Thomas stating that he did not believe the president intended that he be relieved. To support this, he pointed out that he had been dealt with as the department commander regularly since the date of the order relieving him. His effort was futile. He did not receive even the courtesy of a response.[19]

Before many hours passed, reality at last set in, and Harney accepted his fate but not before writing one last angry letter to Thomas. In it, he insisted that his conduct had been dictated by a good-faith attempt to implement his orders notwithstanding the "clamor of the conflicting elements surrounding" him. He reaffirmed that he believed his efforts had been successful, achieving a virtually blood-less victory, while those who "clamored for blood" were unceasing in their efforts to impugn him. Despite this, he had, he wrote, ". . . been relieved from the command . . . in a manner that has inflicted unmerited disgrace upon a true and loyal soldier." He ended by saying that, after his long and faithful service, he thought his ". . . countrymen would be slow to believe that I have chosen this portion of my career to damn with treason my life. . . ." This judgment, he said, ". . . I shall most willingly leave to the unbiased judgment of posterity." There was no response to this letter, either.[20]

Blair and his supporters now had most of what they wanted. Harney was gone and Lyon had now been promoted to brigadier general. All that remained was to get him confirmed in the command he had temporarily assumed upon Harney's departure. With this, the Blair family would have the stranglehold on the state that they desperately wanted. But they could not climb this last hill. Attorney General Bates and Gamble fired all of their guns in opposition to giving Lyon command of the department, basing their opposition on the "uproar created by Lyon's impolitic performances." The president was inclined to agree, finding Lyon a bit too rash to suit him. Instead of appointing Lyon to the command, Missouri was removed from the Department of the West and made a part of Maj. Gen. George B. McClellan's Department of the Ohio.[21]

With Harney's relief, things began to unravel. The Price-Harney agreement was no longer operative, and dissident elements on both sides took advantage of it. Lawlessness increased as each, as well as some independent operators, capitalized on the loss of communication and cooperation between state and federal arms of the government. Price now ordered a steadily growing MSG to prepare for action. Both he and Jackson believed that Lyon intended to attack them. They were absolutely correct.

On June 3, Lyon had informed Washington of Confederate movements in Tennessee and Arkansas. He also alleged that there were "mysterious and industrious" secessionist movements in or toward the southwestern quarter of the state which he believed were aimed at linking them up with Rebel forces from Arkansas and Texas. His plan, he wrote, was to move to southwestern Missouri in conjunction with troops from Kansas to frustrate these activities.[22]

The Conditional Unionists, whose goal was armed neutrality, anxiously monitored these developments. Convinced that there was an alternative to war if only the two sides would talk, three prominent St. Louis citizens, William A. Hall, Davis H. Armstrong, and J. Richard Barret, got busy. First, they met with the governor. Jackson, who was still flirting with the Confederacy and whose troops were unprepared for combat, had already dispatched Colton Greene to Fort Smith in an attempt to convince the Confederates to agree to march north and assist him. He needed time, and now there was an opportunity to gain some. Grasping it under the guise of desiring moderation and of bowing to the wishes of the citizens' group, he asked for a meeting.

The citizens' group then went to Judge Thomas T. Gantt and asked him to act as an intermediary with Lyon. Gantt agreed to do so and approached the new general with the request. The interim department commander agreed to a meeting provided that it was held at the arsenal in St. Louis. Jackson would not have that. His dignity and position affronted, he let it be known that he was not going to be "ordered" around by the abrasive little Yankee.

More discussion somewhat mollified the offended governor and prompted Lyon to agree to a change in his position. The hurdle imposed by lack of agreement on a meeting site was finally cleared on June 8 when both sides agreed to meet in St. Louis—at the Planter's

House Hotel on June 11. Lyon did not miss a final opportunity for a dig at his opponents, though, when he accepted. Although there were neither orders nor warrants for the arrest of any of the State party, his acceptance included an order guaranteeing that the governor and his party would not be arrested ". . . on the journey to and from the city and during their sojourn here up and to midnight on June 12th, 1861." Lyon had served notice that he did not consider them neutral.[23]

At eleven o'clock on the morning of June 11, 1861, the two sides met around a massive mahogany table in one of the hotel's heavily draped and carpeted suites. On one side sat Lyon, who had relinquished his scruffy captain's uniform for the occasion. Today, the man, who liked to copy the rather sloppy style of dress Gen. Zachary Taylor had introduced during the war with Mexico, was dressed in a spotless general officer's uniform, but wore the beat-up old dragoon saber he had carried for years. Next to him was Blair, now both a congressman and a colonel, dressed in dark civilian clothing and a garrison cap bearing an infantry badge. Across the table, Jackson sat, as solemn as an undertaker, dressed in a black broadcloth suit. Beside him was Price, who had forgone his new gray MSG uniform. Instead, he wore his cavalry general's uniform, including plumed hat, high boots, and sword from the Mexican War. Also present were Col. Thomas L. Snead, Jackson's aide, and Major Conant, Lyon's aide.[24]

With few preliminaries, the meeting got down to business. Jackson began with an opening statement outlining his position. In it, he promised to disband the militia, protect all citizens equally, suppress insurrectionary movements, repel all attempts at invasion, maintain neutrality, and, if necessary, request the assistance of the federal government to implement these commitments. In return, he wanted the Home Guards disbanded and a pledge that federal troops would not be deployed beyond their present location. Price hastened to add that this was compatible with his agreement with Harney and he saw no reason that it should not remain acceptable.

Lyon had initially stated that Blair would represent the federal government and that he would act merely as an observer, but this was too much for the scrappy little brigadier. How, he demanded, could the governor do what he proposed without his militia, supported only by a small, tied-down Union force, when he could not do it with his militia fully formed? In Lyon's view, Jackson's proposal rested where he had placed calculus at West Point, "outside the bounds of reason."[25]

After four hours of fruitless discussion, Lyon told Jackson and Price in firm, unmistakable terms that the Price-Harney Agreement was dead and that neutral or separated status was completely unacceptable for their state. At this point, according to Snead, Lyon closed the conference. Speaking slowly and deliberately, while remaining seated, he said, "Rather than concede the State of Missouri the right to demand that my Government shall not enlist troops within her limits, or bring troops into the State, whenever it pleases, or move its troops at its own will into, out of, or through the State; rather than concede to the State of Missouri for one single instant the right to dictate to my Government in any manner, I would [rising as he said this, and pointing in turn to every person in the room] see you, you, you, you, and you, and every man, woman, and child in the State dead and buried." In the dead silence that followed this statement, he turned to Jackson and snapped, "This means war. In an hour one of my officers will call for you and conduct you out of my lines." Then, without another glance or a nod, he strode out of the room "rattling his spurs and clanking his saber."[26]

The other attendees sat for a moment in shock, and then bid each other a courteous farewell. War had come to Missouri.

CHAPTER VII

The Boonville Races

Jackson and Price did not linger in St. Louis. Hastily boarding a train, they set off for Jefferson City expecting Lyon to be in hot pursuit. En route, the two began planning actions to respond to the failed meeting and to deal with the threat Lyon represented. He had made it clear that he intended to fight, and they were ill-prepared to meet him. True, they had Greene seeking help from the Confederacy, but such help was by no means certain and, if it were forthcoming, had to be hastened. Meanwhile, they had to confront any eventuality with limited resources. As they talked, the train sped through the night, stopping only for fuel and water. At last, they reached the capital, where the weary passengers detrained. They found the legislature waiting for them in emergency session.

Planning meetings with administration and legislative officials continued throughout the night, while some of the governor's staff worked feverishly to draft a proclamation for Jackson to issue the following day. In addition to being heavily involved in meetings, Price also had to take some defensive actions. He dispatched troops to destroy the bridges over the Gasconade and Osage rivers and to disrupt telegraphic communications with St. Louis. For his part, Jackson took action to put Price in command of all Missouri troops and to send another urgent request to the Confederacy to supply an army to work in coordination with the MSG. No help, however, could be expected from that source before state forces would have to face Lyon, even if the answer were positive.

Because an attack by federal troops appeared imminent, a decision had to be reached concerning the best defensive position for state troops. Obviously, the attack would probably be directed at the seat of government, and Jefferson City could not easily be defended. Unwilling to risk his force at the capital, Price selected Boonville as the point to meet Lyon's expected attack. Brig. Gen. John B. Clark, a lawyer and U.S. congressman who had served as a colonel in the Blackhawk War and was now in charge of the Third Military District north of the Missouri River, was ordered to march his force to Boonville with all dispatch. Brig. Gen. Mosby M. Parsons, a lawyer, state legislator, and Mexican War veteran in command of the Sixth District, was instructed to move toward Boonville and be ready to support Price. All other districts were ordered to assemble their forces in camp and await directions. Once these decisions were made, work started on the evacuation of the capital.[1]

Jackson's proclamation removed any chance of avoiding armed conflict, if such a chance had existed. The proclamation recited the results of the meeting with Lyon that had just concluded, called attention to what the governor called the "unprovoked and unparalleled outrages inflicted by representatives of the Central Government," called for fifty thousand men to repel an "invasion," and urged all citizens to rally to the state flag. He ended by telling Missourians, "I hold it to be my most solemn duty to remind you that Missouri is still one of the United States . . . [and] it is your duty to obey all constitutional requirements of the Federal Government; but it is equally my duty to advise you [that your] first allegiance is to your own State, and that you are under no obligations whatever to obey the unconstitutional edicts of the military despotism which has introduced itself at Washington, nor submit to the infamous and degrading sway of its wicked minions in this state. No brave hearted Missourian will obey the one or submit to the other. Arise, then, and drive out ignominiously the invaders. . . ."[2] With the publication of the proclamation, Jackson and Price, along with Col. John Sappington Maramaduke and his 1st Regiment of Rifles, boarded the steamer *White Cloud* and embarked for Boonville, which they reached on June 13 after an overnight layover.

Lyon considered Jackson's proclamation a declaration of war. In his view, this was another ample reason, not that he really needed nor wanted any more, to move against the state forces. He had already decided to do so and had actually taken some actions before the St. Louis meeting. Now he began to develop specific plans for dealing with the secessionist forces.

In mid May, Lyon had sent Col. John B. Wyman and his 13th Illinois Volunteer Infantry southwest to Rolla to secure the railhead at that location. With a route to the southwest secure and the Missouri River available for travel to the northwest, Lyon decided on a two-pronged movement. He would send Sweeney, now acting brigadier general of volunteers, with Col. Franz Sigel's 3rd Missouri Volunteer Infantry, Col. Charles B. Salomon's 5th Missouri Volunteer Infantry, Col. B. Gratz Brown's 4th Regiment of Home Guards, and a six-gun battery of artillery to the southwest. Brown would stop at Rolla and use his force to ensure that the Pacific Railroad remained open and that the supply point was protected; Sweeney would continue to Springfield to establish a headquarters there; and Sigel and Salomon would push through Mt. Vernon to Neosho. This action would discourage any Confederate support that might come from Arkansas, while blocking Missouri forces from retreating to that state.

In conjunction with these movements, he would take a force up the Missouri River to strike at Jefferson City. Once he had driven Price's forces from the capital, he would have control of the river and have effectively isolated the northern part of the state. Meanwhile, by forcing the state government to evacuate the capital, he would greatly reduce, or perhaps destroy, its ability to govern effectively. The combined movements would also give him virtual control of all railroads in the state, further curtailing state capabilities. Once he had driven Price out of the capital, he would press him southward and crush him against the southern jaw of his pincers. Failing that, he would at least drive him into Arkansas' northern Ozark Region, which he knew was incapable of supporting a large force for very long. In either event, he would have rendered the state virtually powerless to threaten the government with a credible force.[3]

Lyon's only concern was the status of his own supplies and equipment. He was critically short of both and had told Washington, but little seemed to be happening to alleviate the situation. Immediately following the abortive meeting at the Planter's House Hotel, he had received an open-ended authorization to enlist troops and was informed that five thousand additional stands of arms were being forwarded to him. Although this pleased Lyon, he

Map 1. The campaign for Missouri, summer 1861

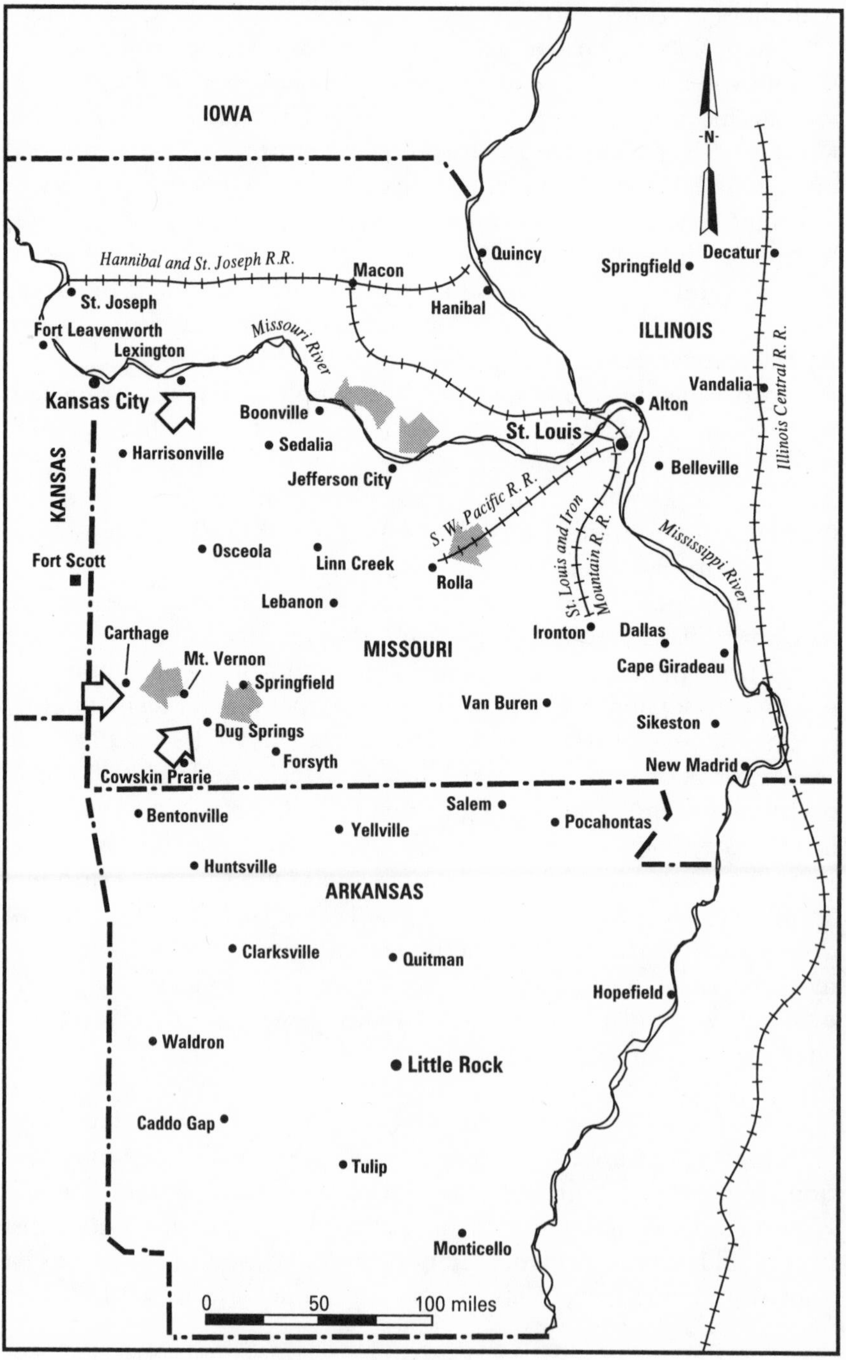

IOWA

Hannibal and St. Joseph R.R.

St. Joseph

Fort Leavenworth
Lexington

Kansas City

KANSAS

Harrisonville

Fort Scott

Carthage

Mt. Vernon

Dug Springs

Cowskin Prarie

Bentonville

Huntsville

ARKANSAS

Clarksville

Waldron

Caddo Gap

Macon

Hanibal

Boonville

Sedalia

Jefferson City

Missouri River

Osceola

Linn Creek

Lebanon

MISSOURI

Springfield

Forsyth

Yellville

Quitman

Tulip

Monticello

Quincy

Springfield   Decatur

ILLINOIS

Vandalia

Alton

St. Louis

Belleville

S. W. Pacific R.R.

Rolla

Ironton   Dallas

Cape Giradeau

Van Buren

Sikeston

Salem

Pocahontas

New Madrid

Hopefield

Little Rock

St. Louis and Iron Mountain R. R.

Illinois Central R. R.

Mississippi River

0   50   100 miles

Chronology

8   Feb   State convention meets at Jefferson City to consider secession.

14 Apr   Fort Sumter surrenders. President Lincoln calls on states for 75,000 volunteers. Governor Jackson refuses Lincoln's request and declares Missouri's sympathies with the South.

6   May   Captain Lyon clashes with St. Louis authorities. Militia begins gathering at Camp Jackson.

10 May   Lyon arrests the militia. Citizens riot in protest.

24 May   State troops under Jackson and General Price refuse to disband.

31 May   Lyon is promoted to general and assumes command in West.

11 Jun   Lyon, Frank Blair, Jackson, and Price meet in St. Louis but cannot agree. Lyon begins move on Jefferson City.

15 Jun   Lyon captures Jefferson City and then pursues Jackson to Boonville. Armies skirmish at Boonville on 17 June. Jackson retreats to Cowskin Prairie and calls for help.

24 Jun   Colonel Sigel arrives in Springfield with his brigade, followed by General Sweeny. Jackson and Price gather troops at Cowskin Prairie.

5   Jul   Battle of Carthage. Sigel withdraws to Mt. Vernon.

13 Jul   Lyon arrives in Springfield and begins maneuvering on Price's force at Cowskin Prairie.

22 Jul   Forces skirmish at Forsyth. Pro-Union Missouri legislature declares loyalty to the United States and elects pro-Union Governor Gamble.

25 Jul   General Frémont assumes command of Union forces in the West. Troops under General McCulloch join Price and Jackson.

2   Aug   Forces skirmish at Dug Springs.

5   Aug   Lyon withdraws to Springfield. Price and McCulloch occupy Wilson's Creek.

10 Aug   Battle of Wilson's Creek is fought. Lyon is killed.

Legend

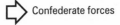 Confederate forces   Union forces

would have preferred to have had assurance that his critical
matériel needs would be satisfied.[4]

He did not let the matériel shortage hinder him, however, and
began marshaling all available resources in preparation to move.
Action was also taken to "armor" with sandbags several steamboats
he had commandeered. Lt. Col. Chester Harding was designated as
adjutant general in St. Louis with authority to act for Lyon and to fill
the critical post of liaison between Lyon and Washington. Schofield
was also detailed to remain in the city to complete the remaining support actions after the main force left, but was to join Lyon as soon as
possible. The first troop movement was started by entraining Lt. Col.
Francis Hassendeubel's contingent for Rolla.

Considering the complexity of the plan that Lyon had initiated,
he was ready to move very quickly. At eleven o'clock on the morn-
ing of June 13, 1861, the left wing of his force under Lt. Col.
George Andrews left St. Louis aboard the steamer *Iatan*. At two
o'clock that afternoon, Lyon and the right wing left on the *J. C.
Swan*, of Camp Jackson fame, followed by the supply steamer
A. McDowell. The remainder of Lyon's force left by rail via the
Pacific Railroad for Hermann, where they were to board the *City of
Louisiana* for the remainder of the trip to Jefferson City. Later that
evening, the last of Lyon's southwestern force under Sigel left for
Rolla. Sweeney had been forced to remain behind temporarily to
complete actions necessary to supply the headquarters he would
establish in Springfield.[5]

Lyon's force consisted of Totten's Light Battery (Company F, 2nd
U.S. Artillery), Lyon's old Company B, 2nd U.S. Infantry, two companies of Regular recruits, Blair's 1st Missouri Volunteer Infantry
Regiment, and nine companies of Boernstein's 2nd Missouri Volunteer
Infantry Regiment. This force moved leisurely up the river, which was
very low, making progress difficult. The troops did not at all mind the
pace, and found the voyage altogether pleasant. One worthy reported,
". . . every Bluff & grocery & log cabin & settlement greeted us cheer
on cheer—men, women & children . . . with handkerchiefs & flags
waving, until we would round a turn & so lose sight of them—We
also cheered ourselves hoarse & returned the Ladies' Salutes."[6]

Expecting to be attacked from shore, Lyon had a sharp lookout
maintained as they neared their destination. All remained quiet, however, and on June 15 the fleet pulled into the wharf at Jefferson City
unopposed. They disembarked, but neither saw, nor were molested
by, state forces. They soon realized that it would be unnecessary to

drive the government out—it had already departed. Once ashore, Lyon ordered a detachment to proceed to the Gasconade River and repair the bridge, and then marched the remainder of his force through the streets of the city to the capitol. There, he raised the U.S. flag over the building, which he occupied. The state's capital was now firmly in the hands of the governor's archenemy, and the state government, if indeed it were still a government, was in full flight. To the south, Sigel had routed a small MSG force at Rolla and plunged on westward. So far, Lyon's plan was unfolding without a hitch.[7]

By afternoon, Lyon, dressed in a long linen duster and wide-brimmed straw hat, typical of the laxness in dress that he had learned in Mexico, occupied the governor's office and pondered his next move. He had word that between two and three thousand MSG troops were dug in, with artillery emplaced to command the river, fifty miles west at Boonville. This obstacle would have to be removed if he were to isolate Jackson and Price south of the river. This development posed no problem to him, however, since striking there, and then driving south, would fit neatly into his grand plan. Detailing Borenstein to occupy the city with three companies of the 2nd Missouri, he placed the remaining six companies under Osterhaus and issued orders to attack Boonville the following day.[8]

Jackson and Price found Clark already at Boonville when they arrived. His force definitely did not cause a surge in expectations. Without exception, his troops were poorly organized, poorly trained, and ill-equipped. They had been installed in newly opened Camp Bacon, which had been established about four miles east of town. Primarily because they were ignorant of what they faced, the troops were in high spirits, filled with confidence that they would do to Lyon what their fathers, under Old Andy Jackson, had done to the British. Price, well aware of what they faced, did not share their enthusiasm and confidence.[9]

Shortly after arriving at Boonville, Price received news that greatly increased his concern. Word came that a large number of federal cavalry and Kansas Jayhawkers were threatening Lexington. Price considered this city a key strategic location, the loss of which would cost the northern part of the state. Fearful for what lay in store for Lexington, he placed Clark in overall command at Boonville and headed there. Upon his arrival, he found no threat but was stricken with a recurring attack of the dysentery he had contracted during the Mexican War. Too ill to continue, he returned to his home in

Chariton County to recuperate, leaving the governor and Clark to cope as well as they could.[10]

Upon Price's departure, Jackson, now surrounded by members of the government and legislature also fleeing capture, exercised his prerogative as chief executive of the State and took command of the Boonville forces. In anticipation of Lyon's imminent attack, he gave field command to his nephew, Marmaduke, with orders to defend the city. The nearsighted, constantly squinting Marmaduke was not a military novice. He had attended Yale, Harvard, and then West Point. Following his graduation in 1857, he had served on the frontier with the 7th U.S. Infantry and had taken part in the Utah Expedition before leaving the service to join the MSG.

Marmaduke knew a bad deal when he saw one. Recognizing that his ill-trained and ill-equipped troops were no match for the force Lyon would bring against him, he strongly advised the governor against engaging the federal force. Initially, Jackson listened to his commander's advice that his force was ill-prepared for combat, but then succumbed to the urging of some civilian hangers-on and ordered him to fight. Marmaduke argued, but Jackson turned a deaf ear, agreeing only to order Parsons up from Pettis City. Unfortunately, or perhaps fortunately, because it is doubtful that his presence would have made a difference, Parsons did not move in time. Forced to go it alone, Marmaduke reluctantly prepared to deploy his troops along the crest of a hill facing the river and await his fate.[11]

Early in the afternoon of June 16, Lyon started his force upriver toward Boonville. Progress was again slow, owing both to low water conditions and to Lyon's caution. Again, the command moved free of opposition and tied up for an uneventful night about fifteen miles from Boonville. Lyon moved them out again at six o'clock in the morning, calling a halt when they reached Rocheport, which was approximately ten miles below their destination. Here, Lyon learned the MSG was prepared to meet him when he arrived at his objective.

Once again, Lyon's force got under way and proceeded upriver until it reached a large island about eight miles below its objective. Anchoring in the lee of the island, Lyon, Blair, and Schofield, who had now joined his commander, disembarked to survey the territory. Scouts were also dispatched in an effort to determine the enemy's position.

The terrain visible to them from the island was a low, flat bottom that stretched about a mile and a half to a sharply rising range of hills. A river road ran through the bottom toward Boonville, getting squeezed closer and closer to the water as the hills moved at an angle to intersect the river in that direction. Just where the hills reached the river, the road turned up the hill, passing through a series of terraces until it broke out on top. A scout informed Lyon that the MSG troops were deployed in line along one of these ridges and across the river road, where it rose from the river bottom. The line was in an excellent position, on high ground, anchored on one end by a grove of trees and on the other by a brick house filled with sharpshooters.

Satisfied with what he had observed and heard, Lyon moved out from behind the island and landed on the Boonville shore. Here, he disembarked all of his force except for one company of infantry and a single gun detachment of artillery. These were ordered to proceed upriver, ensuring that the vessel kept pace with his force onshore. Once in position, and when combat started on land, they were to use the artillery to shell Camp Bacon. Unless they were ordered otherwise, the city of Boonville was to be spared bombardment.[12]

The troops ashore were formed into a column with Osterhaus' troops in the lead as skirmishers, followed by a company of Regulars, Totten's Battery, two companies of Regular recruits, the 1st Missouri, and four companies of the 2nd Missouri. At Lyon's command, the column moved out, probing cautiously for contact with the enemy. After about two miles, the leading elements came under fire from Marmaduke's advanced pickets. Lyon now shifted his formation, deploying Osterhaus to the right, Company B, 2nd U.S. Infantry to the left, and Totten's Battery in the center. Once in position, Totten, the profane, hard-drinking veteran of the Mexican and Seminole wars, threw a few rounds toward the secessionists, and the line began moving slowly forward as the opponents retreated. Shortly, Lyon, who wished to ensure that the lead elements were sufficiently strong, moved up three companies to support Osterhaus, who appeared to be moving toward the enemy's strength, and one to support his old Company B. In about another mile, the federal troops hit a stronger force than the pickets had represented, and firing became general.

The federals, under light but steady fire, advanced slowly along the river road, following it as it turned up the hill. Reaching the crest of the first ridge, they spotted Marmaduke's full force stretched across the road on the crest of the next ridge. Between them and their opponents was a steep valley about three hundred yards wide. Moving off the lower ridge in a ragged skirmish line, they ran into a sheet of fire from the defenders above them. The well-trained federals dropped to a prone position, and directed a steady hail of fire at the crest of the ridge. Later, one combatant made it clear that he thought this was not fair fighting and had caused the disaster that befell them. He said, "This heah business of a-firin' an' a-loadin' while a-layin' on the ground, that's what whupped us!"[13]

But it was not the "layin' down," it was Totten's artillery that ended things abruptly. Behind the troops, he unlimbered his guns and swung into action. Choosing the ends of the Rebel line as his targets, he opened fire. Artillery rounds that fell into the grove of trees sent limbs, leaves, and other debris flying in all directions, while the house on the other end shook as though it were in an earthquake. The occupants of both immediately took to their heels, fleeing for dear life from the artillery barrage. Their companions in line across the road were quickly caught up in the general panic and began voting with their feet. Marmaduke tried to hold them, and succeeded briefly, but Lyon's attack was too much for the green troops. In a few moments, there was a general rout. The forces fleeing the ridge were joined by those remaining in the camp, which was under fire from the steamboat. Governor Jackson and his entourage quickly followed the example of the swiftly departing troops. So precipitously was the field vacated that afterward both sides referred to the skirmish just ended as the "Boonville Races."[14]

Lyon pushed on deliberately after the routed Missourians until he reached Camp Bacon. He occupied it and renamed it Camp Cameron in honor of the Union secretary of war. Some small detachments were sent after the fleeing MSG, but there was no all-out pursuit. Shortly, the mayor of Boonville, grateful that Lyon had spared his town from an artillery bombardment, came forward and surrendered the city. The Battle of Boonville was over.

Lyon had lost two killed, nine wounded (two of whom later died), and one missing. State Guard losses are not known with certainty, although ten were estimated to have been killed. The MSG also gave up sixty prisoners who were soon paroled. Lyon captured two new six-pound artillery pieces, a large supply of badly needed shoes, and a substantial supply of weapons, ammunition, and blankets—losses that the state forces could ill afford. The booty, however, was most welcome to the federal forces that were still suffering from a shortage of the most basic supplies and equipment.[15]

Next day, Lyon received word that he would not be department commander, but instead subordinate to McClellan. While Lyon was dismayed by this turn of events, Frank Blair was incensed. No matter how he schemed and labored, it seemed to him, the matter of control of the state through a cooperating department commander always slipped through his fingers. Montgomery Blair had used every bit of influence he could muster to get Lyon appointed to the post. He had even gone to see General Scott in an effort to get him to rescind the action, but the general-in-chief had refused. The influence of Bates and the president's uncertainty regarding Lyon were too much to overcome.

While the brothers gnashed their teeth in frustration, Old Man Blair was busy determining what was in the offing from McClellan rather than trying to undo a "done deal." He found that McClellan was up to his armpits in the war in the East and did not particularly welcome added distractions. He had little interest in Missouri and let it be known that he was content to let Lyon do much as he pleased in that area. This news greatly mollified Frank Blair and Lyon. They had the substance, if not the form.

On June 18, Price, having recovered from his attack of dysentery, returned to Lexington. There he found brigadier generals James S. Rains and William Y. Slack with several thousand men. Unfortunately, these troops, like those at Boonville, had little organization, training, or equipment. Nevertheless, Price was considering the idea of using them the best he could to protect this strategic point. After receiving word of the debacle at Boonville, however, he abandoned any idea of further resistance along the Missouri River. Instead, he ordered Rains to take command of all troops at Lexington and move behind the Osage River south to Lamar to meet Jackson and Clark. From there, the combined force would continue to move south until a determination could be made regarding future actions. With a small staff, Price would go south seeking support.[16]

The Battle of Boonville, while not much of a fight, was extremely important. The impact on morale was both quick and significant. The North got a boost as they hailed Lyon's victory, while many Missourians viewed the battle as a disaster, and enthusiasm for the secessionist cause cooled substantially, particularly in the central portion of the state. The loss of Boonville by the state forces was also the last step in losing control of the Missouri River, key to control of the state. With the river in its hands, the Union could move rapidly to impose its will across the breadth of the state and block any support to Price from areas north of it. Control of the river meant control of most of the state's population, economic capacity, wealth, and, of great significance, unimpeded access to, and communication with, the West. Finally, the state government, put to flight, had virtually lost its power to govern. As added insult, State Treasurer Alfred W. Morrison and Attorney General J. Proctor Knott both had been taken prisoner, along with a great deal of money and most of the treasury records. Strategically, loss of the Missouri River meant that Missouri was probably already secure to the Union, barring a catastrophic reversal in its fortunes.[17]

CHAPTER VIII

Clash at Cole Camp

L yon probably could have
stopped his advance following the Battle of Boonville with assurance
that, at least for the foreseeable future, the state would be safely in
the Union fold. That, of course, would not have been in character for
Nathaniel Lyon. There were two remaining issues that he believed
required resolution before he could rest.

The first of these was the status of those who had opposed him. In
Lyon's mind, opposition to the federal government was intolerable,
and those guilty of such actions could not remain unpunished. In a
proclamation issued immediately following the battle, he made his
views unmistakably clear. He hastened to assure loyal citizens, and
even those who favored secession but had not acted overtly against
the government, that they had no cause for concern. They were free
to go about their normal business secure in the knowledge that he
would protect them. On the other hand, those who had not obeyed
the law and had resisted duly constituted authority were promised
punishment. Chief among those were the "state officials on the run."
They were no longer recognized as agents of an established government, but simply as enemies of the United States—no more, no less.

The second issue confronting Lyon was the MSG. Although he had
pushed it around rather handily, it could still potentially grow into a

force that could seriously challenge the federal government. Despite its terrible showing at Boonville, it remained a viable threat, albeit a weak and relatively disorganized one. Therefore, in Lyon's view, until it was completely defeated and dissolved, it constituted a threat that could not be ignored.[1]

He neither could nor would abide either of these issues. Missouri had to be kept in the Union, and those individuals or organizations that opposed that concept had to be brought to heel. In his mind, his course was plain—it was his duty to deal with them. Therefore, he moved to complete execution of the plan that he had devised in St. Louis.

Before he could leave Boonville, however, Lyon had to complete several preparations. First, on June 18, he ordered Maj. Samuel D. Sturgis to bring his command from Fort Leavenworth to join him at Clinton. This action would add approximately twenty-two hundred men to his command. Second, he had to wait at Boonville for the 1st Iowa Volunteer Infantry Regiment to join him. This unit, which had recently departed Mason City, Iowa, under orders to reinforce Lyon, contained another thousand troops. Finally, his critical supply situation had to be remedied before he left the river. Supposedly, that situation would be resolved by the resupply boats that were en route from St. Louis. Once he had been resupplied and joined by the 1st Iowa, he would move south, unite with Sturgis, and either destroy Jackson and Price or drive them from the state.[2]

While Lyon waited for supplies and reinforcements, the Missourians streamed south, hoping for help from the Confederate Army. The prospect was not encouraging. At that moment, the Confederacy was struggling to organize in Arkansas and had no appreciable force of its own in the immediate vicinity. The only organized force in that area at the time was an Arkansas militia organization under the command of Brig. Gen. Nicholas Bartlett Pearce, a West Pointer and veteran of the Utah Expedition who had left the army to be a farmer and merchant. Pearce's force could conceivably be used to meet the needs of the Missourians; but it had not yet been mustered into the Confederate service and had no authority to leave the state. Furthermore, it did not appear likely that the governor of Arkansas, H. M. Rector, would give Pearce such authority; and the prospect of the organization being mustered into Confederate service was equally bleak.[3]

Farther south at Fort Smith, Arkansas, colorful Brig. Gen. Benjamin McCulloch, the senior Confederate officer in the region, was attempting to organize and equip his command of Arkansas, Louisiana, and Texas troops that had been charged with keeping the Union out of the Indian Territory (Oklahoma). McCulloch, who had followed Davy Crockett to Texas but had missed the Alamo because of a case of measles, had fought with distinction at San Jacinto in the Texas War for Independence. After the war, he had served in both the Congress of the United States and the Republic of Texas; he also had been a surveyor, an Indian fighter, a member of the Texas Rangers, with whom he had fought in the Mexican War, a commissioner to the Mormons, a gold miner in California, and a U.S. marshal along the Texas coast. In the process, he had become a bit of a legend in his own time. He had no formal military training, but had studied the great captains and had always had a burning desire for senior military command. Secession had finally given him that opportunity. This short, wiry, weather-beaten, and balding man was a good commander. He took care of his troops, who returned his affection and fondly called him "Old Ben." Of him, one of his noncommissioned officers said "there was no compromise, no guessing."[4]

It was to McCulloch that Greene had gone for help. McCulloch listened to the young captain and decided that he had no fundamental problem with helping Missouri. Marching directly to the assistance of the embattled state forces was not what McCulloch had in mind, however. While urging support of Jackson's request for assistance, he recommended that such support be part of a larger overall scheme. His proposal to Confederate Secretary of War Walker was that he be made commander of the Western Military District of Arkansas and authorized to lead a force to occupy Fort Scott, Kansas. Such a move would allow him to accomplish his primary mission of protecting the northern border of the Indian Territory against Union incursions. Meanwhile, it would force the Indian tribes, who were showing considerable reluctance, into active support of the Confederacy. Then, he would be free to cooperate with Missouri's forces to any extent desired by the Confederate government.[5]

While Greene was meeting with McCulloch, Commissioner E. C. Cabell, who had been dispatched to Richmond by Jackson in an effort to gain Confederate support, was joined by Missouri's lieutenant governor, Thomas C. Reynolds. Cabell had already seen the Confederate president and had been denied assistance before Reynolds arrived. Undaunted, the two of them decided they would again beseech Davis for Confederate support. Together, they went to see the Confederate president and laid before him all the reasons why the Confederacy should move with alacrity to Missouri's assistance. Davis listened to their appeal and then, in a grim voice, reminded them that Jackson, at the ill-fated St. Louis meeting with Lyon, had offered to drive Confederate troops out of the state if they crossed the border. To the Confederate president, that amounted to at least disloyalty, which offended this man who prized loyalty above all else. Furthermore, he reminded the supplicants, at the very time that the Missouri governor was doing this, he had been asking for support. In short, the Confederate president was disgustedly, if not overtly, accusing their governor of dishonesty, disloyalty, and duplicity. Both men hurriedly and earnestly assured him that all such activity had ceased. Jackson and Price were now fully committed to the Confederacy and were no longer either interested in, or trying to reach, an accommodation with Union officials. Despite their protestations, Davis remained unmoved. He refused them the desired support.[6]

Scuttling away from Boonville, Jackson and Clark were preparing to move south when they got word of potential trouble waiting for them in Benton County near the village of Cole Camp. Here, Capt. A.H.W. Cook had formed six companies of Home Guards, probably at the direction of Lyon. This force of about seven hundred men lay in the line of Jackson's march and could potentially delay the governor's force sufficiently to allow Lyon to overtake him.[7]

Cook had mustered these troops on June 11 and 12 at the farm of Henry Harms, which he intended to use as his base of operations. Once the troops were mustered, however, it became apparent that they would require a more spacious location for billeting and training. They found it in the nearby farms of John Heisterberg and Harm Harms.

Most of the new troops were accommodated at the Heisterberg farm; they were billeted in the barn, three corn cribs, an open space behind a rail fence just north of the barn, and in a grove of trees just east and south of that structure. The remainder of the force was located about six hundred yards south in Harms's barn. The combined locations, in addition to providing billeting accommodations of a sort, also contained sufficient room to conduct badly needed training which, after a fashion, began immediately. The troops' new home away from home was christened Camp Lyon in honor of the recent conqueror of Boonville.[8]

While Cook was forming his force, about twenty miles to the south in the secessionist hotbed of Warsaw, Col. Walter S. O'Kane was also busily putting together a force. His action had been generated initially by Jackson's call for troops before leaving Jefferson City, but now it was becoming more of a response to his concern about Cook's force. A series of rumors had flooded the area concerning the intentions of this group, and O'Kane was determined to neutralize them before they had an opportunity to implement any of their plans, whatever those plans might be. To accomplish this, he had at his disposal about two hundred and fifty infantry and one hundred mounted troops.

Whether on orders of Governor Jackson, as has been surmised, or solely from a desire to preempt the rumored Home Guard actions, O'Kane decided that the Union force had to be removed. As a prudent and careful commander, he realized that he would probably be significantly outnumbered, a serious disadvantage at any time, but particularly so for an attacker. His only hope of offsetting the imbalance in forces was to obtain full intelligence concerning the number and disposition of the Home Guards that would oppose him and then to surprise them. To obtain the needed information, he sent Sheriff Bartholomew W. Keown, a dedicated secessionist, to visit Camp Lyon, using the need to serve a warrant as a pretext for the visit. While there, Keown was to determine troop dispositions and strength as well as possible.

Keown undertook his mission on June 16, traveling to Camp Lyon with warrants for the arrest of Cook and his quartermaster, Capt. Henry L. Mitchell. Not surprisingly, the subjects took exception to the proceedings and refused to accompany the sheriff. As an alternative to submitting to arrest, Cook promised that the Home Guards under his command would take no action unless attacked by the Warsaw secessionists or were ordered to do so by Lyon.[9]

Keown, who was after something else anyway and had gathered all the information he thought possible, accepted Cook's promise and returned to Warsaw. With the departure of the sheriff, Cook, apparently having failed to penetrate Keown's "cover" and ignoring rumors of an impending secessionist attack, permitted about half of his troops to return home to care for their families and farms.

The Home Guards, under Cook's less than sparkling leadership, were a less than imposing military force. Some of them, who were of German extraction, had acquired various degrees of military experience in Europe before emigrating to this country, but most were as green as their fellow Missourians who had been stampeded at Boonville. Their leaders, as was typical during this period, were elected—at times based on experience and at others on popularity, neither of which was necessarily a sound basis for selecting commanders. Their training, which had only begun, was less than rigorous and often administered by those with dubious qualifications. Their equipment matched their experience and training. They were especially lacking in one critical area, as they had gone into camp with only four hundred muskets and a keg and a half of powder. For unknown reasons, Cook had not insisted, as was the usual case, that the men bring their personal firearms for use until they could be armed by the government. Finally, and critically important, discipline was, to a considerable extent, observed in the breach, much of this due to the copious consumption of some derivative of John Barleycorn, Esq.[10]

While the Home Guards muddled around Camp Lyon in blissful ignorance, down in Warsaw, O'Kane was busily preparing to attack them. He had wanted to keep his plans as quiet as possible, but the hustle and bustle attendant to his preparation and its purpose were clear to all but the most obtuse. One interested observer was John Tyree, who was both a slave owner and a strong Unionist. While in Warsaw on business on June 18, he had ample opportunity to observe this activity and had no difficulty deciphering its purpose. With as much intelligence as he could reasonably gather, Tyree hustled back to Camp Lyon and reported it in detail to Cook.[11]

The camp commander's reaction to this timely warning of an attack was to hold a meeting with his subordinate commanders, put out some pickets, and send couriers to recall the absent troops as best they could. In keeping with the prevailing lax discipline, little effort was made to prepare the forces in camp. The precise reason for this is unclear, but it reflects both the inexperience of the commanders and the nonchalance of the troops. Undoubtedly, the consumption of alcohol contributed to an unwarranted confidence and bravado. One Camp Lyonite, juiced up on the local white lightning, spoke for many of his comrades when he said, "I can whip these rebels single-handed."[12]

Late that afternoon, O'Kane and his troops left Warsaw for Camp Lyon. Until almost midnight, their uneventful march met nothing to cause any concern. Then, as they moved up the Butterfield Trail just south of Fordney School, they bumped into Tyree returning home through the midnight darkness. The cautious O'Kane's suspicions were immediately aroused. It was abnormal for anyone to be traveling the moonlit road alone at that hour. Fearing the meaning of this lone man's travel, he ordered Tyree held and brought to him for interrogation. While O'Kane questioned the unfortunate Tyree, someone held a light close to his face. As soon as his features were revealed, another member of the group announced that he had seen him at Warsaw earlier that day. O'Kane now knew that his chance of surprising Cook had probably vanished into the warm summer night. Disgusted at the turn of events, he grilled Tyree a bit longer. Once he was satisfied that he had all the information his prisoner could give, O'Kane had Tyree tied to a tree and shot.[13]

After this unpleasantness had been completed, O'Kane's troops moved on, turning east just south of Cole Camp to avoid the village. Moving quietly through the still night with their approach concealed by a ridge, the infantry moved directly toward the Heisterberg barn. The cavalry swung south in a wide, half-circle turn that would bring them back north, just west of the Harm barn, positioned to strike the flank of the Heisterberg force. As the attackers moved stealthily forward, trying not to give alarm, they met the outlying pickets. These greenhorns were quickly overwhelmed and bayoneted before they could sound the alarm. At about three o'clock in the morning as the first glow of dawn just appeared in the eastern sky, the attackers reached their objective. The last remaining picket, too terrified by what he saw coming to fire his gun, dropped the weapon and rushed into the barn to sound the alarm.

Whether they had been left open by the fleeing picket or were that way because of heat and crowded conditions inside, the double barn doors were standing wide open. The attackers, following hot on the heels of the picket, charged up to these doors and fired into the befuddled troops who had been sleeping inside. Awakened by the shouting picket and the flashing rattle of musketry, those not killed struggled to get their bearings in the smoke-filled darkness. Compounding the terror and confusion that engulfed the barn's occupants was the realization that their weapons had been stacked outside to give them more sleeping room. Overcoming their panic, the frightened and unarmed men, realizing their mortal danger, grabbed pitchforks, scythes, shovels, or anything else that was handy and fought desperately for their lives.

In their eagerness to get to the barn, the attackers had unwittingly rushed past the rail fence and corn cribs where fifty or so men, under the command of a Captain Elsinger, were sleeping. Roused by the confusion in the barn, these men quickly sized up the situation, formed, and delivered a sheet of fire into the flank of the attacking force. Hit by surprise, the fire was too much for the secessionists, who fell back in some confusion. This momentary respite gave the survivors in the barn an opportunity to escape. They wasted no time and ran into the outlying grove of trees that sheltered another portion of the command. By the time the fleeing men had reached the woods, the attackers had regrouped. They charged once again, but this time they went for both the barn and Elsinger's men. As they were almost out of ammunition, the latter had had to relinquish the advantage they had gained and retreat into the woods.[14]

The troops who had been sleeping in the woods and those who had scampered there for safety now filtered out and began forming to counterattack O'Kane's force. Before they could move, however, the secessionist cavalry arrived and charged into their flank. Unable to withstand the cavalry assault, they again fell back into the grove of timber. The cavalry attempted to follow but found it difficult to maneuver. Although a few of the horsemen remained in the trees, tentatively feeling for the enemy, most returned to the open to support their infantry.

Meanwhile, the men in Harms's barn had been formed up by captains Henry Grother and John H. Mueller. They did nothing, however, and watched the action before them almost as though it were being staged for their benefit. This may have been caused by the fact that O'Kane's men were carrying the U.S. flag; more likely, however, it was the result of immoderate consumption of alcohol just before retiring. Whatever the reason, they simply stood there formed up, until O'Kane's infantry and cavalry turned their attention to them. As soon as they began to take fire, Grother's and Mueller's men withdrew in good order from the field, and the fight was over.[15]

Now that O'Kane was in complete control of the battlefield, he was in no hurry to leave the area. Buildings and the dead, injured, and captured were systematically searched. Anything that struck an attacker's fancy immediately became his possession. The single exception involved 362 muskets that had been captured. These were badly needed by the Rebel forces, and were collected to be redistributed.

After the fight, which had lasted no more than thirty minutes, thirty-five or so of Cook's men lay dead, another sixty wounded, and about thirty had been captured. O'Kane had lost seven men and another twenty-five or so had been wounded. Late that day, the secessionists formed up with their prisoners and moved to Cole Camp, where they spent the night before returning to Warsaw.[16]

Notably absent from the contest and its aftermath was one A.H.W. Cook. The word was that the senior commander of the Home Guards had donned a disguise and departed the scene for a safer area as soon as hostilities had commenced. He later attempted to excuse his actions by saying that he was forced to leave to keep an urgent appointment to consult with Captain Totten, who was pursuing Jackson. Why he had had to leave just at that time, he found it convenient not to explain. Because Totten was near Syracuse approximately thirty miles away, whatever he might have used by way of explanation or justification undoubtedly would have been unacceptable. Even if he had had an urgent need to confer, abandoning his men at the beginning of a fight would be a strange time to do it and would not likely have been accepted by anyone as proper conduct for a senior commander.

The New York Times editorial pinpointed the real issue when it stated, in an example of considerable understatement, "The fitness of Colonel (a title he apparently assumed but there is no record that he officially held) Cook for command is quite doubtful." Actually, Cook fell short as a commander in every respect, from failing to heed properly Tyree's warning to neglecting to fortify the camp and keep the troops alert. And, given that the defenders had two to one odds in their favor when it is generally accepted that the attackers need a three to one advantage for success, it is difficult not to agree with Pvt. Cord Mueller who said, "Had we had a good captain the Confederates would not have had a chance."[17]

Jackson, now free to move south without interference and ahead of the flooding caused by recent hard rains, passed through Cole Camp on June 20. There, O'Kane reported to the governor to give him the pleasing news of the defeat of the Home Guard units in that area. This was also most welcome news to the MSG troops, who were far from jubilant following their poor showing at Boonville.

After crossing the Osage River, Jackson got more news—good and bad. The good news was that he was joined by lieutenants Henry Guibor and William P. Marlow, formerly in charge of Frost's artillery at Camp Jackson. Both officers had accepted parole but now claimed that it was not binding because it had been coerced.

The bad news was brought by the returning Colton Greene, whose unpleasant duty it was to inform Jackson that help from the South was unlikely to be forthcoming. In support of this statement, he gave the governor a copy of the letter that Secretary of War Walker had sent in response to McCulloch's request for permission to assist his northern neighbors. The letter told McCulloch in part, "The position of Missouri as a Southern State in the Union requires much prudence and circumspection. It should only be when necessity and propriety unite that active and direct assistance should be afforded by crossing the boundary and entering the State." In plain English, except in an extraordinary crisis, stay home! Jackson's fury at this response turned white hot when his messenger gilded the lily a bit by telling him that McCulloch and Pearce had five thousand well-trained, armed, and equipped troops just sitting on their hands in northern Arkansas.

Greene did bring a bit of good news along with the bad, however. He informed the governor that Price had arrived at Cowskin Prairie and had been able to add about twelve hundred men along the way. Jackson digested this along with the other news and pushed on, worried about how close Lyon was behind him. He need not have given it a thought.[18]

Lyon was still in Boonville, and it seemed as though he might be there for some time. The 1st Iowa had joined him on June 21, but his supplies and the equipment to move them had not arrived. In addition, rain had come with a vengeance and was creating major problems for him. The Missouri River was running bank full, roads were becoming almost impassable, and he could expect that every stream and river between him and his quarry would be at flood stage or higher.[19] This would not only slow him to a crawl, but it would also hamper any effort that Sturgis might make to join him in a timely manner. Jackson, moreover, would be beyond the Osage, able to move with less interference from the weather.

It was beginning to look as though Fox Jackson would elude Lyon's best efforts to track him down.

CHAPTER IX

The "Fox" Chase

While Fox Jackson and Munroe Parsons made their way south, Lyon fumed at Boonville, trying to get under way. Thus far, McClellan, the new department commander, had not interfered with him, but neither had he been of appreciable help. Perhaps that would change before long, however. Congress was about to reconvene, which meant that Frank Blair had to return to Washington. Once back on the national scene, he might be able to do something about the command situation, which still rankled the Missouri congressman. With this very much on his mind, Blair left Camp Cameron for Washington on June 22, after turning over command of the 1st Missouri to Lt. Col. George Andrews.

Those parts of Lyon's force located at points other than Boonville were moving but were still widely scattered. Sweeney, having dispatched Lyon's supplies, had left St. Louis. He arrived in Rolla on June 23 to find that the wagons he had ordered were not yet available. Not content to wait, he pressed on without them. Sigel and his two regiments were well ahead of Sweeney, and had arrived at Springfield the day after the Irishman left Rolla. Sturgis had left Leavenworth on June 25 and was en route to rendezvous with Lyon at Clinton.[1]

Sturgis was bringing a force roughly equal to Lyon's, consisting of the 1st and 2nd Kansas Volunteer Infantry regiments, four companies of Regular infantry, four companies of Regular cavalry, two companies of Regular dragoons, a company of Kansas Mounted Rangers, a four-gun battery, and a company of Regular recruits. The Regular Army men were among the toughest troops in the U.S. Army; most of them were battle hardened from earlier wars and years of service on an unforgiving frontier. Although the Kansas men lacked the experience of the Regulars, they were nevertheless sound troops—better trained and equipped than the Missourians. In addition, many of them held grudges against Missourians that dated from as long ago as 1854.

On June 23, eleven boatloads of supplies finally arrived at Boonville and were off-loaded. Unfortunately, there was no way to transport them. Quartermaster McKinstry had found his opportunity and struck hard. McKinstry, who had long been at odds with Lyon because of the hardheaded general's proclivity for ignoring supply regulations, had seen an opportunity to clip the senior officer's wings and had taken it. The quartermaster had confiscated all of the wagons that Sweeney had procured for Lyon and had dismissed the teamsters, which forced Lyon to begin scouring the countryside around Boonville for the teams, wagons, and teamsters necessary to move his supply train. He found slim pickings, as Jackson had already taken most of what had been available. Lyon, who had scheduled his departure for June 26, was now faced with another delay.[2]

Meanwhile, the 1st Iowa was getting an education about the army and army life, and it did not like most of what it saw. Although they admired the Regular Army men and attempted to emulate them in many ways, they found the discipline and punishment to which their officers subjected them unreasonable for free men. Despite their dim view of discipline and punishment and, consequently, of many of the Union officers, they did find some to admire. One of them was Frank Blair, called "the bejesus colonel" by Pvt. William P. Heustis, who wished he had a commander like him. Totten, nicknamed "Bottle-nosed Totten" because he always carried a canteen of brandy, also became a favorite for the manner in which he gave orders: "Forward that caisson, goddamn you, sir" or "Swing that piece in line, goddamn you, sir." Pvt. Eugene Ware alleged the men would walk a half mile to listen to him for five minutes anytime.[3]

The new soldiers found the army mule especially aggravating. Ware reported this contrary beast "wanted to bray at precisely twelve o'clock at night" and at that time ". . . one of them in the dark silence would send off a loud, self-conceited, egotistical bray. It would be taken up here and there until the camp was in a perfect uproar. . . ." Ware found the mule's ability to determine the hour of midnight uncanny since, according to him, "They were entirely ignorant of astronomy except as they were in the habit of observing someone coming down whom they had sent up."

Desperate to correct this disturbing habit of the mules, they implemented the advice of Cpl. Joseph O. Shannon, called "Corporal Churubusco" because of his service in the Mexican War. Corporal Churubusco had informed the group that during that fracas they had kept the mules quiet by tying bags of sand to their tails. That struck the Iowans as a perfectly reasonable solution to their problem.

On the next night, they implemented the "cure," and all went well until a mule named "Smollix" went berserk in response to the unaccustomed load at the end of his tail. It was only a matter of moments until Smollix had created bedlam, raising an immediate need to relieve him of his unwelcome burden. Pvt. Jacob M. Grimes, who had not been permitted to assist in the application of the weights, was now asked to quiet Smollix. Grimes succeeded in doing so, but only after some risk to life and limb. By the time he had finished his onerous chore, the entire camp was in an uproar, and several individuals who wore their rank on their shoulders were present at the scene of the "debagging." Suspected of the application as well as the removal of the offending weight on Smollix, and thus of causing the general state of chaos, Grimes was summarily tossed in the guardhouse. To the relief of his guilty messmates, he went quietly, saying he was ". . . too much of a gentleman to tell the damn scoundrels who put up the job."[4]

While the Iowans were adapting to military life with the Regulars, in Arkansas Ben McCulloch received a response to his request to move on Fort Scott. Brig. Gen. Samuel D. Cooper, the Confederate adjutant general, authorized him to "take a position" at that location and also to give Missouri such assistance as would "subserve the main purpose of your command." He was reminded, however, that the overriding object of his command was to "conciliate the Indian nations" and "to obtain their active co-operation . . . in prosecuting the war." In other words, stay out of Missouri, except in case of dire necessity. Assisting that state was clearly low on the Confederacy's priority list, but events were about to change this.[5]

On June 28, McCulloch became fully aware of what was happening to the north of his area of responsibility and that the Missouri forces were falling back, apparently in disorder, in his direction. Information provided by his scouts further indicated that the combined federal forces pursuing them might number as many as eighteen to twenty thousand men, while the poorly armed Missourians numbered only about five thousand. No matter what Cooper had told him, this was a situation he could not ignore. Determined to get a firsthand account of what had happened and what was in the offing, McCulloch sent word to Jackson and Price to meet him at the Arkansas border. He also wrote to Albert Pike, an influential Arkansas newspaperman, lawyer, and writer, who was the Confederate Commissioner to the Indian Nations, seeking his support. In his letter, McCulloch told him, ". . . we must meet and rally the forces of Missouri and turn this invading tide back if possible. . . . Arkansas," he added, "must make the selection between her own soil and that of Missouri for a battlefield."[6]

McCulloch also sent a letter to Secretary Walker telling him that the Missourians had been crushed and were falling back. In addition, he told the secretary, he also had information that Lyon intended to invade Arkansas and the Indian Nations. Under these circumstances, he informed Walker, he was calling on all men in western Arkansas to report to Fayetteville. With this force, he intended to drive the invaders back or, at the very least, prevent them from entering Arkansas. Using this message as a prod to obtain desperately needed supplies and equipment, McCulloch availed himself of the opportunity to tell the secretary that his "embarrassment" since coming to Arkansas had been very great and that he found himself crippled because of lack of support. He asked that something be done now to remedy that situation.[7]

With the Confederacy on notice, McCulloch left Fort Smith with his Arkansas and Louisiana troops on June 30, en route to Maysville to join Pearce. Far behind him the 3rd Texas Cavalry, also known as the South Kansas-Texas Mounted Regiment, led by Col. Elkanah B. Greer, a wealthy planter who had fought in the Mississippi Rifles under Jefferson Davis in the Mexican War, was pushing hard to overtake and join him. The addition of these troops would give McCulloch a badly needed cavalry capability.

As for Price, he was now at Cowskin Prairie, where he had found a suitable place to locate his forces on the edge of the prairie in a woodland belt. Here, he had adequate space to train his troops. In addition, it was only about three miles from Maysville and Pearce's force, should the hoped-for Confederate support develop. Price had named the location Camp Jackson in honor of the governor and, perhaps, in remembrance of the ill-fated Camp Jackson in St. Louis.[8]

Farther north of Price, Jackson and his forces had made rapid progress toward joining the MSG commander. After leaving Cole Camp, where he added some militia, Jackson went to Warsaw. There, he added militia and the four-gun brass battery that had been taken from the Liberty arsenal. By the time Sturgis had left Leavenworth, the rapidly moving Missourians were on the banks of the Osage—fifty-five miles south of Boonville—and had crossed it before the heavy rains began. As the month ended, Jackson was driving hard on Lamar, which was the rallying point established for state forces south of Boonville and north of Springfield.[9]

Lyon was no longer a viable threat to Fox Jackson and his Missourians, at least in the near term. Joining up with Price and, perhaps, McCulloch and Pearce appeared to be only a matter of time; serious interference by the opposition was unlikely. Union strength in the southwestern portion of Missouri was far less than that of the state, even without intervention from Arkansas. The Union force consisted of two regiments under Sigel, who was currently moving southwest; apparently, however, he intended to stay clear of Jackson and Price and Sweeney's small force that was staying in Springfield. Given the disposition of these forces, only Sigel appeared to have the ability to interfere with the MSG, which seemed unlikely. And, should he be inclined to fight, given his strength, he appeared to be no cause for concern. If trouble came, however, Sigel would be the one to give it.

Franz Sigel, a dark, humorless, nervous man, was a native of the Grand Duchy of Baden. Educated at the Karlsruhe Military Academy, he had had a successful career in the German army before leaving it to play a significant role in the Revolution of 1848 against Prussia. When the revolt collapsed, he fled to Switzerland and then to the United States. He obtained employment as a teacher, and, at the beginning of the war, was teaching mathematics in St. Louis. With his military background, he was a natural for the force that Blair and Lyon had created in the River City. Furthermore, he had great influence with the German-American population that flocked to his call, saying proudly, "I fights mit Sigel." Unfortunately, all of this failed to translate into success on the battlefield. At best, he was a mediocre commander, who was once described as being an "odd combination of ineptitude and ability."[10]

On orders from Sweeney, Sigel had moved out of Springfield after a short rest, intending to conduct a reconnaissance toward Arkansas through Mt. Vernon, Sarcoxie, and Neosho. Moving slowly forward in that direction, he arrived at Sarcoxie—about twenty-two miles from Neosho—late in the day on June 28. Here, he received word that Price and eight hundred to nine hundred men were encamped at Pool's Prairie, six miles from Neosho. He was told that Jackson and Parsons were fifteen miles north of Lamar, and that Rains was about a day behind them. With this information, Sigel decided that he would attack Price, capture or scatter his force, and then turn north, attack Jackson and Rains in turn, and open a line of communication with Lyon. This was a very ambitious plan for a man with two regiments.

Shortly after Sigel got under way the next morning, he was informed that Price's troops had moved to Elk Mills, approximately thirty miles south of Neosho. Because they were out of reach, he altered his plans and prepared to move north toward the main force of Missourians. Salomon, who was following him, was ordered to join by forced march; detachments were sent to Cedar Creek and Grand Falls to block roads and gather intelligence; and a company under Capt. Joseph Conrad was ordered to occupy Neosho. The remainder of his and Salomon's regiments, along with Maj. Frank Backoff's eight-gun battery, would advance toward Carthage, with the intention of intercepting the main force of Missourians at Spring River near Lamar and holding them until Lyon and Sturgis, whom he thought were close behind, could finish the pincer maneuver.[11]

The likelihood that this plan would succeed was exceedingly remote. As the month wore to a rain-soaked end, Lyon was still trying to get organized to move from Boonville. Progress was made at a snail's pace—when it occurred at all. A shortage of supplies, despite the eleven boatloads he had received—much of which had been lost in the monsoonlike rains—was a perpetual problem. The troops were unhappy and restless as a result of both this supply situation and the inclement weather. They were frequently confined to their tents all day because of driving rains, and when the rains stopped for brief periods, the men sweltered in stifling heat and humidity. As time passed, they became more and more difficult to control. Although no truly serious incidents occurred, there was a close call when the Iowa troops took exception to a Regular being "bucked and gagged."

In this form of summary punishment, the offender ". . . was seated on the ground; his hands and feet were bound; his knees were drawn up between his arms and a rod inserted so that it ran under the knees and over the arms. A stick was thrust sideways into the offender's mouth and bound there." The Iowans, who had never seen such punishment and considered it "excessive for a free man," crowded around the culprit and demanded his release. The lieutenant in charge ordered them away; but they refused to leave. At this point, the officer drew his sword and threatened them, which simply antagonized the men from Iowa, who hated Regular Army lieutenants as a group, anyway. When they still refused to disperse and began shouting, "Unloose the man," the officer called out a dozen or so of his men and ordered them to fix bayonets. The Iowans responded in kind, and only through the efforts of the senior officers of the volunteers was bloodshed avoided. The Iowans gave in reluctantly; however. They "remembered" the incident, which was added to the long list of "peeves" they had against the Regulars.[12]

The Iowa troops were "ragged and saucy" and disinclined to associate with the other troops, most of whom, even the Regulars, had come from St. Louis. As a group, the "St. Louis" troops were better clothed and equipped than the Iowans, which contributed measurably to the friction between the two groups. To offset this disparity and demonstrate their worth, the Iowans took every opportunity at drill, and later on the march, to show that they were made of better stuff. The fact that they were volunteers, always suspect in "Regular minds" and prone to actions unappreciated by that establishment, caused Lyon to have misgivings about them and not to cut them any slack. The Iowans were fully aware of his views, and they developed a hearty dislike for him as well. By their calculations, not the U.S. Army's, they were due to be discharged in July; despite what they regarded as inferior treatment and their dislike for their general, however, they wanted at least one good fight before they returned home. Lyon would see to it that they got it.[13]

Meanwhile, in Washington, things were improving in the view of the Blairs. Frank and Montgomery had been partially successful with their unrelenting pressure for the reinstatement of the Department of the West with Lyon as commander. The Department of the West was reconstituted on July 1, but not with Lyon as commander. Bates simply would not allow it, for he considered him too "rash and impolitic" for such an assignment, and he had the power to block the appointment.

This state of bureaucratic war finally achieved a temporary truce when an acceptable alternative to Lyon was found. John C. Frémont, returning from an extended stay in Europe, was selected for the post. This compromise was mutually acceptable for the time being. Bates had no objection to him; and the Blairs, who had supported Frémont in the past and felt sure that they could control him, found him acceptable. With agreement between Bates and the Blairs, on July 3, Lincoln appointed Frémont commander of the reconstituted Department of the West and commissioned him a major general.[14]

Frémont, already famous as the "Pathfinder" for his explorations in the western United States, had an impressive list of accomplishments. After an inauspicious beginning by being expelled from Charleston College, he had overcome this stigma and obtained a position as an instructor of mathematics on the U.S.S. *Natchez*. Afterward, he was able to secure a lieutenant's commission in the Topographical Engineers—an achievement virtually unheard of for a non–West Pointer. While serving in this capacity, he had initially received favorable notice for his achievements in exploration. His fame increased as he became more deeply involved in activities in the western United States, where he played a significant role in leading California's break from Mexico. In recognition of his contributions, he was appointed governor. Once again, however, he fell on hard times, when he was court-martialed by Stephen W. Kearny for insubordination as a result of his taking sides against Kearny in a dispute. Frémont was convicted, but to avoid embarrassment, he was permitted to resign by President James K. Polk.

Frémont continued his activities in California, and became wealthy when gold was found on his land. His wealth, large landholdings, and popularity throughout the state again opened the door for the "Pathfinder," who became one of California's first two senators. His fame and appeal to a broad spectrum of the electorate resulted in his becoming the first Republican nominee for president. He lost the election to Buchanan by a narrow margin of the popular vote in 1856. In addition to his own political strength, he also profited from the support of his strong-willed wife, Jessie Benton Frémont, whose father was the redoubtable Senator Thomas Hart Benton, long a power in both national and Missouri politics. This last connection, in particular, made him an outstanding candidate for success in a department centered in St. Louis.

Frémont, who had perhaps become a legend in his own mind, had inherited a situation that would have concentrated the attention of a far stronger leader than he. The condition of his command, according to Governor Yates of Illinois, was a disgrace; it needed everything. An experienced officer with a grasp of the situation would have gone directly to his new headquarters and tackled the monumental problems existing in his command, but not the famous "Pathfinder." Instead, he dallied in the East, "making the rounds," which, to be fair, included an attempt to secure supplies and equipment for his impoverished command. As an excuse for his delay in departing for St. Louis, he said that he was awaiting instructions from General Scott which, if there were ever supposed to have been any, never came.

During his lengthy preparations to go west, Frémont gave little indication that he was concerned for his subordinate, Lyon, who had an army in the field and desperately needed his support. On the contrary, he appears to have virtually dismissed him and was already concentrating on grander things—the expulsion of the Confederates from the Mississippi Valley. And, in these activities, he seemed to have the support of his superiors. At least, he had no reason to think otherwise. In taking his leave of the president, once he decided to depart Washington, he inquired about whether there were any instructions that Lincoln wished to give him. "No," Mr. Lincoln said in a response he would soon regret, "I have given you carte blanche, you must use your own judgment and do the best you can."[15]

On July 1, while Lyon struggled to leave Boonville, Price, whose supply and equipment conditions were even worse, left Cowskin Prairie, still seeking support, to meet with Pearce at Maysville. The Arkansas commander had little to offer him and was actually in no position to do so had he wished. He did agree to lend him six hundred muskets, however, and informed him that McCulloch was scheduled to arrive the next day from Fort Smith. Once McCulloch was on the scene, further discussions regarding the subject of support could be undertaken.[16]

McCulloch's men were grinding their way north through the steep, rocky, heavily wooded hills of the Ozark's Boston Mountains. As they trudged along, mile after weary mile, with rocks abusing their aching feet while heat smothered the rest of their bodies, they found little to distract them from the boredom of their grueling march. Occasionally, however, some light relief was provided by the backwoods folk who gathered to watch them pass. To these folks, who had passed their lives deep in the hills, often with little or no contact with the outside world, much of what they saw both astonished and baffled them.

At one point, one of these worthies, seeing a cannon for the first time, asked a Louisiana captain, "I say, meister, what is this yere thing?"

With a smile, the captain answered, "A cannon."

"A cannon, hey!" said the uncomprehending mountain man. "What in thunder is that fur, I should like to know?"

The captain obligingly explained.

"Well," the now enlightened native said, "that's the durndest gun ever I seed. I say, meister, how much might that ere cannon cost?"

"Oh, about two dimes like these," the captain answered with a grin, holding out two coins.

"Is them ere dimes? Well, I declare," the questioner responded, and then walked off muttering to himself about cannon and dimes, having just acquired more knowledge than he could handle for the moment.[17]

When McCulloch arrived at Maysville on July 2, he did not pause but continued to Cowskin Prairie to meet with Price. Their meeting did not go well initially. McCulloch was uneasy because he had essentially been told to stay out of Missouri and was reluctant to act without specific orders from the Confederacy. "Old Ben" also had great reservations about Price's troops. He had no trouble seeing that they were largely untrained and undisciplined, without the necessary arms and equipment men needed if they were to fight effectively. In addition, they were a ragtag group without uniforms, whose officers were distinguished by a colored piece of cloth pinned to their sleeves. This last reservation was interesting, for it came from a man who had yearned most of his life for senior command and, when he got it, refused to wear a uniform, dressing instead in velvet suits and a wide-brimmed planter's hat.[18]

Price did get McCulloch's attention, however, when he told him that Jackson and Rains were trying to converge north of Carthage with Lyon in hot pursuit. He also had word that Sigel was moving against the governor from the south in an effort to crush him between the two Union forces. Convinced that the Missourians would be cut to ribbons by Sigel and Lyon and that "Missouri [would] fall entirely under the control of the North" without his help, McCulloch decided on his own to intervene. He was also able to convince Pearce to join him in what he considered an inescapable rescue mission. As he prepared to return to his army and move it north, he wired Secretary Walker of his intent, telling him, "It will depend on his [Jackson's] fate what my future movements will be." He concluded by telling Walker that his "great object" was ". . . to relieve the Governor and the force under him."[19]

The next day, Fox Jackson and his generals, Rains, Parsons, Clark, and Slack, unaware that the much needed assistance was about to be granted, were all finally united about twenty miles north of Carthage. Their force was suffering from shortages of everything from food to clothing and weary from a grueling march that had not yet ended. Rain, floods, mud, almost impassable road conditions, and broiling heat had taken much of the starch out of them. Worse still, they were unsure of exactly what lay before or behind them. Although they were not certain of it, the "behind" they did not need to fear; ahead was another matter. Unbeknownst to them, Sigel was coming their way.[20]

Farther north around Boonville, the roads were quagmires, the temperature hovered at one hundred degrees or higher, and periodic rains continued to hammer the area. A harried Lyon, with only a small supply of rations, and short of clothing for the troops, had reluctantly decided that conditions were not going to improve. Transportation remained a major worry with only one two-horse wagon for each company of men to haul somehow all the company property—tents, desk, cooking equipment, three days' rations, and forage for the team. In addition, the wagon would also be required to act as an ambulance for the sick, as there were virtually no hospital arrangements. Nevertheless, Lyon could wait no longer. He had to move.[21]

On July 2, Lyon notified Harding that he planned to start for Springfield the next day with twenty-four hundred men. He again stressed to Harding, who was struggling to help him in St. Louis, his critical need for support and the need for the colonel to pay close attention to activity elsewhere in the state. He asked in particular that vigorous action be taken against the "disorderly," to include suppressing the State Journal, which had been especially critical of him. Having done all that he could, he huddled up with his army that night, while the weather blew up a gale and again drenched the area with heavy rain. At half past three the next morning, Lyon put the command in motion to the south.[22]

Lyon's desire to trap Jackson between his northern and southern forces had been thwarted by his long delay in Boonville, however. Only Sigel was in position to engage the Missourians before they joined with Price and gained open access to Confederate forces in Arkansas. And although they were hardly a competent fighting force, Fox Jackson's men greatly outnumbered the small group that Sigel could throw against them. The "Fox" chase might be interrupted and delayed, but it was far from over.

Brig. Gen. Nathaniel Lyon was commander of the Union forces at the battle of Wilson's Creek and the first general officer to die on a Civil War battlefield. *Kansas State Historical Society*

Maj. Gen. Sterling Price commanded the Missouri State Guard and was the senior Confederate officer at Wilson's Creek. However, to gain the support of the other Southern forces, he deferred command in that battle to Brig. Gen. Ben McCulloch, leader of the Arkansas Confederates. When McCulloch refused to follow the Union forces after the battle, Price took back his Missouri troops but failed to pursue on his own. *Library of Congress*

Brig. Gen. Benjamin McCulloch commanded all Confederate forces at Wilson's Creek. His deep distrust of the ability of the Missouri troops and their commanders led to considerable friction between him and Price, and was a major factor in his failure to pursue the Union's retreat. A self-trained military man, he had always yearned for a senior command, but when he got it he rarely wore a uniform, preferring velvet suits and a wide-brimmed planter's hat.
U.S. Army Military History Institute

Harper's Weekly depicted Lyon's troops fighting their way through a St. Louis mob after their capture of Camp Jackson. This action was a major factor in triggering open rebellion in the state. *Hargrett Rare Book and Manuscript Library, University of Georgia*

After routing the Missouri State Guard at Boonville, the Union army takes up the chase that will lead it to Wilson's Creek. *Hargrett Rare Book and Manuscript Library, University of Georgia*

STRAYED.

From the neighbourhood of Boonville, Mo. on the 18ᵗʰ inst a mischievous JACK who was frightened and run away from his Leader by the sudden appearance of a Lion. He is of no value whatever and only a low PRICE can be given for his capture. Sam.

Pro-Union cartoonists had a field day after the Southern defeat at Boonville. *Library of Congress*

As commander of the Western Department, Maj. Gen. John C. Fremont bore ultimate responsibility for Union army activity in southwestern Missouri. But the famous "Pathfinder" was so mesmerized by his grandiose plan to conquer the Mississippi Valley that he ignored Lyon until it was too late to help him.
U.S. Army Military History Institute

Harper's Weekly's depiction of Capt. David S. Stanley's dragoons charging at Dug Springs. *Hargrett Rare Book and Manuscript Library, University of Georgia*

Capt. Thomas W. Sweeny, who had lost an arm at Churubusco during the Mexican War, was very popular with his troops. He also had considerable influence over Lyon and may have persuaded him against retreating from Springfield and to attack the Southern forces at Wilson's Creek instead. *Kansas State Historical Society*

Maj. John M. Schofield (pictured as a major general) served as Lyon's chief of staff. He objected, almost to the point of insubordination, to Lyon's decision to fight at Wilson's Creek. *Library of Congress*

Col. Franz Sigel (pictured as a major general) was the author of the unorthodox "concentric surprise" battle plan employed by Lyon at Wilson's Creek. Sigel was routed when he mistakenly identified the 3rd Louisiana Infantry as the 1st Iowa Infantry. *U.S. Army Military History Institute*

Brig. Gen. Nathaniel Lyon leading the 2nd Kansas Volunteer Infantry
Regiment into battle at Wilson's Creek, by an artist who was not an eye-
witness. It was during this charge that Lyon was fatally wounded.
Richard Scott Price Collection

Lyon's death, as witnessed by Henry Lovie of *Frank Leslie's Illustrated
Newspaper. New York Public Library, Lenox and Tilden Foundations*

Capt. James Totten's artillery was an important factor in preventing the Southern forces from taking Bloody Hill. The hard-drinking Totten's colorful swearing made him a great favorite of the Iowa volunteers, who "would walk half a mile to listen to him for five minutes." *National Archives*

When Lyon was killed, command of the Union forces fell on Maj. Samuel D. Sturgis. Fearful of losing the army because his troops were getting low on ammunition, he called for a retreat. Appalled, his subordinates pleaded with him to stay: The Union troops were standing firm against the best the South could do. This advice was heeded momentarily by Sturgis, but upon hearing of Sigel's rout, he ordered his men back to Springfield. *National Archives*

CHAPTER X

War Calls on Carthage

Dawn brought clear skies on Independence Day. Lyon's troops were up at half past three that morning. Again, they pushed steadily south through the gently rolling countryside, making good progress over roads still muddy from the recent rain. As the hours dragged by, the sun made the most of the break in the weather and turned the day into an oven. Sweating in the heat and humidity, the men swung steadily past farmsteads left in the care of elderly female slaves, whose secessionist masters made themselves scarce until the area was free of Union soldiers.

As they marched, the Iowans found another way to show their disapproval of both the Regulars and their general. Placed in the rear, they "marched up the heels" of the Regulars all day, much to the chagrin of both. The heat, humidity, and constant pressure from the volunteers wore on the Regulars. When a halt was called for the day on the banks of a small stream forming part of the headwaters of the La Mine River, the Regulars were more than ready. The Iowans noted smugly that only six of their number had straggled during the day compared with more than two hundred of the Regulars.[1]

Miles to the south of them, Sigel's Germans also experienced a tough day of marching. With Salomon joined up, Sigel was ready to tackle Jackson. Early that morning, his command struck out, headed for Carthage. After twenty hard miles through the stifling heat, they stopped for the night at Carter Springs, just southeast of Carthage on the Spring River. By this time, Sigel was reasonably certain that Jackson was about eighteen miles away and thought that he faced a fairly disorganized force of about four thousand.[2]

Sturgis, who was near Clinton, and Sweeney, who was in Springfield, both took the opportunity offered by the holiday to issue proclamations. Each urged loyal citizens to join with them, promised to protect them and their property, and offered amnesty to those who were not within the fold. Sweeney attempted to reassure those who doubted by saying, "It is my duty to protect all loyal citizens in the enjoyment and possession of all their property, slaves included. That duty shall be performed."[3]

The Confederates were also on the move. McCulloch, having decided to act to prevent what he believed was imminent catastrophe for Missouri and the South, marched with Pearce into Missouri to link up with Price. McCulloch brought about three thousand men with him to augment Price's almost symbolic seventeen hundred. The two forces met near the border. After discussions with Price and a look at his troops, McCulloch sent back orders for the remainder of his command to join up by forced march. "Old Ben" and "Pap" then headed for Carthage, stopping for the night along Buffalo Creek about twelve miles from Neosho. Here, they learned that town was occupied by about one hundred Union troops. McCulloch had little concern for that. With local secessionists to lead him, he would quickly sweep up that group in the morning and press on with his rescue mission.[4]

Jackson's force was also on the move early on July 4. With their commander in chief in the lead, they traveled slowly southward through the blistering heat. Still unaware that Sigel was coming on a collision course, the footsore Missourians were more concerned about food and rest than about the enemy. Jackson had dispatched Parsons' quartermaster, a Colonel Monroe, ahead to Carthage to obtain the much needed supplies that he hoped would reach him sometime that night. As the day ended, he halted his troops about eighteen miles north of that city.

Carthage had a long memory in which the border strife with Kansas featured prominently, and that memory was definitely pro-Missouri. Consequently, Monroe and his men found a warm welcome awaiting them when they drove their supply wagons into town. The day was spent in rounding up supplies and loading the wagons for a late-evening start north to rejoin Jackson's force. As the secessionists were nearing the end of their task, word was brought to Monroe that a federal force was approaching the city. The quartermaster could not believe what he was hearing and rode out to see for himself. His doubt evaporated as his unbelieving eyes observed Sigel's advance coming steadily forward. To no one in particular, the dumbfounded Monroe asked, "Where in the hell did those Federals come from?"[5]

Monroe wasted no time in idle speculation. Obviously, the force he had seen was moving to intercept Jackson. The advancing MSG had to be warned immediately and a rider was dispatched at a gallop to inform Parsons of this new development. Monroe did not forget his quartermaster duties, either. He ordered the loading finished at top speed, and then told the teamsters to head north as fast as they could move without sparing the teams. He then returned to his observation point to obtain as much information as possible about the advancing enemy.

Later in the evening, the exhausted dispatch rider thundered up to Parsons's encampment and breathlessly relayed his message to the general. Parsons listened intently. Still smarting from criticism of his failure to move up to support Marmaduke at Boonville, he saw the courier's news as a chance to redeem himself. Before telling the governor about the information he had just received, he ordered his command to prepare to move at ten o'clock that night. Parsons then informed the governor, who called the other generals to a meeting. At first, the information evoked much skepticism; the generals found it difficult to believe that a Union force could be in a position to threaten them. After much discussion and speculation, however, they finally agreed that they had to accept the accuracy of the report. Tomorrow would probably bring trouble in large quantities. Jackson would need his entire force, as well as a bit of luck, to manage it, which meant that he could not afford to have generals with injured feelings off on their own. Therefore, he countermanded Parsons's order, directing instead that the entire command move south at daylight.[6]

Lacking any knowledge of the fight that was shaping up miles in front of them, Lyon's troops rolled out at half past three on the morning of July 5. Before they had finished their breakfast, rain began to fall. As the day wore on, the rain became intermittent, drizzling out of thin, spotty clouds, until later in the afternoon when a huge, boiling thunderstorm rolled up to lash the troops with rain and lightning while thunder boomed across the prairie. The ground beneath them instantly turned into a sucking, clinging mass of thick mud, sometimes hiding beneath pools of rain-beaten water. Everywhere along the line the teams were doubled up to drag the mud-clogged wagons forward. After twelve miles of this, daylight had vanished, and a weary army dropped almost in its tracks to rest.

The next day, a scorching sun replaced the rain. As the troops moved along, the soaked land gave up its moisture to the broiling sun, creating almost unbearable humidity-logged temperatures. This day, the Iowans were given the lead, and they charged out singing their trademark song, "The Happy Land of Canaan." Within an hour, they had opened up a half-mile gap over the Regulars. After two hours, they had a mile lead. An agitated Lyon had to send word ahead to his "Iowa Greyhounds," as he called them, for them to let the column close up. This occurred repeatedly and, each time, as soon as the Regulars appeared, the Iowans would be off again, their voices rising in song. Upon hearing it, Lyon would grumble, "There goes that damned 'Happy Land of Canaan' again." His comment reflected his demeanor—grouchy as a bear and finding fault with everything. The Iowans added this to their store of dislike for their leader.[7]

As Lyon plowed through the mud on his way south, McClellan finally responded to his June 20 request for additional troops. Although by this time Missouri had been placed under Frémont's command, "Little Mac" told Harding ". . . to direct General Pope, by telegraph, to place himself and his brigade at the disposal of General Lyon. . . ."

Harding promptly relayed the department commander's instructions to John Pope, who was not particularly interested. He was busy building his own fiefdom in northeastern Missouri and was not going to be diverted by Lyon, his adjutant general, or a superseded department commander far in the East. As a sop, he did send two small volunteer companies, but otherwise ignored the orders.[8]

While Lyon fought the mud and a lack of support, his opponents were busily engaging in less mundane activity. Scouts returning from a reconnaissance to the north informed McCulloch that he had better hurry if he intended to save Jackson. Without delay, McCulloch prepared to move forward, ordering his infantry, who would slow him down, to remain in camp and await further orders. He also had to dispose of the problem posed by the Union force in Neosho before he could leave the area. He assigned this chore to the mounted troops under Col. Thomas J. Churchill, 1st Arkansas Mounted Rifles, and Capt. James McIntosh, 2nd Arkansas Mounted Rifles. The latter was actually a colonel, but because he had not yet received a formal appointment, he refused to use the rank.

Churchill, a farmer, former postmaster of Little Rock, and Mexican War veteran, waved his troops down the Gates Road. McIntosh, who was known as an aggressive cavalry leader, headed down the Pineville Road. The distance McIntosh had to travel had been severely overestimated, which resulted in his arrival at Neosho well ahead of Churchill. Afraid of discovery if he lingered, McIntosh dismounted his men and marched them to the courthouse, covering it front and back, and sought the federal detachment commander, Captain Conrad. He demanded that officer's unconditional surrender of his detachment and gave him ten minutes in which to decide whether to surrender or fight. After discussing it, the federals gave in. When the bag was toted up, McIntosh's men had captured one hundred thirty-seven prisoners, one hundred fifty badly needed weapons, and seven wagonloads of supplies. Now, the road to Carthage was open.[9]

With Neosho disposed of, Churchill and MacIntosh returned to McCulloch's camp to present "Old Ben" with their booty. It was now very late in the day, and his sense of urgency somewhat abated, McCulloch decided to camp where he was for another night. They would start for Carthage early the next morning, which should be in plenty of time to rescue the governor. But before the night was over, he began to receive reports of heavy cannon fire having been heard in the direction of Carthage during the day. Confronted with these reports, he realized he could delay no longer but had to move immediately. With a sense of urgency restored, his troops were immediately aroused and started forward. They arrived in Neosho shortly before morning. Here, McCulloch allowed them a short rest and then sent them forward again on a forced march to Carthage, which was about twenty miles away.[10]

At daybreak the day before, north of Carthage, Jackson had sent his army forward. Out in front, volatile Jo Shelby, who had developed a real attachment to big horses and plumed hats as a leader of Border Ruffian raids into Kansas, led the way with his troop of mounted rifles. Moving at a deliberate pace, the army had advanced about five miles over the softly rolling prairie, when they spotted Colonel Monroe coming at a gallop.

The quartermaster, his horse in a lather from the already blistering sun, slid to a stop in front of the governor. "Governor, it's that little whipper-snapper Sigel," he announced. "Him and Charley Salomon! They and their Dutchmen marched through Carthage this morning in hope of finding you napping at Lamar."

The usually somber governor allowed himself a grin, looked at his generals, and replied, "Somebody should have told them that we were only cat-napping!"[11]

Sigel had also moved early, headed north, either unaware or unconcerned that McCulloch and Price were coming up behind him. In Carthage, a decidedly unfriendly town, he was able to glean the information that Jackson's men had been in town for supplies the previous day. He also learned that Jackson's army had been approximately eighteen miles to the north on the evening of that day. He doggedly pressed on, sending his footsore troops slogging through the streets under the townspeople's stony glare. On its outskirts, they struggled across Spring River, welcoming the relief it gave from the heat but also cursing the water as they fought to keep their cartridges dry. Once across the river, they plodded forward over the undulating prairie, sweat soaking their gray uniforms as they labored under full packs. They crossed Buck Branch and steadily ate up the miles until they climbed the gentle incline that crested on a rounded hill overlooking the tree- and brush-choked bed of Dry Fork Creek. As the main body topped the rise, some scattered gunfire broke out ahead of them. Their leading parties had bumped up against Jo Shelby's horsemen.[12]

With Shelby out in front, Jackson's Army of Missouri had moved steadily southward, carrying with it the memory of Boonville and its humiliation at the hands of Lyon. Today, they were determined that the story would be different. They were tired of running. It was their state, and no bunch of St. Louis "Dutchmen" would take it from them. Sweating in the heat, they pushed up a gentle slope and, at its crest, looked down on Dry Fork Creek. They halted and stared into the distance ahead. There, barely visible in the shimmering heat, a fat gray worm had already topped the opposite crest and had headed down the slope toward the creek. They, too, heard a rattle of gunfire. Shelby was engaged. That was Sigel coming straight for them.[13]

Sigel wasted no time in clearing Shelby out of his front with a few rounds of artillery fire. Rains, who wanted to protect his cavalry and was aware that Shelby could do nothing alone, ordered him back to the main line. The way cleared, Sigel moved forward again behind the retreating Missouri cavalry.[14]

Jackson had decided to make Sigel come to him, so he deployed his force in a ragged line of battle along the crest. As an army, they were anything but impressive. There were virtually no uniforms; most of the men wore the civilian clothing that they had been wearing when they reported for duty. Their weaponry was little better. Some regulation firearms were present, but they were the exception. Squirrel rifles, shotguns, and even some flintlocks brought from home constituted most of the weapons for this ragtag army. Training and discipline matched the uniforms and firearms. Some had seen service years before during the Mexican War, but most of the training and discipline had been forgotten, and the rest of the men had little idea of either. The disparaging appellation "raggedy-ass militia," sometimes unfairly used in later years by ill-informed Regulars to describe their descendants, suited them perfectly.

Their opponents stood out in stark contrast. They had formed weeks or months earlier and had received considerable training under the tutelage of officers with long military experience. Many of these troops had also been subjected to the ironhanded training and discipline of Europe and had faced combat during revolutions before emigrating to the United States. They had now been under arms long enough for this experience and discipline to have reemerged. To a man, they were equipped with U.S. Army weapons and accoutrements. Volunteers they were labeled, and volunteers they were, but in their neat gray uniforms, they looked like a professional army.

The Missourians stood quietly on the high ground and watched the gray column move down the hill and fan out into the thick vegetation clogging the creek bed. In a few minutes, the first troops broke out of the underbrush in line of battle and halted, while their commander surveyed the force ahead of him. Their thirty-two-wagon support train had been left well back on the south side of the stream, away from immediate danger. Sigel now took a few minutes to encourage them, reminded them of their heritage and the honors they had won on the battlefields of Europe, and told them of his confidence in them. He then turned for a last look through his field glasses at his enemy standing above him with the Missouri state flag flying in the center of their line and the new flag of the Confederacy whipping insolently in the wind at the ends. He knew them and their fighting record. He had no fear of attacking them from the low ground with a smaller force. A few rounds of artillery fire and there would be some "Carthage Races." He gave the order: "Forward."[15]

With disciplined tread, the gray-clad federals slowly climbed the hill, sweating in the broiling sun and probably from the fear of battle. When they were within easy artillery range of the Missouri line, the infantry dropped to the ground in response to shouted commands. Maj. Frank Backoff's two batteries under captains Theodore Wilkins and Christian Essig swung into action. Suddenly, the unnatural stillness that had permeated the field until now was shattered by the sound of federal cannon. Along the skyline, gaps suddenly appeared in the ranks of the Missourians as grape and spherical-case shot ripped into them. The panic that Sigel had expected did not occur, however. The secessionists held fast.

On top of the hill, Capt. Hiram Bledsoe and Lt. Henry Guibor had their artillery poised. Almost as an echo, it thundered a response; the chorus led by "Old Sacramento"—a cannon supposedly cast from church bells. Bledsoe had helped capture it during the Mexican War in the battle for which it was named. It was alleged to have a unique sound when fired that separated it from all others. In any event, this day "Ole Sac" had ample opportunity to exercise its "voice" as the two sides kept the field churned up with the heaviest artillery barrages they could muster. This duel raged on for at least half an hour with no major damage to either side. The grape and spherical case rounds did some damage to the Missourians, but their return fire with round projectiles did little more than make the federals seek shelter in low places. So far, the battle had been mostly noise.

Sigel, aware that he was getting the best of the artillery duel, was undoubtedly beginning to feel that his decision to attack uphill against superior numbers was being vindicated. Determined to take the heights, he ordered a skirmish line formed and prepared to move forward. Then, to his dismay, he spotted Rebel cavalry fanning out along both of his flanks. Although he did not know it, a large portion of this force was unarmed and had been ordered to the side to get them out of harm's way. The others were certainly armed, however, and were intent on doing exactly what Sigel feared.[16]

As the Missourians had prepared to move forward, Rains's horse decided he wanted no more battle. With a snort, the animal wheeled and took off for the rear. Rains's troops watched as their general, who was wearing a bright red sash for identification purposes, galloped wildly away on his uncontrollable steed. Finally, Rains was able to wrestle the horse under control and returned to the front of his troops. Now that the general was back in command after his brief side trip, his cavalry moved out, joining that on the other flank already pressing forward. With all the horsemen finally in motion, the remainder of the line began to move, led by the troops of Col.

Richard H. Weightman, who had served as a captain with the Missouri Volunteers in the Mexican War.[17]

Because he was extremely concerned about the threat that the flanking cavalry posed to his supply train, Sigel ordered his troops to fall back, and they did so in good order. At the bottom of the hill, they again pushed their way through the thick underbrush and sloshed through Dry Fork Creek, heading back toward Carthage. On the south bank, Sigel stationed a strong rear guard and three pieces of Essig's artillery. When the advancing Missourians arrived at the creek, they were greeted by a withering fire from this group. Smoke roiled across the creek bottom as the Missourians fired frantically in return, trying to dislodge the rear guard and close with Sigel's main force.

Finally, Bledsoe galloped up with his artillery and added its fire-power to that of the infantry. Under its cover, some of the Rebels pushed through the underbrush and crossed the creek only to fall back before a scathing fire coming almost directly in their faces. For almost two hours, the opposing sides struggled along this little stream, at times closing to within fifty yards, as they groped through the smoke-shrouded thicket blanketing the creek bank. Finally, the rear guard let go and moved off in the direction of its retreating comrades. As it fell back, Essig leapfrogged his three artillery pieces to keep a steady stream of artillery rounds falling among the pursuing Missourians.[18]

Doggedly following the federals, the Missourians pushed them as hard as they could, while seeking an opening to overwhelm their outnumbered foe. They appeared to have found their opportunity as Sigel's men reached Buck Branch. The Rebel cavalry troops had at last managed to outdistance Sigel's infantry and were waiting for him on the south side of the stream. Behind, the Missouri infantry pressed forward, closing in to surround and crush the federal force. Just as all seemed lost, Hassendeubel asked Sigel's permission to lead a bayonet charge at the cavalry. Sigel, who was startled by this request, seriously doubted that it would be successful, but he really had no alternative. The Missourians were upon him, and unless something were done quickly, it was doubtful that his command could survive. Bowing to the desperate circumstances, he approved.

Hassendeubel ordered three companies of the 3rd Missouri to fix bayonets and form up to charge. At his order, they started at a run, splashing through the shallow stream and jumping up on its south bank. Gaining their footing on the bank, they tore through the thin brush and plunged into the open. Without hesitation, the charged-up infantry then ran straight for the mounted troops, bayonets shining. The look of cold steel was too much for the cavalry. Without a struggle, they wheeled their horses and left in confusion. The door was now open, courtesy of this fantastic charge, so Sigel again got his wagons and troops in motion toward Carthage and safety.[19]

Spring River lay ahead, and Rains wanted to get his cavalry in position to prevent the federals from crossing. He never made it. The hungry cavalry troops paused en route to gobble down handful after handful of ripe huckleberries when they rode into a patch of bushes filled with the fruit. This delay was sufficient to deny Rains his opportunity to force a decision, and it earned his troops the deprecatory title "Huckleberry Cavalry"—a term McCulloch later loved to use in referring to them.[20]

Although this opportunity had been lost, the Missourians nevertheless continued to press as hard as they could. They caught Sigel's force at Spring River, where a hot little skirmish took place, and again at Ornduff Hill. At about five o'clock in the afternoon, the federals entered Carthage with the Missourians in hot pursuit. The hardpressed federals fought fiercely as they made their way through the town, using buildings, walls, and fences for cover.

Col. John T. Hughes of Slack's division now had the lead. He was able to maneuver his troops through the streets and bring the federals under such galling fire that they were forced to abandon the town. Hughes kept hard after them, engaging them in a final firefight at the location where they had camped the previous night. Then, as darkness fell, he let them go, and sent a cavalry company to ensure that they did.[21]

Back in Carthage, a Union scout named Owen Nichols was regaining consciousness as he lay sprawled in the dusty street. A Missouri rifle ball had knocked him out of the saddle. Landing in the street, apparently dead, he lay unmoving as the battle passed over him. Now, as he struggled to his feet, an agonizing pain ripped through his midsection. Terrified that he had been "gut-shot," he tentatively felt his stomach but found no blood. Then, with an almost overwhelming sense of relief, he realized the slug had struck him on his heavy brass belt buckle, leaving him bruised but unbloodied.

Over in the large brick courthouse dominating the town square, the locals were doing their best to minister to the wounded and injured. Among them was a teenage volunteer nurse named Myra Belle Shirley whose father owned a hotel in town. After her brother was killed, this young lady left Carthage to settle in Texas. Years later, she would return to achieve fame of a sort as the notorious outlaw Belle Starr.[22]

While Sigel stumbled on to Sarcoxie and, after a rest, Springfield, Jackson regrouped his forces to move on to Cowskin Prairie. The battle was over, and the Missourians were not interested in pursuit. It retrospect, it really had not been much of a battle, even though *The New York Times* called it "[t]he first serious conflict between the United States and the rebels. . . ." Despite all of the cannonading and small-arms fire, casualties had been mercifully light; combined losses were probably fewer than fifty killed, one hundred fifty wounded, and sixty captured. It had been a real boost for the Missourians, however. They had fought and won a pitched battle with the Union. Some of the sting of Boonville disappeared with Sigel as he marched off into the night. They could never again be taken lightly. They had served notice that they could and would fight—and fight well.[23]

The next morning McCulloch, Price, and Pearce received word that the Missourians had engaged Sigel and emerged victorious. Nevertheless, they pressed on until they contacted the governor later that day. Although he had been a winner the previous day, Jackson was relieved to see them. Undoubtedly, his hope of full Confederate support was reignited at the sight of McCulloch and Pearce. For their part, the Missouri troops were delighted to see the Confederate and Arkansas troops, and enthusiastically greeted them with loud cheers. The impression made by these new arrivals was unforgettable, as they marched in to meet the ragged Missourians. One of Jackson's men later described their feelings toward the troops they believed had come to help them save their state. He said, "[We] were all young then and full of hope, and looked with delighted eyes on the first Confederate soldiers we had ever seen, the men all dressed in sober gray, and their officers resplendent with gilded braid and stars of gold."

McCulloch was unimpressed with what he saw, however, when he reviewed the Missourians. To him, they were still an impoverished rabble, ill-equipped, ill-armed, and ill-trained. To them, the manual of arms was a great mystery and military discipline a foreign concept. Compared with them, his army, which itself was suffering from a shortage of supplies and equipment, was an elite force. He could not then, nor later, view the Missourians as a competent or effective fighting force. He did, however, bring himself to "lend" them 615 muskets and ammunition from his already meager stores.[24]

With the reviews ended and the amenities satisfied, Price resumed command of the MSG and started for Cowskin Prairie. "Pap" knew that it would take a great deal of work to whip this crew into an army and that there was very little time in which to do it. McCulloch and Pearce left, also. They had entered the state only because they believed disaster would befall the Missourians. Without even a tacit blessing of anyone to be there, they turned their troops and headed for Arkansas.

CHAPTER XI

Sortie to Forsyth

hile Lyon struggled with weather, critical supply shortages, and a rather indifferent senior command, Blair continued to rattle the establishment rafters in the nation's capital. He had reluctantly agreed to Frémont but remained uncomfortable with the selection. Blair's firsthand knowledge of the situation in Missouri, as well as his own interests, dictated that a commander in whom he had full confidence and who saw things his way be in charge there. Lyon was that man. Consequently, he continued to agitate at every opportunity for Lyon's promotion to major general and assignment as commander of the department. Bates, Gamble, and Scott were adamantly opposed and remained successful in continuing to thwart Blair's best efforts.[1]

In Missouri, Blair's protégé was driving his army hard toward the south through country that was becoming hillier and more heavily timbered. Periodic storms still hammered the troops and poured more water into the steadily rising streams. Mud remained their nemesis, slowing the wagons and men alike as they fought its sticky pull. The Iowans continued to sing the "Happy Land of Canaan," and fuel their grudge against both Lyon and the Regulars. Life was made easier, however, by the ready availability of freshly distilled, cheap whiskey, which took both the breath and fatigue away. It seemed to the troops that every house they passed had a supply of the colorless, liquid dynamite they called "white-mule" out of respect for its kick.[2]

Lyon arrived at Clinton on July 7 to find Sturgis waiting for him. Given a brevet promotion for his actions in saving his command and most of the government property when he was forced to abandon Fort Smith, Sturgis was a frontier veteran of Indian fighting who had spent time as a prisoner of war in the Mexican War. With him was tough, resourceful Capt. Gordon Granger, winner of two brevets in Mexico and another veteran of frontier fighting. Lyon's troops soon noticed that Sturgis relied heavily on this hard-swearing professional for support. Also along were the two volunteer Kansas regiments— the 1st Kansas under Deitzler, who had risked his life to bring Sharps rifles to the free-state men and had served time in jail on a bogus charge of treason brought by the proslavery forces; and the 2nd Kansas under Col. Robert B. Mitchell, who had opposed both Jim Lane and James Montgomery and had defeated Charles Hambleton of Marais des Cygnes massacre infamy in a race for a state legislative seat. The Kansas officers, as well as many of their troops, had long memories of the depredations of Missouri's Border Ruffians. They had a personal grudge to settle that transcended questions of either the Union or slavery.

The addition of Sturgis' troops brought Lyon's strength to about forty-five hundred, and all of them were on the wrong side of the Grand River that rushed before them in full flood. Fording the river was impossible, so Lyon put the troops to work building a pontoon bridge. While they worked, he seized an old scow capable of holding forty men and started ferrying troops across. By the next day, all of them had crossed, but the price had been high. The river had claimed six men, and Lyon had been forced to abandon a large amount of supplies and equipment. That night, the storms came again, hurling lightning bolts to crash among the trees, while the ground trembled from the rolling thunder.[3]

Beginning early the next day, the troops put in a sweltering twenty-five miles before reaching the Osage River, where it plunged through a thick forest west of Osceola. Like the Grand, the Osage was also a millrace running at full flood, but here, the ferry as well as several large boats had been secured. As Lyon loaded them up and started his army across, a weary sergeant rode up on a jaded mount to tell him that Sigel had been defeated at Carthage and was being pursued by Jackson's army. The courier also told him that, from what he had heard, Sigel's troops had fired ineffectively, so only a few Missourians had been killed or wounded. This was the worst of news. If Jackson got away, Lyon reasoned, he would be free to join McCulloch, and the two of them might be able to overwhelm the force he could bring against them.

Lyon ordered that a small makeshift fort be constructed on the south bank of the Osage as a precaution against a surprise attack, and continued the crossing. Tomorrow, he would move with all speed to relieve Sigel. For now, he sent a courier with a message to Sweeney suggesting that he fortify Springfield and, agitated at the news of the troops' ineffective firing, orders for him to tell Sigel to have his troops "fire low and not at random." Then, he waited as his men struggled to cross safely as the rampaging Osage tossed the ferry and boats about like chips.[4]

Early the next morning, the troops were rolled out and told to dispose of all unnecessary weight in preparation for a forced march to rescue Sigel. Everything that could be packed was placed in the wagons; the rest, even pocket Bibles, was cast aside. Here and there, a deck of cards was stashed away on the theory that its weight, unlike that of pocket Bibles, was insignificant. With the Iowans in the lead, the army headed south behind the blistering pace of the volunteers. Once again, the words of "The Happy Land of Canaan" floated over the marching men. Now, their general seemed to appreciate them. Allowing himself a grin that was more of a grimace, Lyon said, "Lord, God, see them go. . . . the damned Iowans and their Happy Land of Canaan."[5]

And go they did, over muddy roads, down briar- and brush-clogged trails, with the sun beating down on them. The heat caused men to drop from time to time, but they pushed onward, nonetheless. With short stops for rest and a quick bite of anything they could find to eat, they drove through the day and into the night. Darkness did not stop them, although they could see little—stumbling over rocks and into bushes—as they blindly walked along. Morning came and there still was no rest for the weary troopers. Then, in early afternoon, word came that Sigel was safe, and the exhausted marchers dropped in their tracks. They had marched fifty miles in thirty hours. Bill Heustis spoke for most of them when he said, "I wish I had stayed home and sent my big brother."[6]

The next day, moving at a more leisurely pace, they arrived at Pond Springs near Springfield and went into camp. Lyon stopped them short of the city because the supplies he had ordered had not arrived, and he was afraid they would plunder it.[7]

Exasperated with the failure of his supply system, he fired off a message to Harding telling him, "The failure of stores reaching here seems likely to cause serious embarrassment, which must be aggravated by continued delay, and in proportion to the time I am forced to wait for supplies. Shoes, shirts, blouses &c., are much wanted," he continued, "and I would have you furnish them, if possible, in considerable quantities."[8]

The feisty general did not spare Washington, either. He informed them forcefully that he must have reinforcements. He noted that three of his volunteer regiments were due to leave the service by mid August, leaving him with about four thousand men to face a Confederate force that he estimated to number thirty thousand. Therefore, he told Washington, he had to have an additional ten thousand troops fully supplied ". . . or abandon my position."[9]

Washington had more urgent things on its mind than Lyon's problems. In northern Virginia, the Confederates were on the move, and there was deep concern about the Union's ability to protect the capital. Mr. Lincoln, fearing for the seat of government, asked General Scott, "What force is there at Fort Washington?"

In his precise manner of speaking, the general-in-chief replied, "I think, sir, that Fort Washington could be taken now with a bottle of whiskey. At last accounts, it was in charge of a single old soldier, who is entirely reliable when he is sober."[10]

Instead of receiving the ten thousand troops he had requested, Lyon was ordered to send five companies of Regulars and Sweeney to the East. Enraged by this order, Lyon saw villainy at work. In a letter to Harding, he noted that Washington had access to all the troops of the northern, middle, and eastern states for support and that ". . . it seems strange that so many troops must go on from the West and strip us of the means of defense. But, if it is the intention to give up the West, let it be so; it can only be the victim of imbecility or malice. Scott will cripple us if he can." Then, in almost self-pity, he added, "Cannot you stir up this matter and secure us relief? See Frémont, if he has arrived. The want of supplies has crippled me so that I cannot move, and I do not know when I can. Everything seems to combine against me at this point. Stir up Blair."[11]

Lyon also fired off a letter to Washington explaining his situation and the critical need for these Regulars. In detail, he pointed out his manpower situation, noted secessionist activity within the state, reviewed the already unfair allocation of troops, reviewed the critical nature of the situation within Missouri, and outlined his desperate supply situation. He then surmised that the order to withdraw his Regulars had been given without an understanding of these facts and informed headquarters that he "felt justified in delaying execution" of the order pending receipt of further instructions. If the requested troops were lost to him, he said darkly, "Loyal citizens will be unprotected, repressed treason will assume alarming boldness, and possible defeat of my troops in battle will peril the continued ascendancy of the Federal power itself, not only in the State, but in the whole West."[12]

While Lyon's fears for the West may have been well-founded, so were Lincoln's and Scott's concerns for the East. The capital did not fall, but that may have been owing only to good fortune. On July 21, the Confederates routed the federals at Bull Run in the first major battle of the war. Indirectly, that loss was also a blow to Lyon in that the War Department's attention for sometime afterward was directed almost exclusively to the East.

While Lyon was moving to Springfield, Price moved his army to Cowskin Prairie, and Jackson left for the Confederate capital to see whether he could obtain more willing and enthusiastic help. At Cowskin, "Pap" Price faced a monumental task in whipping his congregation of Missourians into a "real" army. To begin with, there was only the semblance of a military organization—a first-priority problem that had to be resolved to create an effective army. And that would be rendered more difficult because of the scarcity of competent officers. In a military outfit too democratic to be effective, officers had been elected—many of whom did not even know how to drill their troops. Most of the officers who did have experience had gotten it at the company level during the Mexican War. The military niche that should have held the concepts and understanding of warfare was virtually a vacuum. Finding competent officers for staff positions was equally challenging. As an example, Snead, who had been with Price in St. Louis, and, by his own admission, did not know a howitzer from a siege gun and had never seen a musket cartridge, was assigned as chief of ordnance. Then, as Price struggled to get organized, he was made adjutant general—a position for which he had the same lack of credentials.[13]

Living conditions at Cowskin Prairie could only be described as abysmal. There were no tents and few blankets. Men slept under wagons or the open sky. There was no commissary, nor was there any money to buy needed provisions. Forage for the horses and mules come from what they could find on the prairie. The men lived on meager rations of cornmeal and stringy beef. The only resource in abundance was lead from local mines. Under the imaginative guidance of Maj. Thomas H. Price, local materials were converted to use in making needed ammunition. Powder bags were sewn by the troops from bolts of flannel, and canister containers were made from tin acquired from a local tinsmith. In addition to the lead, trace-chains, iron rods, and sometimes even smooth rocks were used as shot. In at least one instance, bullets were made by pouring molten lead into a silver thimble from a sewing kit.[14]

Drill and the manual of arms was taught by veterans from the Mexican War who were still able to remember how it should be done. Those who had no arms were formed into squads with instructions to follow behind the troops when combat came and to scavenge arms from the casualties without regard to army affiliation. Training in firearms was turned over to Col. John Q. Burbridge, one of the regimental commanders. Nothing if not practical, Burbridge worked them hard and taught them how to make the most of their buck and ball ammunition. He told them to aim at the enemy's breeches button, which would help overcome the tendency to shoot high and almost always resulted in a fatal wound. Besides, he noted, it generally gave the wounded man time to make peace with his Maker before he went to meet Him.[15]

Back in Arkansas, McCulloch still stewed about what he had seen in Missouri. Nothing he had observed about the Missourians had encouraged him, including their commander, whom he would dismiss as an "old militia general." He shared his concerns with the Confederate War Department, writing, "I find that [Price's] force of 8,000 or 9,000 men is badly organized, badly armed, and now almost entirely out of ammunition. This force was made by the combination of different commands under their own generals. The consequence is that there is no concert of action among them, and will not be until a competent military man is put in command of the entire force." There is little doubt who he had in mind as the "competent military man."[16]

Although McCulloch was basically accurate in his overall analysis of the army of Missouri, he did fail to consider one salient fact—the bravery and fighting ability of the individual Missourian. These men were from the stock that had whipped the British at New Orleans with Andy Jackson. Their kin had stood with Crockett, Bowie, and Travis at the Alamo and fought with Sam Houston at San Jacinto. They had also fought well alongside McCulloch himself in Mexico. Most of them, in fact, sprang from the same roots as McCulloch. He would soon be reminded of these facts when he watched them hurl themselves into the cauldron of combat against their fellow Missourians and the hated Kansans along the banks of Wilson's Creek.

He had a different view of his and Pearce's troops. With his army standing firmly across the Springfield Road north of Bentonville, Arkansas, he watched his troops drill with growing pride and confidence. Of them, he said, "They are a fine body of men and through constant drilling are becoming very efficient. I place a great deal of reliance upon them." He was almost equally confident of Pearce's Arkansans. Although the Missourians were a different matter, he did note that they "were clamorous and fretful at the delay. They wanted to drive the vandals from their homes." And he had in mind a plan that would do just that.[17]

He urged the Confederate government to strike now with the forces they had in hand in Missouri, northern Arkansas, and western Tennessee. A three-pronged attack into Missouri offered an opportunity, he believed, to overrun the state quickly and take St. Louis. His plan was for Maj. Gen. William J. Hardee, in command of a brigade at Pitman's Ferry, Arkansas, to move against Ironton, Missouri, in conjunction with a thrust into southeastern Missouri by Brig. Gen. Gideon J. Pillow from western Tennessee. McCulloch and Price would simultaneously attack Lyon from the southwest and either defeat him or tie him up until Hardee and Pillow could join to crush him. The combined forces would then grab St. Louis and secure the upper Mississippi River and the mouth of the Ohio River for the Confederacy. This grandiose concept was seriously considered by the South, but it came to naught. Maj. Gen. Leonidas Polk refused to approve it, when he discovered that Jackson had been inflating the strength of the MSG, although he did later send Pillow against New Madrid. Without approval of the plan by his senior, only a shadow force in front of him at the moment, and his own organization only partially staffed, Hardee was not interested. He told McCulloch that he was short twenty-seven hundred men and, until he had them and a full complement of artillery, ". . . [he would] with every desire to aid and cooperate with the West, be compelled at this time to forego [sic] that gratification."[18]

While Price trained and McCulloch planned, Lyon, still fighting administrative and supply problems on all fronts, decided to take some action. Earlier, the Rebels had set up a camp at Forsyth, Missouri, and had successfully defended it against at least one attempt by Home Guards under Capt. Charles Galloway and Lt. F. M. Gideon, Sr., to retake the town. Springfield was full of stories, mostly exaggerations, of widespread secessionist activity in that area and claims that the town was serving as a Rebel training camp and MSG recruiting center. This situation offered the perfect opportunity for Lyon to both defeat a Rebel group and demonstrate the ability to strike deep into the Ozark Mountains, which was widely regarded as a secessionist sanctuary. Lyon ordered Sweeney, with twelve hundred men and two guns, to capture the town and disperse the Rebel force, which was rumored to be five hundred strong, occupying it.

The morning of July 20, Sweeney started forming up his force. It consisted of five hundred fifty men from the 1st Iowa under Lt. Col. William H. Merritt, an unassuming lawyer who knew nothing about the military; two companies of cavalry under Capt. D. S. Stanley, a veteran of the frontier and Kansas who had turned down a colonelcy in the Confederate Army; the 2nd Kansas Infantry under Colonel Mitchell, which was augmented by a very undisciplined company of Mounted Kansas Volunteers that was commanded by Capt. Samuel N. Wood. Galloway and about eighty of his Home Guards also joined them.[19]

At noon, this group was given the order to march. They struck out through blazing heat, raising a dust cloud that became almost suffocating. After seven miles of this, they stopped to spend the night on the banks of the James River. After dark, the sky turned black and then flickered with lightning, as thunder crashed and rain pummeled the weary men, forcing them to crawl into any shelter they could find.

Next morning, with yesterday's dust now a sea of mud, they struck out again. Progress was slow as teams strained to drag the wagons through the clinging mud. The men slogged along, as the miles passed slowly behind, until they reached the little village of Ozark. Here, they found some large stores and a mill. They helped themselves to new boots from a "secesh" store and watched as the cavalry brought back a wagonload of whiskey that had gotten stuck in the mud when it attempted to leave town ahead of the invading troops. After a lunch of raw meat and crackers, they fell in again at the call of the bugle. Instead of moving out, however, they found the first sergeants prepared to dole out a ration of the captured whiskey to each company.

While this was being accomplished, Sweeney, much liked by the troops, rode among them. When he found a group crowding out of line, he shouted, "Right dress! Get back there, get back! Right dress there, right dress! I'm pretty drunk, but I could right dress if I were you." He wasn't, of course, but the troops loved it. After the whiskey was distributed and downed, a contented body of troops marched a few more miles and then camped for the night. As darkness fell, a drizzle began that made sleep difficult.[20]

"Boys, you have a hard day's march ahead of you today; save your strength all you can. You may have a little fight before tonight." With these words, Sweeney started his troops along their way on the morning of July 22. Saving strength was difficult. Their path led them up and down hills covered with dense growths of blackjack, hickory, and occasional bunches of pine trees, and through creek and hollow bottoms where oak, walnut, and random cottonwoods blotted out the sun. Small, crystal-clear streams running bank full had to be crossed with aggravating regularity, which soaked both feet and pants. These hills abounded in sharp flint rock called "chert," which often made walking difficult as it slid under feet or its sharp edges sliced into leather and sometimes skin. They occasionally passed by isolated, dirt-poor homesteads, whose inhabitants, for the most part, either disappeared before their arrival or silently watched them pass.

At one place, an old woman rocking to and fro on a porch was asked if there were many secessionists in that area. "No," she responded, "not so many as you might think; there are lots more Union men here than secesh." Then, as if to encourage them, she continued, "I've been reading the Bible right smart all my life, and I knowed there was going to be a war. It's prophesied in the Bible. And I've told some of these people that if they go to war they will get whipped, because it's prophesied in the Bible. The North always whips the South in the Bible, and, besides, this war was foretold and the North is to whip the South."[21]

The troops splashed across Bull Creek, Blue Creek, and into Swan Creek, which ran past one side of their objective. Swan Creek meandered waist deep down a valley in such a crooked course that the troops said they had to wade it lengthwise because every few minutes they had to cross it again. As the day wore down into early evening, scouts who were sent out to find the enemy ran into a picket post manned by three men. They managed to nab two of them, while the third ran away to warn his comrades of the approaching danger.

The captured men were hauled before Sweeney, who subjected them to an intense interrogation. Determining that there were only about one hundred fifty Rebels in Forsyth, the one-armed commander ordered Stanley to take his cavalry and the mounted Kansans ahead to surround the town. As soon as the mounted troops had departed, one of the prisoners said to Sweeney, "If that is all you have, you will get badly whipped for we have a thousand men in Forsyth."[22]

This altered story brought a rush of concern to Sweeney. Realizing that he may have sent his mounted troops against overwhelming strength, he hurriedly sent a messenger after them to tell them the revised number. Stanley was to be instructed to try merely to hold the enemy in check until the infantry and artillery arrived, if he found the enemy force to be as large as now asserted. The infantry that had already completed twenty-six grueling miles heard their commander order, "Forward double-quick. Go it, boys,—don't stop 'til you catch 'em."[23]

Stanley led the mounted troops down the valley at a gallop. Some distance from the town, he swung off through a grove of oak trees to avoid fire from Rebels thought to be stationed on a bluff overlooking the town. At the edge of the tree line, the horsemen found a field of corn with stalks high enough to hide a mounted rider. They charged ahead down the muddy corn rows and across Swan Creek directly in front of the town, which was completely deserted except for some secessionist riflemen. Here, Stanley halted momentarily and formed his troops into line. With a shout the U.S. troops charged headlong into town along the main road, while the Kansans swung to the side to enter it from the right. The Rebels greeted the charge with a blast of musket fire that dropped Stanley's horse and wounded two or three other horses and men. The Union men weathered the storm without breaking stride, however; and the cavalry pushed hard after the retreating Rebels, while the Kansans, to Stanley's disgust, stopped to loot a large store of supplies found in the courthouse. The secessionists for their part dashed for safety. Some crossed the White River, which lay behind the town, and sought shelter in the trees, while others scrambled into the timber and climbed some steep bluffs to the east of town.[24]

The group that had fled across the White River now opened fire again from the trees that sheltered them. Stanley ordered his force forward to deal with this threat. The cavalry moved, but the Kansans had swapped interest in combat for interest in loot and refused to participate. The enraged captain was forced to manage the chore with what he had. Moving toward the river, the cavalrymen sprayed the offending timber with heavy rifle fire. About a hundred rounds were enough to convince the Rebels that they had nothing to gain from further challenging the Union troops. With this issue settled, Stanley turned back to town where the Kansans and Galloway's Home Guard were busily digging through the stores in the courthouse.

Now, Lt. George O. Sokalski and the artillery came bouncing up, followed by the infantry, puffing after three miles of double-quick. Sweeney ordered the artillery to unlimber and be brought to bear on the town. Sokalski thought the order was to fire on the town. In moments, a twelve-pound howitzer coughed, and a round went whistling directly into the upper story of the courthouse, scattering bricks, supplies, Kansans, and Home Guardsmen. As the startled plunderers frantically vacated the building, two more rounds came sailing into it, fortunately causing no casualties among the terror-stricken occupants. Stanley described the scene with considerable relish, saying, "Never did rats desert a burning brush pile as did those plunderers this courthouse. They did not run out, they tumbled out, and ran, each man for his horse, mounted and spurred out of town. This afforded me both fun and satisfaction, as these fellows had quit the fight for plunder."[25]

As the infantry deployed as skirmishers and moved forward, the Rebels, who had occupied the high bluffs, opened fire. With slugs slapping the mud around the slowly moving infantry and the artillery battery, Sokalski turned his attention to this new threat. Swinging his guns around, he raked the bluffs with three rounds of grape. This was sufficient to terminate hostilities. The Rebels packed up and headed south toward more friendly environs. The infantry now moved forward unimpeded to occupy the town.[26]

It was now almost dark, and the deserted town was completely at the mercy of its captors. Sweeney ordered the troops to take only items they could use, such as clothing and food, and to leave everything else as they found it. For the most part, these orders were obeyed, except that part of the troops sought solace in a barrel of Port wine they had discovered, until an officer stopped them. They then moved out of town, leaving it largely undisturbed, and went into camp. At this time, according to Lt. John Du Bois, ". . . Captain Wood of the Kansas Rangers slipped back on some pretense and plundered everything he could find." The next morning, Pvt. Eugene Ware of the 1st Iowa reported that he had gone into town early hoping to find something of value but had found it completely stripped.[27]

At noon that day, Sweeney started his force back toward Springfield. The troops were loaded down with all sorts of supplies that had been stored in the courthouse, as well as approximately two tons of lead that had been dropped into the town well in an effort to save it. The arms and ammunition captured were distributed to the Home Guards, and the remainder of the booty was taken to Springfield.

Although Sweeney's report mentions the capture of only five prisoners, he had more than one hundred with him. Most of these were civilians who had been "fingered" by some of the locals as having secessionist sympathies or as having been involved in disloyal activities. Prisoners were the last thing Lyon needed, so all of them were promptly paroled upon swearing loyalty and swearing not to bear arms against the Union in the future. Most of the oaths were later disregarded, on the ground they had been obtained under coercion and were, therefore, not binding.[28]

About two miles from town, the Rebels had laid an ambush; but it proved unsuccessful when they fired at too great a range to do damage. They were hastily dispersed by a couple of rounds of canister. Harassment by Rebel cavalry continued, however, as the federal troops moved leisurely back toward Springfield. Scattered horsemen fired on the flanks from a distance and occasionally pressed the rear of the column. This proved to be an aggravation only, which kept the troops on edge and disrupted sleep at night. They were of sufficient concern, however, for Heustis to again lament, "I wish I was home. Why didn't I send my big brother."[29]

On July 25, the troops arrived in Springfield, after having stopped for a swim in the James River to offset the one hundred degree temperature and to wash off the dust that covered them. Their mission had been a success but, besides demonstrating the ability to strike where they pleased, they had accomplished very little. The Rebels had even been spared the pressure of pursuit, as they had been allowed to fade into the woods and then return on the heels of the departing troops. As for defiant Forsyth, its residents replaced the flag-pole that the federals had chopped down and had the Confederate flag flying almost before the invaders were out of sight. The sortie boosted the morale of the federal troops, who derived satisfaction from having whipped a bunch of Rebels in their own den. In fact, one said, "They enjoyed every bit of the trip."[30]

CHAPTER XII

"A Worse Enemy to Me"

Frémont finally arrived in St. Louis on July 25 to assume active command of the Department of the West. He found a quiet city, unimpressed that the "Pathfinder" was now in its midst with considerable control over its future. There were no crowds to greet him, no banners lining the way, and no cheering throngs as he made his way through the streets. His wife, Jessie, later said of the city's response to the new department commander, ". . . it was a hostile city and showed itself as such."[1]

The naïve, flamboyant general lost little time in alienating it further by setting up for business in the three-story Brant Mansion, which he had selected for his headquarters. Pomp and ceremony were key ingredients of Frémont's style of operation, and the headquarters soon assumed the look of a flashy stage set. His staff, many of whom were Europeans with almost unpronounceable names and no understanding of the country they were in, strutted around in glittering uniforms bedecked with gold braid the locals called "chicken guts." Confederate Gen. Albert Sidney Johnston, upon hearing of Frémont's headquarters and reading a list of his staff positions and the men who filled them, commented, "There's too much tail on that kite." Private Ware was more direct, calling his new commander an "empty, spread-eagle, show-off, horn-tooting general."[2]

In fact, Frémont was simply overwhelmed by the problems that faced him in Missouri, although the possible loss of the state in the near term was not one of them. Those remaining were sufficiently monumental, however. The population of the state was bitterly divided, guerrilla warfare and outlaw activity were rampant, political machinations of every description were consuming the state leadership, war profiteering was a growth industry, and the Confederates appeared ready to invade both in the southwest and southeast. The enormity of the task before him would have staggered a man of greater capability than the "Pathfinder." He was a boy sent to do a man's work, who lacked even the perception of what needed to be accomplished.

Instead of moving swiftly to come to grips with the major problems confronting him, Frémont went into virtual seclusion and began to work on a "grand plan" that had little, if anything, to do with them. A bodyguard of three hundred of "the very best material Kentucky could afford; average height 5 feet 11 1/2 inches, and measuring 40 1/2 inches around the breast," ensured the general could plan undisturbed. Isolated from the world and his subordinate commanders, except for when he chose to let them intrude, he labored over his ambitious and, at that juncture, unrealistic plan to split the Confederacy by taking Memphis, Vicksburg, and New Orleans. This effort left him little time or inclination to worry about his troops already in the field. Furthermore, the leaders of those troops found it difficult to obtain an audience with him or to get his attention through correspondence. And, when they did get access to him, the results were uniformly unsatisfactory. Brig. Gen. Ulysses S. Grant described the way such meetings went: "He sat in a room in full uniform with his maps before him. When you went in, he would point out one line or another in a mysterious manner, never asking you to take a seat. You left without the least idea of what he wanted you to do."[3]

Frémont, for all of his naïveté, love of pomp, and consuming desire to execute his "grand plan," was not entirely oblivious of the challenges confronting him. And at least to the extent that they threatened his principal goal, he was extremely concerned about the ability of his department to deal with them. He was particularly worried about the loss of Cairo, which would completely foil his grandiose scheme for splitting the Confederacy. Lyon was also a concern, but Frémont's fixation on the Mississippi and lack of understanding of the national significance of the scrap embroiling his western force prevented his acting decisively either to support or retrieve it.

To some extent, his lack of commitment to decisive action in the West is understandable. Springfield offered little strategically, while Cairo was potentially crucial. It could be reasonably argued that loss of this critical point would lead to the certain loss to the Union of Missouri, Kentucky, Tennessee, and perhaps other Border States. That might also mean losing the war. On a personal level, Cairo and the Mississippi potentially offered glory and enduring fame to the "Pathfinder"; Springfield offered little of either. On the other hand, while only speculation existed concerning Confederate designs on Cairo, the Missourians in rebellion had a substantial force in the field in the southwest, and the Confederates apparently were prepared to join them. At the moment, this was the only force seriously and actively threatening Union domination of the state. Unless contained, it might eventually lose the state for the Union and probably cause an impact on some Border States in the same way as would loss of Cairo. The "Pathfinder" either did not care, or did not think seriously, about this eventuality, which resulted in disastrous consequences for his southwestern forces.

Because Nathaniel Lyon was not a man to relinquish a quest once undertaken, the approach of the new department commander boded ill for him and his army. The New Englander's situation was quickly becoming critical. His troops were in desperate need of shoes and clothing, he had no money, the troops had not been paid, ammunition was running short, and he was steadily losing troops as enlistments ran out. In an effort to stem his hemorrhaging combat capability, he had Harding present his needs to the new commander at the first opportunity. When Harding got his chance, he carefully presented his commander's case for support, based on both the importance of his mission and the simple necessity of caring for the troops. In addition, he urged the department commander to take the long view by revealing that Lyon hoped to make Springfield a base for supporting an invasion of Arkansas. Frémont heard him out but, as he was engrossed in his own plan and in establishing his headquarters, did nothing.[4]

Next, Lyon dispatched Capt. John Cavender to give the department commander a firsthand briefing on the situation in southwestern Missouri and, if possible, to persuade him that it was necessary to respond promptly with the urgently needed support. When Cavender arrived, he was given a brief audience and then told to return later in the day for more detailed discussions. When he returned, he found the headquarters closed, but was finally able to talk to Capt. John C.

Kelton, Frémont's adjutant. Kelton eased Cavender's concern by telling him that action had already been taken to pay the troops and to provide Lyon with needed reinforcements. Satisfied with this information, Cavender headed back to Springfield. Neither money, although Frémont had requested two months' pay from the War Department, nor troops ever arrived.[5]

In many ways, Frémont considered himself in as desperate straits as Lyon. He also was short of arms, manpower, and money. To his chagrin, he learned that the resources that he had acquired in New York, before finally coming West, had been diverted to Virginia in the aftermath of Bull Run. Frustrated by this development and unable to get a response from the War Department, the "Pathfinder" went directly to Montgomery Blair, outlining his situation and asking the cabinet officer to use his influence to get him the needed assistance. Because he realized that he had perhaps "broken the rules" and, if not, that he might be asking others to do so, he sought to encourage the postmaster general by telling him, "This is a day for men, not rules, to govern affairs."[6]

His effort was futile. Blair wired him, "I find it impossible to get any attention to Missouri or Western matters from the authorities here. You will have to do the best you can and take all needful responsibility to defend and protect the people over whom you are specially set."[7]

Frémont now acted on the advice that he had given Blair. On July 30, he wrote directly to the president, which he justified by saying that it had previously been authorized by Lincoln, described the particulars of his situation, and asked for help. He informed his leader that he had found his new command in disorder, faced insurrection in every county, and had the enemy advancing from the south from several points. He was in desperate need of support, particularly arms and money. He could get manpower but, at present, could not support it. As a part of the letter, he told Lincoln that he desperately needed $100,000 of the unappropriated $300,000 in funds in the St. Louis Sub-Treasury. He had asked for the money and had been turned down. Now, he told his commander in chief, he intended to take it, saying, "I will hazard everything for the defense of the department you have confided in me, and I trust you for support." When the president did not respond, he took it as approval and acted.[8]

Meanwhile, Lyon was keeping the pressure on in the hope of obtaining relief from his situation. Following Cavender's and

Harding's failures to acquire the necessary support, and having heard nothing from his commander, he appealed to Congressman (Colonel) John S. Phelps for his help. The congressman immediately took steps to meet with Frémont, who greeted him cordially. Phelps repeated the litany of needs that had been previously presented. Then, in the hope of jarring the department commander into action, he gave him the additional message that Lyon wanted delivered: "The safety of the state is hazarded; orders from General Scott strip the entire West of regular forces, and increase the chances of sacrificing it."[9]

To the congressman's astonishment, instead of a sympathetic hearing and assurance of support, he got a mild lecture on the "real" situation. Frémont informed the legislator that no troops could be spared for Lyon because all available troops were needed to protect Cairo should Gideon Pillow decide to move against it, which seemed likely. Furthermore, the general told him, Lyon's situation was by no means as serious as he believed. It was impossible for Ben McCulloch to obtain and subsist a force of the size he was purported to have in the Ozarks. Anyone familiar with that region could not fail to recognize its resources were totally inadequate to support anything like that level of activity.

Phelps was stunned and then outraged at what he heard. He took leave of the general and, without delay, set off for Washington to enlist the aid of Frank Blair. Together, they were able to persuade the president that the assistance Lyon sought was crucial and to agree to provide it. But it would arrive too late.[10]

Lyon's next emissary, Dr. Frank Porter, did not fare nearly so well as the first two. The "Pathfinder" had apparently heard all he wanted to hear from Nathaniel Lyon's advocates. The good doctor was bluntly informed that Lyon had been given the guidance he needed. "If General Lyon makes a fight at Springfield," Frémont told him, "he must do it upon his own responsibility; General Lyon has his orders to fall back." In short, the little Yankee was on his own.[11]

Although Frémont had not adequately addressed the issues confronting him, he had accomplished a good deal in a short time by gaining control in St. Louis, reorganizing the Home Guards, seizing key rail lines, stopping Confederate enlistment activities in the city, and taking positive antiguerrilla actions in northern Missouri. Even so, in most respects, the Department of the West was still extremely unsettled, and the major problems in which it was embroiled were proving to be intractable. Frémont, who dealt effectively with smaller issues, simply did not have the experience, perspective, resources, nor ability to deal effectively with the sweeping problems facing him. He had contented himself with concentrating on his grand scheme, while leaving other problems and the troops in the field largely to their own fate. Consequently, his department careened along, under uncertain command and barely under control. The situation was further exacerbated because of the inattention of a central authority enmeshed in what it considered more serious problems. And, finally, the department's neglect and suffering were increased by unwise, and sometimes illegal, actions of subordinates who had their own axes to grind. Even Jessie, who never wavered in blind support of her husband, hung a small cloud when she wrote a friend, "It's making bricks without straw out here and mere human power can't draw order out of chaos by force of will only."[12]

In Springfield, Lyon worried about his situation and kept up a steady demand for "soldiers, soldiers, soldiers." The news of Bull Run brought added discouragement and with it the realization that he probably would not get the support he so desperately needed. He pressed the issue constantly, nonetheless. Schofield wrote Harding on July 27 of their need for clothing—especially shoes—noting that many of the men were barefoot and unable to march. He also again hammered home forcefully their need for reinforcement, adding that he feared the Union loss at Bull Run would prevent it. "If so," he wrote, "the next news will be of our defeat also."[13]

Lyon wrote the same day expressing his "deepest concern" over his need for troops and asking Harding to press Frémont for support as a matter of "vital importance." He was clearly frustrated over the fact that the troops had not been paid, arguing that those ending their three-month enlistment, who were about to leave, would reenlist if paid. Failure of the department to act meaningfully and promptly would, he wrote, create a circumstance in which ". . . all that is gained may be lost." He closed by telling Harding, "If the Government cannot give due attention to the West, her interests must have a corresponding disparagement."[14]

In addition to his other troubles, Lyon's troops were growing restless, fed up with bureaucratic wrangling and what they perceived to be their ineffective utilization. They were constantly on alert, answering the long roll of the drums frequently during each day in response to enemy activity in front of their pickets. Their standing orders were to remain ready to march at a moment's notice. Yet nothing ever seemed to happen. With enlistments running out, the troops lost any patience they may have once had with this constant "exercising."

Ware said his group, whose enlistment, according to their calculation, not the army's, had run out on July 20, was willing to stay, but only if they were going to have a fight. This represented the view of many of the men, but others simply wanted to go home.

Discipline was also in danger of breaking down under the stress of this "active inactivity." A case in point arose when the 1st Iowa was given a "fly-blown, putrid quarter of beef" rejected by the Regulars. They were already unhappy and became incensed by both the quality of the ration and the implication that what was not good enough for Regulars was good enough for them. A group of the Iowans formed and confronted their officers with a demand that their grievances be heard and "hell raised" about the quality of their rations. Fortunately, their lieutenant was able to talk them out of any action by giving them a patriotic pep talk about the critical need of the country for their services.

In typical soldier fashion, their anger turned to humor, and they buried the beef with full honors. As they laid it to rest, Corporal Churubusco solemnly read a passage from the "Revised Army Regulations." Then, Bill Heustis, acting according to Ware "with the air of an archbishop," closed the ceremony by saying, "My dominicca rooster can whip your dominicca rooster—you bet, you bet."[15]

All the troops were not content to wait, however. On July 26, about two thousand of them, including some Home Guards, whose enlistments had expired or were about to expire, headed back to St. Louis under Lt. Col. W. L. Wolff. The irrepressible Sweeney, who had been elected brigadier general by this group, once again found railroad tracks instead of a star adorning his shoulder as he became a brigade commander without a brigade.[16]

While Lyon waited in vain for supplies and reinforcements, Capt. Clark Wright and his Dade County Mounted Home Guards were busy gathering intelligence and scouring the country for supplies. On July 27, Wright sent Lyon the unwelcome news that the Confederates were on the move in his direction. Some intelligence indicated that their intent was to attack Lyon in Springfield, but Wright discounted that, maintaining their movements were primarily for the purpose of securing provisions and forage. He closed by informing Lyon that he had a man in Rains' camp and was scouting as far west as Lamar and as far south as the Rebel camp. He expected shortly to be able to inform him fully about intended Rebel actions.

An excited scout arriving the next day on an exhausted horse lathered with sweat caused Wright to revise drastically his intelligence estimate. Rebels, the shaken scout informed him, were on the move in considerable strength. There were between one and two thousand troops at Carthage, six hundred at Sarcoxie, and sixty at Bowers' Mills—all moving north intending to attack Springfield. Wright, who was at Greenfield and directly in the path of the reported Rebel advance, dispatched a messenger to Lyon with this new information and asked to be reinforced. Lyon responded by ordering a regimental-size force forward to his support and began planning to deal with this impending threat. When the reinforcements arrived at Greenfield, they found that the threat had not materialized and made a tired march back to Springfield.[17]

They had hardly arrived home when Lyon, who had still not heard directly from Frémont, received more bad news. First, he learned that Pillow's troops had landed at New Madrid. This, he justifiably feared, ended any hope of his reinforcement. A Confederate move to capture Cairo was one of Frémont's greatest fears and was the major reason that he had not resupplied and reinforced Lyon in response to the latter's repeated earlier requests. Now that this worst case had materialized, any inclination he may have had to respond favorably to Lyon was submerged in his anxiety to prevent the loss of Cairo. Every hand in St. Louis was turned to collecting the wherewithal to succor what Frémont perceived to be the beleaguered Brig. Gen. Benjamin M. Prentiss commanding at Cairo, who had been sending him "scare" messages for days. Scraping up the thirty-eight hundred troops he could find, Frémont staged a parade and, with much hoopla, loaded them on boats and set off downriver at their head to save Cairo. The southwestern commander was left to his own devices. Lyon could advance, retreat, or stand fast as he saw fit the "Pathfinder" had more important fish to fry.[18]

The second bit of bad news was a report from his spies that a large Rebel force was moving toward him from Cassville. This came as no great surprise, as Lyon had been expecting something of the sort ever since Sigel had failed to stop Jackson at Carthage. Based on the intelligence that he had received and his preconceived concept of likely Rebel actions, he concluded that there were three columns moving toward him—McCulloch, Price, and the force Wright had reported approaching Greenfield. His fear all along had been that the Missourians and the Confederates would be able to join their forces and confront him with overwhelming strength. This was precisely what he saw developing. Because he could not hope to overcome the combined force, which he had badly overestimated at thirty thousand, he determined to take them on one at a time. His initial attack would be directed at the main column and then, if successful in that effort, he would defeat the other two in turn. He had no inkling that the feared combining of forces had already occurred.[19]

Lyon was now beginning to show signs of wear from the strain. Ware reported that the commander never seemed still, always looked worried, and acted angry all of the time. He never seemed to sleep, was constantly on the move, poking his nose in here and there, making adjustments, correcting deficiencies, and worrying himself and the troops to distraction. Private Heustis commented, "Old Lyon is busier than a snake-doctor." Weight that he could ill-afford to lose slipped from him, and his whiskers and hair looked rattier than ever. A volatile personality, given to jerking on his hair and beard, he had a violent temper, but rarely lost control of it even when it was raging. Now, at the end of a staff meeting devoted to discussing his almost untenable support situation, the threat looming before him, and deciding on his course of action, he exploded. Banging the table with the hilt of his sword, he shouted to all who could hear, "God damn Frémont! He is a worse enemy to me, and the cause of the Union, than Price and McCulloch and the whole damn tribe of rebels in this part of the State!"[20]

Lyon was about to learn that he had overstated matters a bit, although undoubtedly his commander had left him in the lurch. A worse enemy had already formed in front of him. How serious that would be was about to be demonstrated.

After returning from Carthage, McCulloch continued to be reluctant to join with the Missourians in an offensive operation, despite their pressure on him to do so. His reluctance stemmed from several sources; chief among them were: his having been told by Price that the Missouri forces were "badly organized, badly armed, and now almost entirely out of ammunition"; his own observations and concerns about the ability of the Missourians and their commanders; and his continuing doubt that he really had authority to operate in Missouri. But he also found Lyon's position in Springfield almost too tantalizing to resist. Here, if he moved with determination, was a beautiful opportunity to destroy the Union Army in southwestern Missouri or, at worst, to isolate it completely from its base of support in St. Louis. In either event, it would be eliminated as an effective force and open the way for the Confederacy to assert itself with finality in the "Show-Me" state.

The temptation was finally too much for the Texan, who reversed his thinking on the advisability of engaging in joint operations with the Missourians. To enable them to take the field, both he and Pearce supplied Price with all of the ammunition they could spare and the three reached an agreement to commence an operation against the Union force in Springfield.

The one remaining burr under McCulloch's saddle blanket was the large number of unarmed and partly unorganized men accompanying Price's army. "Old Ben" was convinced that this group would cause major problems unless positive action were taken to eliminate its capability. To eliminate the potential trouble this group posed, he now refused to move unless Price ordered this group to remain at least one full day's march behind the last unit of the joint force. When Price ostensibly agreed, McCulloch was as satisfied as he could be, given his doubts about the Missourians in general, and indicated his willingness to advance. At Price's request, the Texan designated Cassville, Missouri, as the point at which the forces would concentrate.[21]

Price left Cowskin Prairie on July 25 and arrived at Cassville on July 28. Here, he was met by Brig. Gen. J. H. McBride and his Ozark troops. Even among the ranks of the tatterdemalion MSG, these troops were unique. For the most part, neither officers nor men had the slightest knowledge of anything military. They were democratic to a fault—freely lounged around their general's tent and addressed him as "Jedge." Because the staff consisted primarily of country lawyers, what protocol existed was copied from what they knew about courtroom practice and etiquette. Sergeants formed their companies by calling, "Oh, yes! Oh, yes! all you who belong to Captain Brown's company fall in here."

It would have been a serious mistake to have equated the looks and lack of military demeanor of McBride's men with their fighting ability, however. Typical of mountain folk, they were dead shots with the squirrel rifles they had brought with them and equally adept at using the razor-sharp knives strapped about their waists. In a fight, fear was a foreign concept. These mountaineers quickly settled in with the remainder of Price's army to await the arrival of the rest of the force.[22]

The still uneasy McCulloch arrived the next day, and immediately found two causes for additional concern. First, he was distressed to find that the Missourians were still armed principally with shotguns and ordinary rifles. Why he would have expected anything else is unclear, but the situation merely fueled his doubts about his allies.

Worry was all he could do, however, as there was nothing that could change the situation.

The second cause was something he could change. Price had reneged on his word regarding the unarmed troops, and permitted them to travel as an integral part of his armed force. McCulloch promptly confronted "Pap" about this violation of their agreement. Price pacified him by promising that the unarmed folks would march as agreed when they left Cassville. Then, while they waited for Pearce, Price deferentially asked McCulloch to draw up the order of march when they moved on Springfield.[23]

The Missouri troops, excited about becoming a part of the Confederate force they had so admired after Carthage, mixed freely with McCulloch's men. As they "shot the bull" soldier style, the Missourians related what they had heard about Lyon. "Boys," they told McCulloch's men, "old Lyon swears he will drive us into the gulf and drown us!"

That did not go down smoothly with the Texan's men. "Damn Lyon! He'll find that 'Old Ben' don't work in the lead with a cuss!" one Rebel responded. Old Ben's boys had not the slightest doubt that their leader would take the measure of this upstart Yankee once they closed on him.[24]

Pearce arrived on July 30 with Woodruff's and Reid's batteries, completing the consolidation of the Rebel forces. With Pearce's arrival, McCulloch wrote to Secretary Walker to inform him of their situation and plans. He estimated that the combined force would consist of about twelve thousand effectives—his and Pearce's well armed, the Missourians less so. He also informed Secretary Walker of the sacrifice he and Pearce had made to supply the Missourians with ammunition and their consequent need for prompt resupply, especially if the fighting dragged out. His intention, he said, was ". . . to move towards Springfield as rapidly as possible with the entire force and hope soon to put the Missourians again in possession of it."[25]

The Texan then issued instructions for the combined forces to begin to move the next morning. The line of march would be down the Telegraph Road, which ran between Springfield and Fort Smith via Fayetteville, Arkansas, and was commonly called either the Wire Road or State Road. This road followed closely the old Butterfield Overland Mail stagecoach route and, for part of its length, wound along and across Wilson's Creek. The combined force would march in three divisions with Rains's cavalry acting as advance guard and providing protection for the flanks. The First Division, commanded by McCulloch, would consist of the 3rd Louisiana Infantry, 1st Arkansas Mounted Rifles, 2nd Arkansas Mounted Rifles, 3rd Arkansas Infantry, McRae's Arkansas Infantry Battalion, Weightman's MSG Infantry Brigade, and Woodruff's Pulaski Arkansas Battery. The Second Division, commanded by Pearce, would consist of the 4th Arkansas Infantry, 5th Arkansas Infantry, 3rd MSG Division, 4th MSG Division, 6th MSG Division, 7th MSG Division, and Reid's, Guibor's, and Bledsoe's batteries. Because this division contained most of the Missouri troops, Price would accompany it. The Third Division, commanded by Brig. Gen. Alexander E. Steen, would consist of the 1st Arkansas Cavalry, Carroll's Cavalry Company, Major's MSG Cavalry Battalion, Rives's MSG Cavalry Battalion, Brown's MSG Cavalry Battalion, and Campbell's MSG Cavalry Company.[26]

Another group of approximately two thousand unarmed troops were to remain a day's march to the rear of Steen's Division. Price, as he had promised, confirmed this by issuing an order directing "All persons now in the army, but not forming part of it, and all unarmed men, . . . [to] keep at least one day's march in the rear of the Third Division." Despite his earlier promises, however, he countermanded the order as soon as McCulloch moved out. In his new order, he directed all organized but unarmed infantry units to march in the rear of the Second Division and all organized but unarmed mounted units to march in the rear of the Third Division. Those unarmed personnel not organized into units would remain a day's march in the rear of the Third Division.[27]

On the morning of July 31, as scheduled, McCulloch, in front of the leading element of the First Division, swung onto the Wire Road and headed toward Springfield. Unknown to them, there would be a bloody stop at Wilson's Creek before they reached their destination.

CHAPTER XIII

Rains's Scare

During the afternoon of August 1, Lyon moved his force out of Springfield, leaving the city's protection in the hands of a few Home Guards and civilian volunteers. He headed south taking with him about fifty-eight hundred troops and three batteries of artillery consisting of sixteen guns. Before departing, he fired off another request to Frémont for reinforcements, but did not expect the request to be honored. Still unaware that the Confederates had consolidated and unsure of their location, he was determined to learn what was happening and to defeat them if possible.[1]

August had come to Missouri with all of its summer fury. Gone were the rains that had aggravated but cooled the troops only a few days earlier. Now, unrelenting heat, cloaked in stifling humidity, held the men firmly in its grasp as they tramped forward through a cloud of smothering dust churned up by their plodding feet. They had gone only a short distance when lack of water and the accompanying thirst began to take a toll. Little relief was available, even when they found small streams or springs, as most of them had suddenly gone dry in the terrible heat. So desperate for water were the suffering men that five dollars was offered for a canteen filled with spit-warm ditch water.[2]

Nor were heat, dust, and thirst their only concerns. Now that they were headed toward combat, some of their earlier brash courage was beginning to fade. Marching over the open prairie, they felt safe enough, relaxed as much as the heat would permit and, when the opportunity arose, joked a bit. It was a different story when they reached the dark, brush-choked draws that appeared before them with increasing frequency. They were well aware that somewhere out there a Confederate force lurked, waiting to attack. And, who knew? Maybe it was in the next draw, simply biding its time, awaiting their arrival. This hung in their thoughts each time they left the open to plunge into a draw, their bodies tensed and thirst momentarily forgotten in anticipation of a Rebel bullet slamming into them from its limb-choked recesses. After ten miles of this misery, they reached Wilson's Creek and a welcome supply of fresh water. Lyon, who had now been informed by his cavalry that the opposing force was only eighteen miles from Springfield, called a halt and allowed them to go into camp.[3]

McCulloch arrived at Crane Creek that same evening and went into camp there. Pearce stopped short of McCulloch at Flat Creek and Steen pulled up some distance behind that location. Rains, out in front with the advance guard, stopped in the vicinity of McCullah's Store, or Curran Post Office as it is sometimes called, with some troops as far forward as the vicinity of Dug Springs.

During the night, Rebel scouts returned from patrol to report the Union force directly in front of the Confederate line of march. This information reached McCulloch early the following morning. He immediately sent the information to Price, telling him that he would remain at Crane Creek until the Second and Third Divisions joined him.

Upon receiving this intelligence, Price directed Pearce and Steen to move as rapidly as possible to join McCulloch. At midmorning, Pearce's troops arrived at Crane Creek while Steen, who halted near water about three miles to the rear, did not close until late in the afternoon.[4]

As soon as Pearce arrived with the Missourians in his division, McCulloch found to his disgust that the unarmed and camp followers had not been kept in the rear as promised. Because most of this group was with John Clark's Missouri State Guard Division, McCulloch asked him to send them to the rear. To his disgust, Clark refused, even after "Old Ben" explained that they would use supplies needed by the fighting men and were also likely to panic when fighting started. McCulloch, who had no authority over Clark, had to accept the latter's refusal, but it increased his distrust of the Missourians and his doubts about the capability of their commanders.[5]

The Union troops were under way again early on August 2. Lyon had also been informed during the night that his quarry was in front of him and that the Rebel forces might have combined. Once more the federals trudged forward under a blazing sun. After about six miles of sweat-soaked and dust-choked marching, they arrived at Hayden's Farm near Dug Springs at midmorning and halted. Here, Lyon's advance elements reported enemy cavalry about a mile in front of the main Union force.

Lyon now found himself in a dilemma. Although he had undertaken this march to attack the enemy, he was beginning to doubt the condition of his command. He later reported they had subsisted mostly on meat for the past three weeks, and that large numbers were suffering from diarrhea. At this point, in his view, the volunteers, who he described as poorly disciplined and inadequately clothed, were unfit to engage the enemy.

The next available water in sufficient quantity to support Lyon's force was approximately four miles ahead at McCullah's Store. That position was already occupied by Rains' troops, which Lyon estimated to number three thousand. Unwilling to face a force of that size at the moment, he prepared to stay at Dug Springs and remain disengaged. That was not to be, however, as the Rebel cavalry ahead of Lyon had observed his halt and decided to do a bit of probing to determine his intentions.[6]

As the Rebels moved up, Lyon's advance, made up of Totten's Battery and four companies of Capt. Frederick Steele's battalion, prepared to meet them. Two companies were deployed as skirmishers on either side of the road with the artillery in the center. As they prepared to move forward to engage, Totten fired a round toward the demonstrating Confederates. That was enough. They immediately dispersed, heading to the rear.

Steele, a New York–born West Pointer who had won two brevets in the Mexican War, moved to take the advantage now offered. He ordered his troops forward. For a mile and a half, they moved slowly along the narrow valley floor, skirting raised spurs, covered with scrub oak and brush, that stuck out from the enclosing hills like grasping fingers. The road at this point rose up a hill where a thick growth of timber closed in on it. At the crest, almost a mile ahead, Steele could see enemy cavalry moving into and out of the trees as they crossed and recrossed the road. Here, he received orders from Lyon to halt and hold his position unless the pressure on him became too severe.

Steele positioned Company E, 2nd U.S. Infantry, commanded by 1st Sgt. George H. McLaughlin, to the left on the crest of the last spur before reaching the foot of the hill. Behind him, Lt. Warren Lothrop and his company of general service recruits positioned themselves on the crest of the next spur prepared to back up McLaughlin. On the right, a company of mounted rifles under Lance Sgt. John Morine deployed as skirmishers at the edge of a cornfield that lay along the edge of the hills and up the valley toward the Confederates. First Sergeant William Griffin backed him up with Company B, 2nd U.S. Infantry. A bit farther back, Captain Stanley and his cavalry troop waited.[7]

When word reached Rains that his troops were engaged, he moved that portion of the advance guard not already committed, approximately four hundred men and two field pieces, forward. After about three miles, he came up on the opposing units who were lightly sparring with each other. The field pieces were deployed and began a slow fire that was largely ineffective because of the heavy growth of timber and inexact knowledge of the precise location of their targets. A group of sharpshooters was also deployed to discourage any "forward exploration" on the part of the Yankees. He then sent word back to McCulloch that Lyon was in front of him with a large force and that he was engaged with the Yankee advance at Dug Springs.[8]

The Texan responded by ordering Captain McIntosh, whose colonelcy was still not officially confirmed, forward to evaluate the situation. McIntosh took about one hundred fifty of his Arkansas troops and moved toward the reported combat. After about seven miles, he came in contact with Rains's command. Here, he deployed his men to screen them from the enemy and went forward alone to join Rains at his command position. Rains told him that the enemy was directly in front, but McIntosh was unable to confirm anything about the size and deployment of the Union force from that location. Leaving Rains, he rode ahead to make a personal reconnaissance. Moving laterally along the front from this forward position, he was recognized by some of his old troops who had remained with the Union. A few of them yelled in recognition and sent some not very well directed shots in his general direction by way of greeting. In response, he swept off his hat, bowed, and trotted back to join Rains.[9]

McIntosh told Rains he had seen a train or encampment some distance to the rear but found no evidence that he was threatened by a substantial force. He reminded the general that he had not been instructed to engage the enemy in force but was simply to determine their position and strength. Once he had accomplished that, he was expected to fall back late in the evening and take up a strong defensive position. In the event that he were attacked in force once he had positioned himself, he would be reinforced if he needed additional support. McIntosh then reiterated that Rains was not to attack Lyon's troops. With that, he started back to report his findings to McCulloch.[10]

At approximately five o'clock that afternoon, some minor activity by the Union on Rains's right made him think that they were attempting to outflank him. In response, he ordered Col. Jesse L. Cravens with one hundred fifty men forward to block the supposed flanking movement. They had pushed only a short distance through the trees and thick undergrowth when McLaughlin's company, seeing this as an attack on their position, opened fire on them. The engagement was short. It took only a few minutes of hearing the sound of bullets slapping leaves, snipping off twigs, and occasionally loosing the banshee wail of a ricochet, for the Missourians to decide this was not going to work, and they fell back.

Rains now ordered a general advance of his entire force supported by the two field pieces that had been pecking away at the Yankees all afternoon. He also dispatched a messenger to catch McIntosh and inform him that he was fully engaged by a heavy force. Again, the brunt of Rains's effort was against the Union's left, which he still apparently mistakenly believed was trying to outflank him. Soon, the struggle became intense, and both sides fired through the cloaking growth, which did little damage but created a great commotion. The pressure would soon become too great for McLaughlin, however, forcing him to fall back on his reserve. At this point, Steele ordered two more companies of infantry forward.[11]

Stanley had left his position to the rear of the Union's right, moved across the road, and taken a position on a spur to the left and slightly forward of the new Union line. As he watched, the Missourians streamed past in front of him and ran headlong into a blast from Totten's artillery. Breaking under the artillery fire and a sudden forward movement of Steele's infantry, they turned just in time to have

Stanley's cavalry slash through their formation and shatter it. This last was too much. The Missourians panicked and ran wildly to the rear to avoid the hotly pursuing Yankees, who now had their eyes on about two hundred abandoned horses. Before they could reach the horses, however, orders from Lyon arrived ordering them to retreat. Fearing that he was being cut off from another direction, Steele did so, forgoing the capture of the abandoned cavalry mounts.[12]

Behind the Union retreat, the Missourians were running pell-mell for safety. McIntosh barely had time to swing his troops in line before the rout struck him. Try as they might, he and his troops could stop only a small portion of the panicked Missourians; the rest rushed on to ford Crane Creek several miles behind. Capt. William E. Woodruff, commander of the Pulaski Arkansas Battery, reported the spectacle they presented: "General Rains' unattached Missourians in seeming hordes, came rushing south across the ford at Crane Creek, with any imaginable numbers and style of vehicle and people, mounted and on foot. . . . The disorder was terrifying and had well nigh panicked the unattached and unarmed Missourians."[13]

The 3rd Louisiana, in a forward position that provided a full view of the panic, had heard nothing from McCulloch. Taking no chances, the regimental sergeant major had the long roll sounded. At that moment, McCulloch dashed forward, according to Sgt. Willie Tunnard, ". . . fairly foaming with rage—exhausting his whole vocabulary of vituperation. . . . which was not a meager one." The Texan's rage reached even a higher plane when he was told that McIntosh had been killed. McCulloch placed great value on the Floridian whom he used as a vice commander. His loss would be irreplaceable. As McCulloch brusquely questioned troops trying to ascertain exactly what had happened to McIntosh, he bumped into an old man who said he has seen someone fitting McIntosh's description.

"Well, what was he doing?" McCulloch snapped.

"Cussin' the Missourians," was the laconic reply.

Relieved laughter swelled through the group at this, for it left no doubt about the well-being of the missing captain. McCulloch turned to ride off, saying, "The enemy have stopped to take dinner. Come on, boys, we will go and take dinner too."[14]

The battle of Dug Springs, such as it was, was over. Casualties were light on both sides, and virtually nothing material was achieved by either. The rout had won the Union an important psychological victory, however. McCulloch had never placed much confidence in the Missourians, and the infinitesimal bit he had once summoned up had now evaporated. As far as he was concerned, he had accurately described them when he said they were "splendid roasting ear foragers but poor soldiers." After the debacle, McCulloch missed no opportunity to derisively refer to the engagement just finished as "Rains's Scare" or to disparage the Missouri "Huckleberry Cavalry." His distrust of them and their leaders would have a significant impact in the days to come.[15]

On July 31, Hamilton Gamble was elected provisional governor of Missouri, confusing further an already confused political scene by giving the state two diametrically opposed governments, each claiming to represent the will of the people. On August 3, he issued a proclamation urging all citizens to work for peace and assuring them that military intervention in their affairs would soon end. Backed by Lincoln, he also offered amnesty to any in rebellion who wished to give it up and return home peacefully. Jackson retaliated on the fifth by declaring Missouri an independent Republic. Neither action appeared to impress anyone, especially Frémont, who essentially ignored both and continued with his own agenda.

Gamble had not approved of Lyon's actions, but now that they had occurred, he recognized the urgent need that he receive the support he was requesting. Consequently, the new governor made every effort, "by application in writing and in person," to get Frémont to grant promptly Lyon's requests. He wasted his time. The best he could get was an assurance from the Pathfinder's adjutant that ". . . they [Frémont and his staff] are just notified Lyon & Sigel have men enough. . . . [although] . . . they purpose to send more men in that direction as soon as possible." There is no evidence that there was any truth to either assertion.[16]

Lyon moved slowly forward again on the morning following the "dust up" at Dug Springs. The weather was again scorching hot with the temperature soaring well above one hundred degrees. The troops, many of whom were marching with bare, bloody feet and all with cracked, parched lips, had to be urged on by Lyon. About three miles after leaving Dug Springs valley, they came upon a small Confederate patrol from Marion preparing its noon meal at the spring near McCullah's Store. A few rounds from Totten's artillery put this group to flight. Lyon then moved in to occupy the camp, sending the 2nd Kansas about two miles farther on to take a position to guard against surprise. Here he waited, hoping for better intelligence concerning the Rebel army.[17]

Pvt. Daniel Matson reported that, while the troops were resting near the spring after the brief skirmish, a group of about fifty horsemen rode through the command from rear to front and stopped for water. As their horses were drinking from the small stream running out of the spring, the leader of the group asked one of the resting men to give him a drink. As the soldier handed him the water, the horseman asked, "Whose command do you belong to?"

"General Lyon's," the soldier responded. "What do you belong to?"

Finishing his drink, the horseman answered, "General McCulloch's." With that the group sank spurs to their mounts and dashed away.

Lyon, who had been resting nearby, heard the response, leaped to his feet, and shouted, "Surrender! Fire!" He was too late; the intruders were already out of range.[18]

Scouts sent out by Lyon now returned reporting that they had been unable to establish the exact location of the Rebel force. They had developed what turned out to be erroneous information that the Confederates were being augmented by a substantial force from Sarcoxie. The inability to establish McCulloch's and Price's location, although he now knew they had combined, caused him to worry that they might be moving to cut him off from Springfield. Because that city was protected by only a small, ill-trained force, he was also concerned that they might move directly on it and take it, and thus completely isolate him. News of the phantom force from Sarcoxie was also a worry because its size and intention were a complete mystery. A final concern was the state of his supplies, which were running critically low.

With this information in hand, he called his commanders to a council of war. The options available to them and the potential threats facing them were carefully and fully examined. The officers then engaged in a full and free discussion regarding the action that should be taken. Finally, Lyon asked them individually for their recommendations. Each was ready to fight if he could be assured that they could face the main Confederate force. If not, they recommended retreat because of the critical supply situation. A frustrated Lyon accepted their recommendation.

Before moving, however, the discouraged general sat down and wrote to Frémont. In his letter, he reviewed his actions to date and his tenuous situation, his inability to obtain exact intelligence, and his fear of being cut off by the enemy. He again stressed his acute need for support, noting the 1st Iowa Regiment was due for discharge on August 14 and Sigel's and Salomon's regiments August 9 through August 18. This would leave him only thirty-five hundred men with which to face a force that he estimated to be fifteen thousand. Although he acknowledged many of the opposing troops were ill-conditioned and ill-armed, their sheer numbers were too much for his current force and could not possibly be faced with the anticipated reduced force. "Prudence," he wrote, "now seems to indicate the necessity of withdrawing, if possible, from the country, and falling upon either Saint Louis or Kansas." He ended by saying, ". . . I am under the painful necessity of retreating, and can at most only hope to make my retreat good." On the morning of August 4, having held his position at McCullah's Store for over twenty hours, he reluctantly ordered a retrograde movement toward Springfield.[19]

While Lyon waited at McCullah's Store, the Confederate forces held fast at Crane Creek. Price was beside himself. Convinced that the main Union force was in front of them and that they had a great opportunity to destroy it, he urged McCulloch to attack. The Texan refused. His distrust of, and disgust with, the Missourians was complete. Further, he said that he doubted that he had the authority to operate in a "neutral" state and was waiting for guidance from his superiors. Price kept after him, pleading that they were about to lose a golden opportunity. Finally, after the discussion had become very heated, the Texan indicated he might be willing to attack, but only if he were given overall command of the Rebel forces.

"Pap" Price was incredulous. In his view, he had much more experience than McCulloch, having seen extensive duty as a brigadier general in the Mexican War and had certainly held a more responsible position in civilian life as the governor of a state. In addition, this was his state for which they would be fighting. Furthermore, he was older and held higher rank than the Texan.

"Old Ben" quickly resolved the rank issue, which could have become quite sticky. He simply refused to recognize Price's seniority in rank because his stars had been bestowed by a state, while McCulloch's star had come from the Confederate government. Furious at the effrontery of this "Texas lawman," Price stalked out of the tent and returned to his own headquarters.[20]

The next morning, having considered the matter and recognizing that he had to have McCulloch's support, Price returned to the Texan's tent. After some brief preliminary comments, Price, in a "loud imperious tone," demanded, "Do you mean to march on and attack Lyon, General McCulloch?"

"I have not received orders yet to do so, sir," McCulloch told him. Then he added, "My instructions leave me in doubt whether I will be justified in doing so."

Price, in the supercilious tone he often used in speaking to McCulloch, as if the latter were inferior, pointed out the reasons that he, Price, should command: his age, experience, senior rank, larger force, and the location of the activity. But nevertheless, he continued, ". . . if you will consent to help us whip Lyon and to repossess Missouri, I will put myself and all my forces under your command. . . . We can whip Lyon . . . and all the honor and glory shall be yours. . . . If you refuse to accept this offer, I will move with the Missourians alone, against Lyon. . . . You must either fight beside us, or look on at a safe distance, and see us fight all alone the army which you dare not attack even with our aid. I must have your answer before dark, for I intend to attack Lyon tomorrow."

McCulloch, who later said that the Missouri officers tendered command of their troops without being asked, remembered the army's lack of commissary supplies and decided all of this was a ploy to blame him if retreat were necessary. Still, he did not wish to reject the offer summarily. Buying time, the Texan told Price that he was expecting direction from his superiors and would give him an answer by the specified time.[21]

Whether or not McCulloch was really expecting correspondence from the East, it came. In late afternoon, Maj. Andrew J. Dorn arrived with a message from Maj. Gen. Leonidas Polk in Memphis. Polk informed McCulloch that Pillow was advancing into Missouri. Given the Texan's previous urging of a combined attack, he had no "wiggle room" left. If Pearce would agree, he would assume command of the combined forces. Pearce agreed.[22]

As soon as Price was informed of McCulloch's decision, he issued an order announcing the agreement, but reserved the right to take back command of his troops at his discretion. The news was not well received by the Missourians. They were well aware of McCulloch's contempt for them and regarded the agreement as an insult to their leader. They made no effort to hide their displeasure and expressed their opinion that "Pap" had ". . . won more battles in Mexico than McCulloch had ever seen."[23]

That same evening, McCulloch received some reinforcement when Col. Elkanah Greer, a Texas planter who had fought under Jefferson

Davis in the Mexican War, rode in at the head of his 3rd Texas Cavalry Regiment. The unit was almost on its last legs, however. Afraid that they would miss the fight, Greer had pushed them hard for the last five days since leaving Van Buren, Arkansas. Their march through the Ozarks had been grueling—up one hill and down another, over rocky roads that still permitted dust to churn up in the blasting heat—with brief and infrequent rest. In describing their arrival, one of the watchers reported, "They were strewed along under every tree, some sick and vomiting and others weary with fatigue."[24]

While the troops waited in camp for their leaders to decide on a course of action, rumors of every description made their way through the ranks. One of the most persistent was that Lyon was in the process of surrounding them. This threat failed to impress one of the 3rd Louisiana troopers who said, ". . . it didn't make much difference which side he attacked them on, as they were so far from home that all points of the compass seemed alike to them, and if Lyon wanted to attack us in the rear, and he were McCulloch, he would give him a pass through his camp *and then lick him like hell.*"[25]

Having finally decided to take full command, McCulloch decided to move quickly, hoping to surprise Lyon. He ordered the command to be ready to march at midnight. At the appointed hour, the command moved forward, poised to pounce on the unsuspecting Yankee army at McCullah's Store. It was gone.

Chagrined that he had been the one to be surprised, the Texan ordered his force to continue in the hope of catching Lyon before he reached Springfield. Through the sweltering night, the troops moved as quickly as they could, but to no avail. After seventeen miles, they reached Moody's Spring nearly exhausted, and McCulloch permitted them to halt and go into camp. The next day, they moved forward again and went into camp along both sides of Wilson's Creek, about twelve miles from Springfield, where they had ample water and forage.[26]

Frémont had returned to St. Louis from leading the "Cairo Expedition" on August 4. Now, for the first time, he seemed to realize that his army in southwestern Missouri was in serious trouble. He wired General Scott, "Force large in front of General Lyon." He also took belated steps to reinforce him. Col. James Montgomery and his 3rd Kansas Volunteer Infantry Regiment were ordered directly to Springfield from Leavenworth while Col. John D. Stevenson and his 7th Missouri Volunteer Infantry Regiment were ordered there from Boonville via Rolla. He could hardly have found reinforcements far-

ther away and, besides, these troops had been at their respective locations all along. They moved, but the pot was too near a boil. Before
they could arrive, Lyon would be long past needing them.[27]

As McCulloch futilely pursued, a very discouraged Lyon hustled on
back toward Springfield. His troops, like the Rebels, suffered greatly
from the heat and dust as they marched over the dry, dusty roads
under a blistering sun. For the most part, their return was uneventful
with only a casual brush with some secessionist outriders from time
to time. Still, the hard-bitten Lyon found time to earn a bit more
enmity from his 1st Iowa.

Ware had spotted an open cracker barrel in a wagon. He boarded
the vehicle and dived into the nearly empty container. While in this
position, he heard, "What the hell are you doing in there?"

Standing up, he came face-to-face with Lyon. "Getting something
to eat," he answered the general.

"Get out of there," Lyon snapped. "Where's your company?"

"On ahead," Ware told him.

"Trail arms and double-quick to your company—Go!" Lyon
barked.

Ware did so but reported the incident to his messmates. They
added it to the store of dislike they had built up for their high-strung,
frizzle-bearded little commander.[28]

Although Ware may have been "bit in the butt" in this incident, in
another he made out like a second-story man. Near a springhouse
along the way, he saw a Regular Army trooper place his shiny new
Springfield rifle against a log, while he went inside to get a drink.
Ware decided the position in which the rifle was left "was not altogether satisfactory" to him, so he moved it about four feet and
replaced it with his worn-out but shiny old weapon he called "Silver
Sue," and went in to fill his canteen.

"What do you suppose that Regular Army soldier did?" he asked.
"Why, he rushed out of that springhouse and without saying a word
he just picked up 'Silver Sue' and ran off with her. It was one of the
coolest pieces of robbery that I ever saw, and being at the springhouse made it cooler. He ran on and disappeared in the dust. There
was no alternative for me—I had to take the only gun that was left. I
smothered my indignation and also disappeared in the cloud of dust.
That evening I traded my silver watch that had been on a strike for
some time to a Regular for two packages of ammunition—80 rounds
that would fit my new gun which I called 'Orphan'. . . . I called it
'Orphan' because it had been so cruelly deserted." He concluded the

story with a bit of smug satisfaction, having upgraded his weapon at the expense of the Regulars.[29]

Arriving back in Springfield on August 5, Lyon left Sturgis about four miles outside town to guard against surprise. He then sealed off all access to the city, not against entry, but against departure. The grizzled New Englander was determined that McCulloch would not obtain any intelligence about his intentions or troop dispositions if he could prevent it. That accomplished, he had to make up his mind about his next move. The status quo was obviously not an option.[30]

CHAPTER XIV

"We'll Saber Hell Out of Them"

In the area along Wilson's Creek that was selected as the site of the Confederate encampment, the creek flows southward until it bumps into the flank of Oak Hill, which would soon be rechristened Bloody Hill. It then angles toward the left for a short distance, turns back southward, and wanders off to find the James River. Just before it turns southward after bumping into Oak Hill, its steep banks subside, it widens a bit, and the water depth drops sufficiently for a ford. At that point, the Wire Road crosses it on a northeasterly course for Springfield. In 1861, the more or less level areas along the creek bottom contained a number of farms growing corn, fruit, oats, some vegetables, and hay that offered ample opportunity for the troops to obtain supplementary rations and forage for their animals. The remainder of the area is broken into steep, sometimes blufflike, hills, broken ridges, and spurs, all covered by a heavy growth of scrub timber and considerable brush. At irregular intervals, rough gullies or small ravines slash a crooked, thicket-lined course toward the stream. Near the southern end of this stretch of Wilson's Creek, Skeggs Branch and then Terrell Creek cut their way through the rocky ground to join the main stream.

As viewed from the north, just south of Gibson's Mill and well out in front of the main army, Rains positioned his troops on the right bank of Wilson's Creek. Behind him, down the creek on the left bank with the Wire Road running beside them, McCulloch's division camped. Pearce's outfit was located still farther down the creek on the same side as McCulloch. Price set up camp on the other side of the creek just below the spot where the Wire Road crosses it. The cavalry camped immediately behind him. Just to the north of Price's headquarters and overlooking it, the land rises slowly to the crest of Oak Hill.

Making use of the shade of the trees lining the creek bank and the cool water the creek offered, the troops settled down. With activity at a low ebb, the troops lounged around, providing welcome rations for the ticks and chiggers, while their leaders tried to decide their next move. As the army waited, more and more men drifted in to swell its ranks, eager to participate in the big show they saw coming. Bugler Blocker of the 3rd Texas was a bit amused at some of the new volunteers, saying, ". . . old gray headed men came in, armed with their old squirrel rifles, a pouch of bullets, a string of patching already cut out, and a powder horn full of powder, to help the boys whip the Yankees when the fight came off."[1]

Unlike most of his troops, McCulloch was considerably less than a happy camper. His confidence had been shaken by the conduct of the Missourians and by being surprised at Lyon's departure from McCullah's Store without his knowledge. His ability to obtain any reliable intelligence about the enemy had been extremely limited. Now, owing to Lyon's action in sealing Springfield, it was virtually nonexistent. As soon as they had gone into camp, he had dispatched scouts toward the city and foragers to other areas. All returned empty-handed regarding the status of enemy forces. As remarkable as it seems, McCulloch could not even determine whether the streets of Springfield were barricaded. The Texan blamed much of this on Rains, although he had himself joined scouting parties with no more luck than the hapless Missourian.

The Texan's unhappiness was exacerbated by Price's unrelenting insistence that McCulloch press forward and attack Lyon, which "Old Ben" would not do without more information about the size and disposition of the federal forces. In his view, the Missourians, with great knowledge of their own country, should have been able to provide him the desired intelligence. They had not done so, despite promises that they could and would. Now, in response to their entreaties, he let them know that he was not inclined to launch a blind attack on Springfield. In fact, he was beginning to think that retreating to Arkansas might be a more attractive alternative. He even mentioned this possibility once or twice, although he later claimed it was only to needle the Missourians into obtaining the information he needed. But it was still a viable alternative. Therefore, when Price pressed him too hard, he bluntly told the Missourian ". . . he would order the whole army back to Cassville rather than bring on an engagement with an unknown enemy!"[2]

On August 8, Price finally received some definitive word from Springfield. Two ladies, who were devoted to the Southern cause and anxious to aid Price, had succeeded in obtaining permission from Lyon to leave the city. Once free, they hurried toward the Confederate camp, traveling a circuitous route through Pond Springs to conceal their intentions. Upon arrival at Price's headquarters, they informed the general ". . . that Lyon was greatly perplexed; that he was in constant expectation of being attacked; that he had kept his men under arms all the time; and that he was getting ready to abandon Springfield."[3]

Price hurried to McCulloch's tent to report this latest information, and vouched for the trustworthiness of the ladies. The Texan listened to the information but indicated no interest in responding to it. The Missourian pressed him for an answer, insisting that it was imperative that they attack at once. McCulloch told him he would think about it and give him an answer that evening. Price reluctantly accepted the answer and returned to his headquarters.

After the Missourian departed, McCulloch decided to try once more to obtain the intelligence that he felt he must have. First, he dispatched Capt. A. V. Reiff with a company of Arkansas cavalry to reconnoiter as close as possible to Springfield and to map a route through Union lines. Next, he called McIntosh to join him. After some discussion, McIntosh assembled some scouts and, with McCulloch accompanying them, rode out of camp headed north.

McCulloch returned late in the evening but failed to call on Price as he had promised. Instead, he went to his tent and turned in. Unknown to Price, Reiff had informed the Texan that Lyon was much weaker than they had thought. What the Texan saw on his own went unreported. Price was left to stew in his tent.[4]

Early the next morning, Price, determined to wait no longer, dispatched Snead to McCulloch's headquarters to demand the answer promised the night before. Snead hurried there, but almost as soon as he arrived, Price galloped up to the Texan's tent, obviously enraged. Without ceremony, he demanded, "General McCulloch, are you going to attack Lyon or not?" McCulloch gave a quiet, noncommittal response.

Price would no longer be put off by noncommittal answers. In a loud, almost insulting tone of voice he said, "Then I want my own Missouri troops, and I will lead them against Lyon myself if they are all killed in action, and you, General McCulloch, may go where the devil you please!"[5]

The Texan realized that his hand had been called. Despite his previous thoughts and comments, the idea of retreat was not very attractive under the current circumstances. Furthermore, in view of Price's demand, he could no longer threaten the Missourian with it. He had to take a stand, one way or the other, but he wanted a bit more time. To calm Price and to give himself the needed time to think, he told the irate Missourian that he would convene all the generals at Price's headquarters that afternoon for a council of war. Somewhat mollified, "Pap" left, returning to his tent to await that afternoon's meeting.

As promised, all the general officers were at Price's early in the afternoon. McCulloch was still opposed to an attack because of his doubts about the accuracy of his intelligence and his overriding distrust of the Missourians' ability to perform effectively in combat. Once the generals had gathered, the Texan patiently explained his great unwillingness to attack and thoroughly discussed most of the reasons for it, omitting mention of his lack of confidence in a portion of the command. Price would have none of it, telling him again ". . . if orders were not forthwith issued for a forward movement, he would resume command of the Missouri troops and himself give battle to Lyon, be the consequences what they might."

Unwilling to split the force and commence what would probably be a disastrous retreat, McCulloch resignedly yielded to Price's demands, which had been supported by the other Missouri generals. The decision made, he laid out a plan that required the army to march in four columns, converging on Springfield just at daybreak to rejoin and attack the city. He then dismissed the generals with orders to be prepared to move at nine o'clock that evening.[6]

Publication of the orders for the attack caused a great deal of excitement throughout the camp. Preparation began immediately, as men scrambled to prepare for tomorrow's momentous happenings. Ammunition was of great concern. General Pearce said, "The scene of preparation . . . was picturesque and animating in the extreme. The question of ammunition was one of the most important and serious, and as the Ordnance Department was imperfectly organized and poorly supplied, the men scattered about in groups, to improvise, as best they could, ammunition for their inefficient arms. Here, a group would be molding bullets—there, another crowd dividing percussion-caps, and, again, another group fitting new flints in their old muskets. They had little thought of the inequality between the discipline, arms, and accoutrements of the regular United States troops they were soon to engage in battle, and their own homely movements and equipments"[7]

Finally, it was done, but the men continued moving restlessly about, trying to wear off the anxiety building inside them. Some even engaged in a little impromptu dancing. Few seemed to give much heed to the fact the Angel of Death was waiting just up the road in a Yankee uniform.

Precisely at nine o'clock, the order to move out was given. The troops had scarcely begun to move when a light rain started to fall. Immediately, a halt was ordered, and the men were told to rest on their arms in formation. Lack of proper equipment for the army had stopped the march almost before it had started. The Confederates had very few ammunition boxes; instead, they carried their ammunition in cloth sacks. McCulloch knew that movement in the rain would result in the loss of much of their ammunition, which could not be replaced short of Fort Smith. Thus, to continue the advance would result in rendering the army virtually incapable of combat. Even Price did not object to the halt.[8]

The army remained in this position for the remainder of the night. Wracked by uncertainty and suspense and extremely uncomfortable, the men lay in wait. Swarms of mosquitoes brought out by the rain attacked them by the millions, making an already miserable night almost unbearable. Pickets that had been called in were not replaced, either through oversight or because their officers expected to move momentarily. Even the horses remained hitched to the artillery, awaiting a decision to move or retire. And while the Rebels lay in discomfort, ignorant of the intentions of their officers, to the north their fate marched steadily toward them.[9]

Upon arrival in Springfield on August 5, Lyon found that his expectation of nothing had been fulfilled. He had received no supplies, no reinforcements, and no word from his commander. The weight of his burden and being abandoned by those who should have been supporting him were beginning to grind him down. He no longer appeared to be the cocksure little scrapper that he had in the past, for matters were not going his way, and it showed.

At last the tough little Yankee, for whom retreat was close to anathema, was forced to begin to consider and accept the idea that he might have no alternative. The odds were fully stacked against him— his command was slowly dissipating as enlistments expired, an enemy that outnumbered him at least two to one was in front of him and moving to attack, and he had no hope of securing reinforcements on time. Still, if retreat were unavoidable, as it appeared, Nathaniel Lyon would not go quietly and unobtrusively, for that would have been totally out of character. Instead, he thought that, if he had to retreat, he would leave behind at least a bloodied Rebel nose.

His pugnacious attitude was not all just Yankee pride and stubbornness. A retreat in any direction would expose the federal army to attack by the Confederates while they were strung out in line of march. The best they could expect was to be "nibbled to death" by the gray cavalry that would be able to strike almost at will, as Lyon had a very small mounted force with which to counter them. A retreat, unless something were done to disrupt the Rebel force, would certainly result in heavy losses in both manpower and matériel, and might result in the loss of the entire army. That was unacceptable to Lyon. And, of course, there was always the possibility that an attack to disrupt the enemy would result in a decisive victory.[10]

Lyon now ordered Sturgis and Andrews to prepare their brigades for an attack on the Rebel advance guard. They were to be ready to march at six o'clock on the evening of August 6, striking the enemy by surprise under cover of darkness.

Then, in early afternoon, Capt. Job Stockton sent word from Grand Prairie that he had made contact with the Rebels just west of Springfield. In response to this information, Lyon dispatched two companies to support Stockton. He then ordered Sturgis and Andrews to anticipate an order to march at ten o'clock that night. He also called out part of the 1st and 2nd Kansas and Osterhaus's battalion to prepare to march in support of Sturgis and Andrews. The entire army continued to be kept on a high state of alert, and was required to respond to roll call several times throughout the day.[11]

Lyon was beginning to show signs of fatigue and an inability to concentrate on the major problem at hand. In addition to the tactical and strategic concerns about the employment of his force, he was besieged by "civilian problems." Noncombatants crowding the city were clearly on the verge of panic. Large numbers of them were preparing frantically to evacuate, while a constant stream of new refugees poured in from the outlying countryside. Members of this frightened group, including various city officials, were constantly interrupting Lyon with demands for one thing or another, which made it nearly impossible for him to concentrate on his immediate task. Aware that he needed to maintain the image of a strong, caring federal presence, he valiantly tried to maintain a concerned demeanor and to respond as best he could to all demands.[12]

So preoccupied was Lyon by these and other distractions that he failed to notice the time slipping away. The proposed departure hour arrived and passed without being acknowledged. At midnight, Lyon finally departed his headquarters, sending orders ahead for Steele to scout forward and locate the enemy pickets. Three hours later, at the head of the second force he had alerted, he arrived at the departure point. Consulting his watch, he realized for the first time that the night had slipped away. He held a hurried consultation with his commanders and canceled the attack. The entire force was ordered back to Springfield, with a small force ordered to set up an ambush at the city's edge to prevent a surprise attack. As they rode along on the return journey, Lyon told Schofield ". . . that he had a premonition that a night attack would prove disastrous, and yet he had felt impelled to try it once, and perhaps would do so again, 'for my only hope of success is in a surprise.'"[13]

There was, indeed, little light on the general's horizon to give him hope. Later, in a black mood, he confided to an associate, "I begin to believe our term of soldiering is about completed. I have tried earnestly to discharge my whole duty to the Government, and appealed to them for reinforcements and supplies; but, alas, they do not come, and the enemy is getting the advantage of us."[14]

Throughout daylight hours, Rebel scouting activity and rumors of enemy activity kept the federal force in a constant state of agitation, which repeatedly forced the men to stand ready in the broiling August sun. Lyon recognized this situation could not be allowed to continue indefinitely. He had to do something quickly. On the evening of August 7, he called his officers to a council of war. During this meeting, which stretched late into the night, their situation and

options were discussed in minute detail. Deitzler and Mitchell wanted to fight. Sturgis and Schofield counseled retreat—the latter so
forcefully that it bordered on insubordination. As the discussion wore
on, it became obvious that retreat was the sensible thing to do. But
there was disagreement even about that, as some wanted to go to
Rolla, while others opted for Kansas. Lyon listened fitfully to the discussion, at times seemingly forcefully restraining himself from speaking. His later comments reflected that he was thinking about retreat,
but only after a bit of a fight. In his opinion, a "stubborn contest
would be a better guarantee" of a successful retrograde movement.
"A bold dash, if skillfully made," he explained, "would astonish the
foe and bewilder his judgment, even though it might not succeed in
routing him."

The officers were not persuaded by this nor by additional arguments that a retreat would leave loyal citizens unprotected to suffer
all manner of indignity. To retreat without resistance would also
reflect poorly on national arms and commitment, their commander
told them, but to no avail. Finally, the meeting broke up but no final
decision had been reached. As they left, Lyon gave orders for the
army to prepare to break camp. Clearly, Lyon was not convinced, but
he appeared to be "leaning" in the direction of retreat. What he
would do before retreating, if anything, he had not revealed.[15]

Sweeney, who was by no means comfortable with the meeting and
what he perceived to be its results, hurried to call on his commander,
who had returned to his quarters in the Boren House. When Sweeney
arrived, Lyon came out on the back porch, and the two began an
emotional discussion. Sweeney argued forcefully against a retreat, to
some extent reiterating Lyon's earlier remarks at the meeting by
pointing out its negative impact on the citizenry and the great boost it
would give the morale of the opposing army. In a bit of rebuttal,
Lyon stated that their supplies were short. Furthermore, the possibility could not be ignored that the Confederates would surround them
and prevent any effort to replenish them. It was possible that they
could simply be starved out. At this, the emotional Irishman turned
red in the face, waved his remaining arm, and in an impassioned
voice said, "Let us eat the last bit of mule flesh and fire the last cartridge before we think of retreating."

The reticent Lyon smiled at this outburst and promised Sweeney he
would think about it. The captain had hardly left the porch when
Surgeon (Captain) Florence M. Cornyn, a longtime Blair man,
appeared. He, too, urged that any thought of retreat be abandoned.

Again, the general assured his visitor that he would think about it and returned to his quarters.[16]

Apparently, the two visitors were sufficiently convincing to push the commander firmly in favor of a fight, if indeed he had ever considered anything else. The next morning, Maj. Alexis Mudd, Sigel's quartermaster, came into Lyon's headquarters and asked, "When do we start back, General?"

"When we are whipped," came the snappy answer. "Not until then."[17]

The next day was brightened by a wagon train of supplies, which included shoes, that arrived from Rolla. Ware was not particularly impressed, however, saying, ". . . I know of no benefit it brought our regiment except a few shoes, and a lot of love-letters from home and the girls. . . ." Still, it was a boon for those who had been hobbling barefoot across the rough countryside. There were no reinforcements nor any mention of them, however. Outside the city, the sniping, light skirmishing, and picket fighting continued. Inside the city, the troops were becoming restless, worn by constant alerts and the brutally hot weather. The volunteers were extremely unhappy, and made it clear that they would stay for a battle and no longer. Lyon called another council of war.[18]

When the officers had gathered, Lyon opened the meeting, saying, "Gentlemen, there is no prospect of our being reinforced. . . . It is evident that we must retreat. . . . Shall we endeavor to retreat without giving the enemy battle beforehand, and run the risk of having to fight every inch along our line of retreat, or shall we attack him in his position, and endeavor to hurt him so that he cannot follow us? I am decidedly in favor of the latter plan. I propose to march this evening . . . throw our whole force upon him at once, and endeavor to rout him before he can recover from his surprise."

That was it. The die was cast. The order was accepted, but the officers asked for a short delay, as much of the command was fatigued and needed rest before marching out again. Before Lyon could give a final answer, Sigel took the floor. He was for fighting and did not oppose the delay, but he had a plan he wanted implemented. His proposal was that the army be split in two with Lyon commanding one element and he commanding the other. He then would take his element, circle the enemy, and strike him from the rear simultaneously with Lyon striking him in the front in what he called a "concentric surprise." The officers present where unanimous in their rejection of this idea. Lyon then told them that they would depart the next evening at dusk and strike the Rebels at first light on August 10.

The next morning, Sigel again approached Lyon with his plan for a "concentric surprise" and, during a long meeting, convinced him to agree. Having finally gotten his way, Sigel started to leave, but then hesitated and asked his commander whether he ". . . should attack immediately [when in position] or wait until . . . appraised of the fight by the other troops."

"Wait until you hear the firing on our side," Lyon told him.[19]

Given the views of his other officers and considering Sigel's poor performance against Jackson at Carthage, it is surprising that Lyon agreed to a plan that required him to divide his meager force and that essentially allowed Sigel to act unilaterally. On being questioned about it later, Lyon is alleged to have responded, "Frémont won't sustain me. Sigel has a great reputation, and if I fail against his advice it will give Sigel command and ruin me. Then again, unless he can have his own way, I fear he will not carry out my plans."[20]

Schofield, still convinced that retreat was the correct option and that history would sustain him in his opinion, was obviously surprised when Lyon told him of the plan. "Is Sigel willing to undertake this?" he asked.

"Yes, it is his plan," came Lyon's curt response.[21]

Fred Steele minced no words when Lyon told him about it on the march that evening. Shaking his head, the Regular Army man told his commander, ". . . you have made a mistake, our command is too small to divide, and Sigel is not to be trusted with a separate command."[22]

At noon, Lyon finally heard from his commander. The letter, written August 6, had been sent by special locomotive to Rolla and then by fast messenger to Springfield. For the first time, Frémont was showing concern for the situation of his field commander. No copy of this letter has been found, but Schofield, who was allowed to read it, said it contained instructions that ". . . *if Lyon was not strong enough to maintain his position as far in advance as Springfield, he should fall back toward Rolla until reinforcements should meet him* [italics Schofield's]."

It was too late. Lyon had made his decision and would not back down now. For weeks he had made known his needs and literally begged his commander for the support he considered rightfully due him. He had been left on his own. Now, he would make the best of it. Calling Schofield, he prepared a response to Frémont. In it, he told his commander, "I find my position extremely embarrassing, and am at present unable to determine whether I shall be able to maintain my ground or be forced to retire. I can resist any attack from the front, but if the enemy move to surround me, I must retire. I shall hold my ground as long as possible, though I may without knowing how far, endanger the safety of my entire force. . . ." Not a word that in a few hours he intended to throw the entire game on the table to win or lose it all.[23]

Springfield was in turmoil. As the day wore on, Lyon and his staff were busy putting the final touches on their plan of attack. Sweeney had ridden in to complain about "Sigel's Plan" and Cornyn added his support, but Lyon refused to change. The civilian population was in an uproar in response to widespread rumors that the army was preparing to abandon them and retreat. Amidst this civilian excitement, the troops scurried around throughout the afternoon drawing ammunition, preparing rations, and acquiring any other supplies or equipment they felt was needed for the coming battle.[24]

Late in the afternoon, cavalry under Stanley and Wood defeated a patrol of Price's cavalry and took several prisoners. From them and through intelligence obtained by a patrol led by Capt. G. Harry Stone, Lyon confirmed the Confederate force's position, that it was fully united, that the Rebels were in no better shape than he for supplies, and that the Southerners planned to attack Springfield the next day.[25]

As the sun edged toward the western horizon, the troops were placed in formation, prepared to march. As they waited for the command to move, they saw the scruffy little general, who would take them in harm's way the next day, ride up slowly. After a brief discussion with his officers, he rode slowly from outfit to outfit and stopped at each to speak to them in subdued tones. His message was the same at every location: "Men, we are going to have a fight. We will march out in a short time. Don't shoot until you get orders. Fire low—don't aim higher than the knees; wait until they get close; don't get scared; it's no part of a soldier's duty to get scared."

Men who needed inspiring, not lecturing, were unimpressed. Heustis, undoubtedly still wishing for his big brother, spoke for most when he asked, "How is a man to help being skeered when he is skeered?"

Ware had an answer that reflected great insight into the tough little Yankee. He thought the speech was just the kind Lyon would make. "His idea was duty," he said, "every soldier was to him a mere machine; it was not the 'duty' of a soldier to think, and hence he was not to get scared until his superior officer told him so. Lyon might have spoken a few sentences," he continued, "that would have raised his men up to the top notch and endeared himself in their memory for all time; but that was not Lyon; he did not care to endear himself to anybody."

The men much preferred the speech Sweeney gave to his cavalry. The ebullient Irishman jiggled his empty sleeve as he gave them the word—short and to the point. "Stay together, boys," he said, "and we'll saber hell out of them."[26]

They were now ready to move. Behind local scouts, Pleasant Hart and Parker Cox, Lyon's portion of the command left about five o'clock in the afternoon with Company B, 1st U.S. Infantry, under Capt. C. C. Gilbert, a veteran of Vera Cruz in the Mexican War, leading the way. This company was a part of the 1st Brigade, under Sturgis. The brigade consisted of four companies of the 1st U.S. Infantry, commanded by Capt. Joseph B. Plummer; the 2nd Missouri Infantry Battalion, commanded by Osterhaus; Company I, 2nd Kansas Mounted Infantry and Company D, 1st U.S. Cavalry, administratively under Sweeney; and Company F, 2nd U.S. Artillery (6 guns), commanded by Totten. Next, came the 3rd Brigade under Andrews, consisting of the 1st Missouri Infantry, commanded by Andrews; four companies of the 2nd U.S. Infantry, commanded by Steele, and Du Bois' Battery (4 guns), under 2nd Lt. John V. Du Bois. The 4th Brigade under Dietzler, consisting of the 1st Kansas Infantry, commanded by Dietzler; the 2nd Kansas Infantry, commanded by Lt. Col. Charles W. Blair; the 1st Iowa Infantry, under Merritt (their commander Col. John F. Bates was hospitalized in Springfield); and a group of Home Guards commanded by Wright completed Lyon's force.

Lyon's group of about forty-four hundred men would proceed generally west down the Little York Road until opposite the leading elements of McCulloch's left flank. At that point, it would make a sharp left, cross Grand Prairie, and assume a position that would permit it to strike the left front of the enemy column.

Sigel left about half past six that evening. His 2nd Brigade was composed of the 3rd Missouri Infantry, commanded by Lt. Col. Anselm Albert; the 5th Missouri Infantry, under Salomon; Company I, 1st U.S. Cavalry, commanded by Capt. Eugene A. Carr; Company C, 2nd U.S. Dragoons, under 2nd Lt. Charles E. Farrand; and Backoff's Battery (6 guns) under lieutenants Edward Schuetzenbach and Frederick Schaefer. The strength of this command totaled about twelve hundred.

Sigel would move down the Yokermill Road. After traveling a sufficient distance to pass the Rebel front, he would swing southwest, move along the Rebel right flank the length of their column, and then turn north to position himself in the enemy rear, blocking the Wire Road, which was the Rebel's only escape route. If Sigel's and Lyon's movements were completed as planned, McCulloch would be caught by surprise in a pincer and annihilated.[27]

Because surprise was the goal, little noise would have been expected, but just the opposite was true. No sooner were they under way than the 1st Iowa let loose with their "Happy Land of Canaan." Their singing worried Lyon—not because of the noise—but because he felt their levity might indicate an inability or unwillingness to fight. Whatever the case, he remarked that he would soon give them an opportunity to show what they were made of. He need not have worried.

The light rain that spotted the area shortly after dark ended early in the evening, having done little other than smother the earlier high temperature and partially settle the dust. The troops moved easily along in the cooler temperature under a sky filled with ragged clouds—their way illuminated by starlight as there was no moon. Had the earlier rain not grounded their opponents, the two columns might well have passed in the night with neither detecting the other.

After a time, the Kansans joined the Iowans in singing. Perhaps both groups were trying to hide their fear of the approaching battle, although Ware denied they had any such feelings. Joking also took place in the ranks as they marched along. Ware said, "The boys gave each other elaborate instructions as to the material out of which they wanted their coffins made. Bill Heustis said he wanted his coffin made out of sycamore boards, with his last words put on with brass tacks, which were: 'I am a-going to be a great big he-angel.'"

About midnight, the noise trailed away as the marchers saw cavalry passing mounted on horses whose hooves had been muffled. They also noticed that blankets had been wrapped around the wheels of the caissons and wagons to muffle the sound. About one o'clock in the morning, the sky ahead began to glow from the reflection of enemy campfires. They had met no pickets; nor had scouts in front found any. Lyon's hoped for surprise seemed a certainty. At this point, he gave the order to halt, and the troops dropped on their guns, glad for a break before the fighting started. Ware went right to sleep, saying, "I had made up my mind that if we were going to have a battle I certainly would not get killed, but might need all of my strength and ability in getting away from the enemy's cavalry."[28]

At the head of the column, Lyon and Schofield prepared to share a rubber blanket. Schofield thought Lyon looked "down" and ". . . was oppressed with the responsibility of his situation, with anxiety for the cause, and with sympathy for the Union people in that section." As they got situated, Lyon looked at Schofield and said, "I am a believer in presentiments, and I have a feeling that I can't get rid of that I shall not survive this battle." He paused for a few seconds, then added, "I will gladly give my life for a victory."

The two men huddled on the blanket, leaning back against the rocks to feel the warmth from the heat they radiated. As they sat there, waiting for the dawn and sufficient light to attack, Schofield inquired about his commander's comfort. "I'm quite alright," the tough little Yankee answered. Then, reflecting the determination that had driven him to this point and with which he would go forward at daybreak, he added, "Back in Connecticut, where I come from, I was born and bred among rocks."[29]

Surrounding and within the little Ozark valley ahead of them rested a wildly disparate group of fighting men who would meet "the varmint" in the morning. Emigrants from Europe, dirt farmers, Texas cowboys, cane-break Cajuns, politicians, plantation owners, business men, Border Ruffians, Kansas Jayhawkers, mountain men, hillbillies, gentry, and hard-bitten frontier army men composed these armies. Men among them such as Frederick Steele, Danridge McRae, David Stanley, and James McIntosh, along with sixty others, would wear general's stars. Others, such as James Butler "Wild Bill" Hickok, Frank James, Cole Younger, and William C. Quantrill would gain fame or infamy in other pursuits. But first, they all had to dance with the devil the next day amid the scrub oaks and thick brush along Wilson's Creek.[30]

CHAPTER XV

"The Cannings Is A-Firin'!"

Daylight finally appeared, beginning with some faint streaks of light in the east, and then slowly pushing away the darkness, as the sun grudgingly climbed above the horizon. A very light breeze was blowing softly across the prairie, carrying with it coolness that belied the scorching heat full day would bring. With the first light, Lyon ordered the troops roused. Their sergeants quietly woke them, saying, "Get up! Fall in. Keep silent. Not a damn sound, do you hear?"

As soon as they had fallen in, he formed them into line of battle with Plummer's four companies on the left, Andrews's regiment in the center, and Osterhaus's battalion on the right. The remaining forces formed up behind them in reserve, with Company D, 1st Cavalry and Wright's Home Guards designated to watch the wagon train and halt stragglers. With the line formed, he started his army forward shortly after five o'clock that morning.[1]

A mile or so ahead of him, Col. James Cawthorn, leading the Rebel advance guard, was nervous, perhaps because he realized that there were no pickets out. To allay his concern, he ordered a patrol out at daylight. They had proceeded almost a mile, when they bumped into scouts leading the federal force. The patrol hurriedly returned with this surprising news. Cawthorn immediately dispatched word of the federal movement to Rains and ordered Col. De Witt Hunter, with about three hundred men, forward to determine whether or not the federal force was in strength.[2]

On Cawthorn's left and slightly to his rear, Col. B. A. Rives was camped with another three hundred men. One of his men, a Captain Croucher, who had been scouting a short distance out in front, raced in to tell the colonel ". . . that the enemy was approaching and was within less than 400 yards."

Rives immediately ordered twenty scouts out to determine the strength and intention of the Union force. Simultaneously, he instructed his teamsters to move the wagons back to a safer location and told the remainder of the force to form a line of battle. Before any of this could be accomplished, the Yankees poured over the hill and opened fire. This sudden assault was too much; Rives ordered his unit to fall back on the main force.[3]

As soon as Rains heard the report of activity in his front, he dispatched Col. John F. Snyder to determine what was going on. Shortly, the colonel returned at a gallop. Sliding his horse to a stop, he told Rains, "The Federals are coming in great force! Their soldiers and cannon cover the whole damn prairie!" Rains promptly waved Snyder to the rear with orders to notify Price as quickly as he could.[4]

Meanwhile, Hunter moved forward close to the Short Farm when, from the top of a ridge, he spotted the main federal force. At about the same time, Lyon spotted him and ordered Totten to open up. A two-gun section under Sokalski unlimbered and opened fire. In the face of the artillery rounds, Hunter relinquished any thought of engaging the federals and began to fall back toward his unit.

Cawthorn, upon hearing the artillery, deployed the remainder of his force, about six hundred men, to block any advance. When Hunter reached Cawthorn's position, he was ordered to dismount his troops, move the horses to the rear, and place his men in the already established battle line. On his left, Rives, already under fire, was retreating.[5]

Lyon hurried his troops forward at the double-quick as soon as Hunter began to retreat. Reaching the crest of the hill in front of them, the federals saw that they faced a deep ravine, and on the up-slope behind it were Cawthorn's massed troops. Lyon now ordered Deitzler to bring his 1st Kansas in line to the left of the 1st Missouri.

Map 2. The Wilson's Creek battlefield, 1861

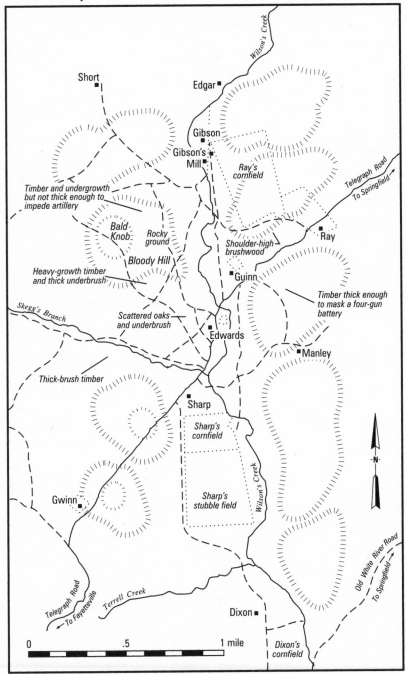

Wilson's Creek

Short

Edgar

Gibson

Gibson's
Mill

Ray's
cornfield

Telegraph Road
To Springfield

Timber and undergrowth
but not thick enough to
impede artillery

Bald
Knob

Rocky
ground

Ray

Shoulder-high
brushwood

Bloody Hill

Heavy-growth timber
and thick underbrush

Guinn

Timber thick enough
to mask a four-gun
battery

Skegg's Branch

Scattered oaks
and underbrush

Edwards

Manley

Thick-brush timber

Sharp

Sharp's
cornfield

Wilson's Creek

Gwinn

Sharp's
stubble field

-N-

Old White River Road
To Springfield

Telegraph Road
To Fayetteville

Terrell Creek

Dixon

0   .5   1 mile

Dixon's
cornfield

On hearing the order, Deitzler, undoubtedly savoring his chance for revenge for the indignities Kansas had suffered at the hands of the Border Ruffians, stood up in his stirrups and shouted to his troops, "Boys, we've got them, damn them!"

As the 1st Kansas rushed forward at the double, Totten, who had limbered his cannon, hurried behind them to provide artillery support, but he never had the opportunity. Without hesitation, the Kansas and Missouri regiments came down on Cawthorn, forcing him to retreat quickly up the slope and over the crest of Oak Hill. The excited pursuers, charging hard after the Missourian, topped the crest and saw the entire Confederate army sprawled across the valley in front of them.[6]

Sigel had moved at first light, also. Carr's troops, out in front, had advanced a mile or so when they spotted forty Rebels busily stripping fields of any vegetables they could find. Without firing a shot, they captured the lot, which prevented their sounding the alarm. Later, one of the prisoners explained the ease of their capture by telling Farrand that they had mistaken the federals for reinforcements who were expected from Louisiana.

A short distance farther along, Sigel's command came out on top of a low hill. From this point, he had an unobstructed view of the Confederate cavalry camp sprawled out just west of Wilson's Creek. Sigel immediately ordered four guns of Backoff's battery unlimbered and positioned to fire on the Rebel camp. He then directed Salomon to move forward, with cavalry protecting his flanks, to block the Wire Road. Sigel then deployed the remainder of his force in line and waited for Lyon to start the battle.[7]

McCulloch and McIntosh had gone at daybreak to Price's headquarters. They found him just sitting down to a breakfast of coffee, beef, and cornbread, and, at his invitation, joined him. They had just started to eat when Snyder galloped up on his lathered horse and shouted, "Lyon with twenty thousand men and a hundred pieces of artillery is within a mile of this camp!"

"Oh, pshaw, that's another of Rains's scares," McCulloch said laughing. "Tell General Rains I will come forward myself directly."

In another minute or two, a second messenger thundered up and confirmed the first report. "Oh, nonsense!" McCulloch snapped. "That's not true."[8]

Price stood up and walked outside, looking up at Oak Hill. Everywhere in front, he saw men scrambling wildly through the brush, running toward the main camp, while looking back over their shoulders. Behind them, standing out in the light of the newly risen sun, were the lead elements of an army moving purposefully toward his camp. McCulloch and McIntosh joined him in time to see a flash on the crest of the hill and to listen to the following roar of Totten's cannon. Like an echo, a responding blast bellowed in their rear as Schuetzenbach and Shaefer answered Lyon's call to war.

Price ordered the long roll sounded and told Snead, "Have my horse saddled, and order the troops under arms at once." Without formality, McCulloch and McIntosh ran to their horses and took off at a gallop to rejoin their commands. Fortunately for all the commanders, the troops were already under arms and had been all night.[9]

Across the creek, a Sergeant Hite rushed up to Pearce. Breathlessly he gasped, "General, the enemy is coming!"

"Where?" Pearce demanded, and then watched as the sergeant pointed toward the high ground across from the Ray springhouse. There, he, too, saw the lead formations of the Union force.

The previous day, the meticulous Arkansan had made a detailed survey of the area to determine where best to deploy his force should the need arise. He now ordered them to take the previously surveyed positions. To the south and east of Wilson's Creek, Reid positioned his battery in a flat area looking toward the Union line of attack, which also allowed him to cover the mouth of Skeggs Branch. In order, toward the north and the ford on Wilson's Creek, Pearce placed the 5th Arkansas Infantry, commanded by Col. Tom P. Dockery, 4th Arkansas Infantry under its adjutant, Col. Frank A. Rector (its commander Col. J. D. Walker was ill); and the 3rd Arkansas Infantry, commanded by Col. John R. Gratiot. Captain Woodruff's Pulaski Arkansas Battery was placed to the north of Gratiot, in a defilade position relative to Totten, just slightly under the crest of a knoll near the Guinn House. Capt. Charles A. Carroll's cavalry company was ordered to stand by in reserve at Manley Hollow. Weightman's MSG Brigade was positioned to the right of the Arkansas organizations. Because of his forethought, Pearce quickly had the high ground on the eastern bank of Wilson's Creek covered from the mouth of Skeggs Branch to the ford.[10]

Captain Woodruff, whose teams had remained hitched during the night, was quickly in position, his guns commanding the Wire Road. It took seconds to unlimber these weapons and line them up on the opposing artillery, now tossing shot and shell freely into the milling troops below and ahead of it. As soon as the weapons were positioned, Woodruff opened up. This unexpected artillery barrage

Map 3. The Battle of Wilson's Creek, 0500-0600

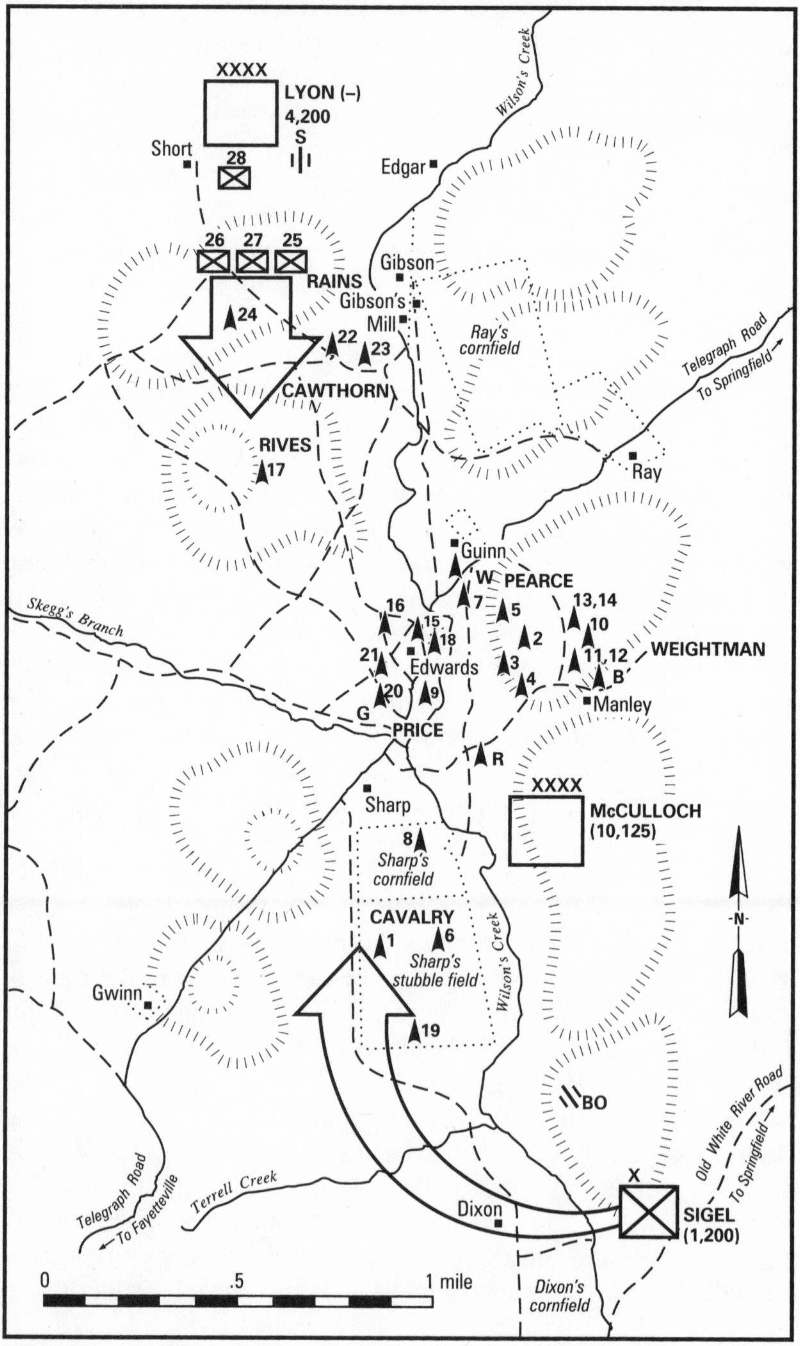

Chronology

- Lyon attacks the north end of the Confederate camps and captures Bloody Hill.
- Sigel attacks and captures the cavalry camps in Sharp's cornfield.
- McCulloch and Price learn of the attacks and begin to react.

Confederate Forces

W	Woodruff	11	1st Missouri State Guard
R	Reid	12	2d Missouri State Guard
B	Bledsoe	13	3d Missouri State Guard
G	Guibor	14	4th Missouri State Guard
1	1st Arkansas Cavalry	15	Hughes's Infantry
2	3d Arkansas Infantry	16	Thornton's Infantry
3	4th Arkansas Infantry	17	Rives's Cavalry
4	5th Arkansas Infantry	18	Burbridge's Infantry
5	3d Louisiana Infantry	19	Major's Cavalry
6	1st Arkansas Mounted Rifles	20	Wingo's Infantry
7	2d Arkansas Mounted Rifles	21	Foster's Infantry
8	South Kansas–Texas Mounted Regt.	22	Peyton's Cavalry
9	Kelly's Infantry	23	McCowan's Cavalry
10	Brown's Cavalry	24	Hunter's Cavalry

Federal Forces

S	Sokalski	26	Osterhaus
BO	Backoff	27	1st Missouri
25	Plummer	28	1st Kansas

Legend

:::::::	Fields	⇨	Federal axes of advance
■	Farmhouses	⑊	Artillery
⚙	Elevated areas	▲	Confederate camps

diverted a portion of Totten's Battery from the encampment in front of them as they swung to meet this new challenge. As the artillery duel heated up, Lyon's advance slowed to a crawl.

With the Union advance virtually stopped, cringing under Woodruff's fire, Totten opened up on the man who had been his student only three months ago. He found that the student had learned his lessons well. Defiladed as Woodruff was, Totten had difficulty bringing his fire to bear on him. The Union cannoneers were forced to aim at flashes and smoke while their target remained free to sweep the crest of the hill on which Lyon's force was positioned. With the exception of Maj. John A. Halderman's battalion of the 1st Kansas, which was taking casualties, much of Woodruff's fire was ineffectively passing over his targets. According to Ware, however, he caused some havoc among the artillery. At any rate, it was a sufficient problem to cause Lyon to stop his advance entirely and bring up Du Bois' Battery, positioning it to the left of Totten where it could bring Woodruff under fire.[11]

While the cannoneers dueled, out in the valley, reaction varied to the sudden appearance of the Union army. Up the creek from Woodruff's rapidly firing battery, a Confederate trooper, hurrying into cover on John Ray's farm, where he had camped the previous evening, found Ray's children, Olivia, Livonia, and Wesly, herding horses near the springhouse. Barely slowing his pace, he commanded the children to go immediately to a safe place, telling them ". . . there's going to be fightin' like hell in less than ten minutes."[12]

Elsewhere, an officer was leisurely enjoying his morning coffee when a messenger rode up and told him to form up his troops. "Is that official?" the relaxed officer asked.

Almost before the sound of his voice died, an artillery round decapitated a sapling nearby. Leaping to his feet, the officer exclaimed, "Well, by God! That is official," and scrambled to find his men.[13]

In other places, panic was the order of the day. Many of the advance guard were falling back in disarray. The greatest problem and heaviest contributor to the confusion threatening to sweep the encampment was the behavior of the unarmed and unattached. As McCulloch had feared, this group was completely panicked as they rushed toward the rear in utter confusion.

Many in this fleeing crowd crashed into the 3rd Texas Cavalry. According to Private Barron, the road was "so completely filled with the mass of moving trains and men rushing pell-mell southward" that his unit was able to cross it only by making a "heroic effort." Pvt. Henry Clay Neville of Arkansas also reported that these men were "a great encumbrance" and that Price ". . . had to get his unarmed men out of the range of the Federal guns before the other troops could do much effective service in resisting the attack." Pearce also complained, claiming that this fleeing mob had almost caused a disaster because McRae's battalion ". . . was literally run over by this rabble trying to get out of the way." There was also great confusion, disorder, and some panic among the remainder of the encampment. One Texan later said, "There was perfect panic at first, and not more than two regiments fought in any order."[14]

"Old Pap" had no trouble recognizing the problem and was busily controlling it. As the pressure that Lyon had been applying to the Rebel lead elements eased, Price began to gain control of his troops. Taking advantage of the time Woodruff was buying them, Price's division commanders busily formed up their infantry and moved forward to block the Union advance. Slack, without waiting for orders, moved up first and engaged the enemy on the left of Cawthorn's beleaguered unit with Col. John T. Hughes's and Maj. C. C. Thornton's infantry. Other units now began to arrive: Col. John Q. Burbridge of Clark's Division fell in on Slack's left; Col. Joseph M. Kelly, supported by Guibor's Battery of Parson's Division, moved up on Burbridge's left; Churchill's 1st Arkansas Mounted Rifles moved in left of Guibor; and, finally, McBride, with Col. Edmund T. Wingo's and Col. Robert A. Foster's infantry, fell in left of Churchill to anchor the left flank of Price's line. Weightman's infantry of Rains's Brigade moved up to fill an opening that had developed between Slack and Cawthorn. When these actions were complete, Price had a line of battle in position to meet the federal attack.

Facing Price, left to right as the battle shaped up, Lyon had Plummer, Osterhaus, 1st Iowa, DuBois's Battery, 1st Kansas, Steele's Battalion, Totten's Battery, 1st Missouri, 2nd Missouri Infantry Battalion, and Sokalski's Section of Totten's Battery. The 2nd Kansas was held in reserve.[15]

McCulloch had raced back to his brigade at the sound of the opening cannon shot. He found the 3rd Louisiana already formed up, but standing in position. Anxious to get his line formed, he shouted at Col. Louis Hébert, a West Pointer, former chief engineer of Louisiana, and their commander, "Colonel, why in hell don't you lead your men out?" An observer reported that the question did not have to be repeated.[16]

The Arkansas Infantry Battalion, commanded by McRae, and the 2nd Arkansas Mounted Rifles, commanded by McIntosh, were ordered to follow the 3rd Louisiana into line on the right of Woodruff's Battery. Before this disposition could be completed, Woodruff sent word to McCulloch that a Union force had crossed Wilson's Creek and was moving toward his position. In response, McCulloch ordered Gratiot's infantry to shift into position to protect Woodruff's Battery and told McIntosh and Hébert to take their regiments and McRae's battalion to stop the advancing federals. At McIntosh's command, "This way, boys," the Confederate force moved out.[17]

Plummer, who had been ordered to support Gilbert on the Union left, soon caught up with his Company B, which had bogged down in a swampy area in a ravine at the foot of Oak Hill. After a bit of a struggle, Plummer got the force back on track, crossed the creek, probably without orders, and entered Ray's cornfield with the objective of silencing Woodruff's Battery. Without regard for the Confederate forces now deploying to head them off, Plummer's battalion struggled toward the guns through a wilderness of high corn that had been planted broadcast instead of in rows. The tall, thick corn made navigation difficult and resisted penetration, as the troopers struggled to pass through the field and gain a "snake" fence made from rails at its far end. From the protection of its cover, they hoped to ward off the Confederates moving toward them and then take care of the guns.[18]

Ahead of them, Rebel troops moved toward the cornfield along a narrow road, choked with brush on both sides. As they neared the snake fence Hébert started to form them into a line of battle. While they were still trying to form, a fusillade of Yankee musket balls ripped into them from behind the fence. Hurriedly, they left the road and plunged into the heavy undergrowth where they finished forming and then started forward. In front of them a federal climbed up on the fence and yelled, "We are friends."

Drum Major R. Patterson, with one fluid move, swung up his rifle and dropped him. As the victim fell, Patterson said, "No, you don't, I have seen you before."[19]

On the left, just where the fence intersected the road, a sergeant, who had not taken cover, watched as two more of the enemy climbed on the fence. As he raised his weapon to take aim, one federal yelled, "Don't shoot, we are friends."

At that moment, Lt. John B. Irvine stepped into the road and someone called to the sergeant, "Get out of that, you damned fool, you'll be killed."

Galvanized into movement, the sergeant jumped for the roadside as one of the federals shot Irvine in the throat. When the lieutenant dropped, the Yankee said in a loud voice, "I got that son-of-a-bitch," and dropped off the fence as a swarm of bullets swept it.[20]

The opposing forces were now only a few feet apart. The crash of musketry became almost deafening as bullets whipped through the bushes and tangled corn. Here and there, men silently dropped, dead where they landed; others cried out, as leaden pellets found their marks. Some men dropped to the ground for cover, while others moved purposefully through the brush or along the fence looking for a target. A cloud of gunsmoke was slowly enveloping the area, further reducing visibility that was already limited by the crowded corn and vine and briar-tangled bushes. Slowly, the federal troops fell back from the fence, taking cover in the corn, as the Confederates moved up to take their turn at using it for cover.

"Sergeant," a dog picked up somewhere along the way and now a mascot of the 3rd Louisiana, ran wildly through the brush, barking at the top of his lungs. As he rushed ahead, one of the troops hollered at him, "Get out of that, Sergeant, you damned fool, you'll be killed." At that moment a bullet found him, killing him in midstride.[21]

Now, almost as if by mutual consent, there was a pause in the firing, and the bit of breeze remaining slowly pushed aside the smoke. Pvt. William Watson, a Scotsman with the 3rd Louisiana, described the scene he witnessed: "When the smoke cleared away a little we could see the enemy plainly. They stood as firm as ever, but their ranks were thinned and their dead lay thick . . . some of them had been slightly wounded in the head, but they still stood in their places, while the blood running down their faces gave them a ghastly but fierce and determined look."[22]

The respite was brief. McIntosh hurried along the line and shouted, "Get up, Louisiana, and charge them! Do you all wish to be killed?" With that, he yelled, "Charge!" and vaulted over the fence.

At the sight of McIntosh leaping the fence, a loud yell rippled down the line. Without a moment's hesitation, the men from Louisiana and Arkansas sprang to their feet, bayonets fixed, jumped over the rail fence, and charged in a mad rush toward the remaining federals. This was too much for the Yankees, who began to fall back rapidly under the Rebel pressure. But even in retreat, the federals still had fight in them. "They broke," Watson said, "the greater part retreating toward their centre on Oak Hill. . . . one young officer stood holding a small flag or marker along their line. I ran to seize the flag from him. He with his sword inflicted a slight wound on my wrist. I closed with him, but found the poor fellow was already severely wounded, and he fell fainting to the ground still holding the flag."[23]

As the retreating Yankees were driven out of the cornfield into a recently harvested oat field, Du Bois, who had moved into position to give Woodruff fits and had caused him to have to reposition his battery, spotted the federals' plight. Swinging his guns into position, he loosed a blast of canister into the Rebel ranks that broke their charge. It was now the Confederates' turn to retreat. The Arkansas troops, led by Lt. Col. Benjamin T. Embry, and one battalion of the 3rd Louisiana, under Lt. Col. Samuel M. Hyams, raced to cover along the east bank of the creek. The remaining Louisiana troops, under Maj. William F. Tunnard, sought safety behind the Ray House. Du Bois now swung his cannon toward the latter group, but after firing a couple of rounds, he saw a yellow hospital flag flying by the building and ceased fire. Hébert now caught up with this portion of his command and moved them off to the rear.

Plummer continued his withdrawal across Wilson's Creek, retracing his route back to where they had charged through Cawthorn's camp earlier that morning. Here, the captain, who was severely wounded and no longer able to lead, turned over his command to Capt. Arch Hanson. Gilbert, who had split off from the battalion during the retreat, also recrossed the creek and joined Steele's troops.[24]

On top of Oak Hill, Lyon's advance, which had initially waited to hear Sigel attack and then had been stopped by Woodruff's artillery fire, was ready to move forward again. As soon as he had heard Sigel's artillery, Lyon had assumed that the action was going as planned. Consequently, he moved the 1st Iowa up on the left of Du Bois and placed Steele on his right and slightly behind the 1st Kansas, whose units were split apart by a deep ravine running down the hill. At this point, the Confederates, who were out of the effective range of most of their firearms, were about three hundred yards in front of the federals. This left Price with the problem of deciding whether to advance or to wait for Lyon to come to him. With Totten's artillery playing among the trees, and brush hiding Price's line, and his battle line now set, the federal commander made the decision for the Missourian by ordering his troops forward.

The thin rattle of musketry that had been rippling through the morning air now rose to a thunderous crescendo. As the Kansas and

German-Missourians moved down the hill into the exploding shells being lobbed at them by Guibor, the Rebel Missourians started up the hill to meet them, bowed under the slashing fire of Totten's guns. Now, full vent could be given to the pent-up hatred that had simmered for so long. Here was a chance to even the old scores and settle, once and for all, the enmity that existed between them. It also was the start of the bloodletting that day, which would change the name of Oak Hill to Bloody Hill.[25]

Immediately to the left of Totten, the 1st Missouri watched a formation approach that was led by an officer carrying a Union flag. When these men were identified as Rebels, Capt. Gary Gratz, furious at this example of Confederate perfidy, stepped out in front of his company and shot the flag bearer from his horse. The wounded man hit the ground, bounced up, and staggered back toward his lines. Gratz jumped forward a few steps, shot again, and killed him. The federal was immediately shot at least five times for his trouble and dropped to join in death the man he had just killed.[26]

Smoke rolled across the hillside, blinding both sides. Men dodged around the trees and peered through the masking undergrowth, firing at shadows weaving in the smoke in front of them. Cannon fire from both sides ripped through the timber, showering the combatants with falling branches and flying splinters. Men shouted, cursed, and screamed as they waded through rifle and shotgun blasts.

At brutally close range, the opposing forces hammered away at each other, but neither side gave ground. Suddenly, Burbridge's regiment broke through and started to forge ahead up the hill. Before they had made much progress, however, Sigel's artillery from back in their rear dropped a salvo in their midst, which forced them to retreat. Several times, the Rebels were able to force the Yankees back, but each time they regrouped and came doggedly forward again.

In the center, Andrews's unit was taking severe punishment from Guibor's battery. The colonel, desperate to get some relief, shouted for his troops to form up and charge the Missouri battery. Before they could respond, McBride struck them savagely on the right in an attempt to outflank them. Andrews forgot Guibor and turned to meet this challenge, watching as a bitter fight raged along his right flank for several minutes before his men were able to stem McBride's effort.

Lyon was in the thick of things, leading his horse as he walked along. While he was working with the 1st Kansas, trying to restore order after they threatened to buckle under the Rebel attack, an

Map 4. The Battle of Wilson's Creek, 0600-0800

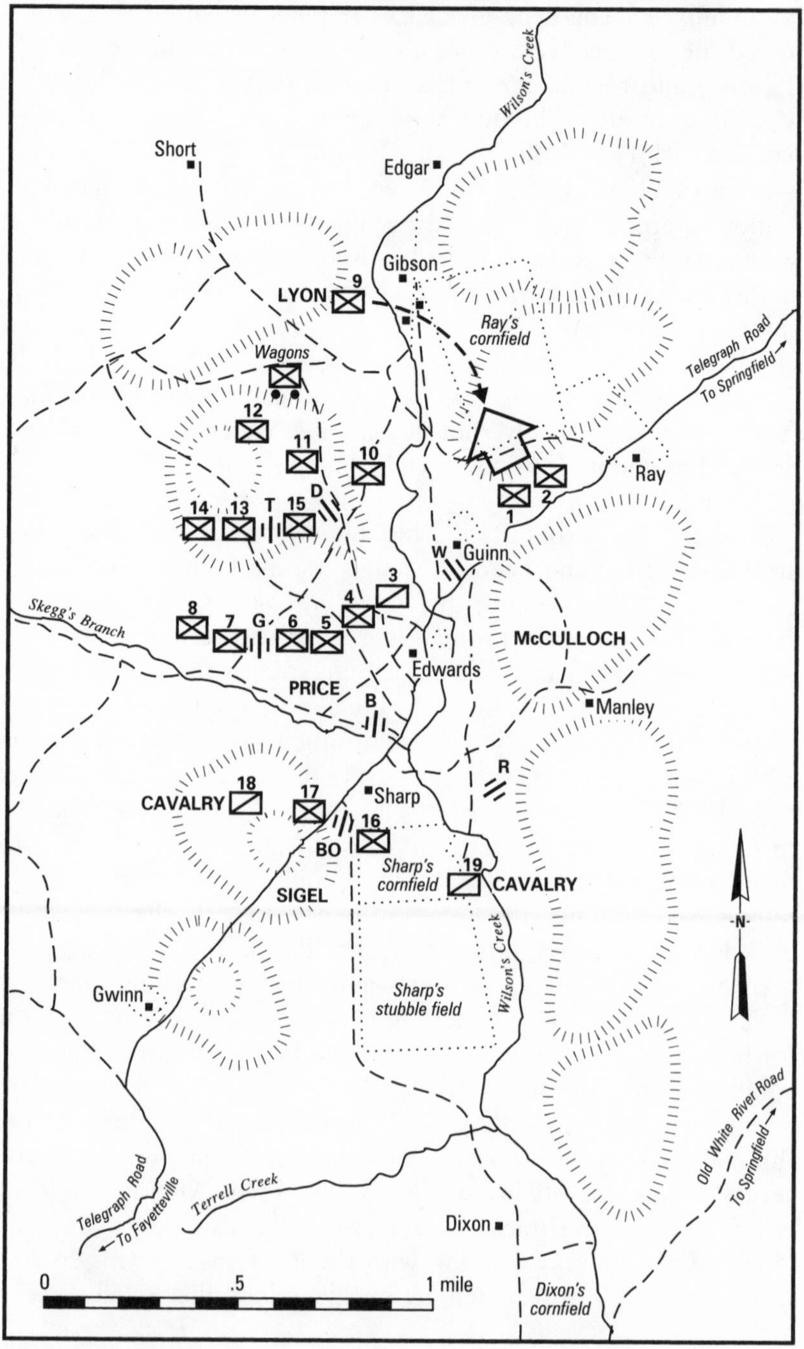

Chronology

- Sigel clears Sharp's field, blocks Telegraph Road, and waits for Lyon.
- Price stops Lyon's attack and begins to build a line of battle.
- Plummer crosses Wilson's Creek and tries to silence Woodruff's guns.
- McIntosh attacks and defeats Plummer.

Confederate Forces

W	Woodruff		4	Weightman
R	Reid		5	Slack
B	Bledsoe		6	Clark
G	Guibor		7	1st Arkansas Mounted Rifles
1	2d Arkansas Mounted Rifles		8	McBride
2	3d Louisiana Infantry			
3	Cawthorn			

Federal Forces

T	Totten		13	1st Iowa
D	Du Bois		14	2d Kansas
BO	Backoff		15	Steele
9	Plummer		16	3d Missouri
10	Osterhaus		17	5th Missouri
11	1st Missouri		18	Carr
12	1st Kansas		19	Farrand

Not shown:

McCulloch's Brigade, organizing east of Wilson's Creek near the ford on Telegraph Road.

Pearce's Brigade, organizing just west of Manley's house.

Company D, 1st U.S. Cavalry, and Home Guards, which were deployed near the wagons.

Cavalry from the Confederate camps, which wandered in confusion within the Confederate lines.

Legend

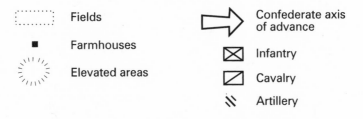

Fields		Confederate axis of advance	
Farmhouses		Infantry	
Elevated areas		Cavalry	
		Artillery	

artillery round exploded, which killed the horse and wounded the general. Capt. Francis J. Herron witnessed the incident and later said, ". . . the animal sank down as if vitally struck, neither plunging nor rearing. Lyon then walked on, waving his sword and hallooing. He was limping, for he had been wounded in the leg. He carried his hat, a drab felt, in his hand and looked white and dazed. Suddenly blood appeared on the side of his head and began to run down his cheek. He stood a moment and then walked slowly to the rear."[27]

Simultaneously, the firing began to subside. As Lyon walked past Andrews, the colonel, glad to feel the pressure against him ebbing, but believing they needed help from Sigel, asked him, "Have you seen or heard from our other column?"

Lyon, who appeared to Andrews to be suffering, shook his head and continued to the rear.[28]

As the fighting raged down the slope, Price also moved back and forth along his line, steadying it here, urging the troops forward there. His presence provided a calming influence on his raw troops, which combined with their hatred of their foe to keep them from buckling. As the troops watched their sliver-haired, obese comman-der, they cheered him, and then begged him to get back for fear of losing him.[29]

On the left, the 1st Iowa watched as the enemy advanced across a small meadow and took shelter behind a low rail fence. After a few moments, the attackers broke holes in the fence and charged toward the artillery. The Iowans responded by greeting them with a hail of fire—every man loading and firing as rapidly as he could. Shortly, the entire front was shrouded by a thick cloud of gunsmoke. Then the fire died down and the smoke drifted off to reveal a lone Rebel sit-ting on the rail fence waving a Confederate flag.

Officers hastened to stop several troops who were preparing to shoot him. They felt that the man's bravery was such that it would be "ungentlemanly" to fire on him. Reluctantly, the Iowans watched, itching to put a stop to his impudence but restrained by their officers. One of Totten's Irish sergeants, a short fellow with a bright red mus-tache, had no such qualms. He swung a twelve-pounder around, aimed it at the Rebel, and pulled the lanyard. The flag flew into the air as the enemy soldier disintegrated. The Iowans cheered.[30]

All along the line now, the firing was dying away to a mutter as the secessionists retreated down the hill to regroup. Above them, their enemy was grateful for a break. As the cloud of gunsmoke draping the hillside continued to drift away, a scene of terrific slaughter was revealed. Bodies, dead and wounded, were scattered everywhere. The screams and groans of shattered men filled the smoldering air as the sun bore down on them. Pleas for water could be heard, as dying men sweltered in the intensifying heat, but no aid was available. On both sides, men were regrouping for another try.

In Springfield that morning, Col. Marcus Boyd, commander of the Home Guard unit left to protect the city, had assigned an eager, but perhaps not too sharp, captain to take a position some distance out on the road leading to the city. The officer's orders were to watch the countryside carefully and, if he saw or heard anything unusual, to return, but in any event, to report at thirty-minute intervals. Shortly after the sound of the battle's opening artillery salvos muttered like thunder in the distance, the captain came racing in, whipping his horse with a piece of lath. He pulled the mount to a halt in front of Boyd, saluted, and crisply reported what every soul in the city already knew, "Colonel Boyd, sir! The cannings is a-firin'!"[31]

CHAPTER XVI

"Two Dutch Guards and Nary a Gun"

Sigel's opening rounds sailed over Wilson's Creek, striking the loosely organized mounted troops like a thunderbolt. Men cooking breakfast or caring for their mounts looked up in shock as the opening rounds slammed into the valley. Others tumbled from their blankets, still half asleep and disoriented, and found themselves in the midst of chaos. Troopers ran in every direction, horses reared and plunged, and officers shouted orders in an attempt to form their troops and quell panic.

Fortunately for the Rebels, the excited, unskilled artillerymen were mostly shooting over their heads. Dr. Samuel H. Melcher, 5th Missouri assistant surgeon, described the situation with perhaps a bit of anti-German bias when he said, ". . . our guns being on an elevation, and the Confederates being in a field which sloped toward the creek, the shots passed over their heads, creating a stampede but doing little, if any, damage to life or limb. In vain I and others urged the artillerymen to depress the guns. Either from inability to understand English, or, in the excitement, they kept banging away till the whole camp was deserted."[1]

Carr, who had occupied a position on high ground overlooking the Confederate encampment, tried to help the artillery. He dismounted his men and ordered them to open fire on the scrambling troops below. The range was too distant for the small-arms fire to be effective, but it did contribute to the discomfort and confusion of the Rebel cavalrymen.[2]

The inaccuracy of the fire did little to lessen the fear of many of the green soldiers who were undergoing their combat baptismal. In Capt. S. M. Hale's Company D, 3rd Texas Cavalry, two men, who had been notable braggarts concerning what they would do in combat, came to him quivering in fear. "Captain Hale, where must we go? We are sick," they told him.

"Go to hell, you damned cowards!" Hale growled. "You were the only two fighting men I had until now we are in battle and you're both sick. I don't care [where] you go."[3]

Others were less affected. A Private Brazille, who was in the process of preparing a breakfast of fresh corn he had just "foraged," would not be rushed. Calmly holding his position, ignoring the roar of the artillery and the whistle of rounds flying over the valley, he watched the remainder of his organization depart. Finally, with the corn done, he gathered it up and started after his friends. Instead, he met a patrol of Yankees moving into the valley. The officer leading the patrol halted him and asked where he was going.

Through a mouthful of corn, Brazille informed the officer, "I'm gwine to ketch me a Dutchman, I am, you bet!"

With a shake of his head, the "Dutchman" took his weapon and sent him off a prisoner.[4]

Clearly, the troops could not remain in the open. Either by order or instinct for survival, they headed for safer ground, which resulted in some units becoming separated. Greer, with part of his 3rd Texas Cavalry, headed north and crossed Wilson's Creek at the ford; he then discovered that part of his unit had remained behind, but he could not return because the ford was jammed with wagons, horses, and fleeing people. While he was trying to recross, McCulloch sent him word that the main force of the enemy was up the creek. Greer then decided to give up the attempt to regroup his unit, crossed the creek, and headed up Skeggs Branch. Behind him, Maj. George W. Chilton took command of the separated battalion, got it into the sheltering trees, and formed it into line of battle.

Churchill's 1st Arkansas Mounted Rifles and Col. De Rosey Carroll's 1st Arkansas Cavalry had also been caught in the open.

These units rushed pell-mell for the cover offered by the inviting woods to the west of their camps. Soon after gaining this shelter, the officers had settled their men down and placed them in formation. As each unit formed, its commander led it out to the Wire Road and headed in the direction of the main line of battle.[5]

Sigel, satisfied that he had scattered the opposition in front of him, started moving forward to rejoin Salomon. Concerned that he might not be able to move all of the artillery where he was headed, he left the four pieces that had been in action in position. While Carr remained in his "high ground" position, the remainder of the command moved down the hill, forded Wilson's Creek, dismantled the fences around Dixon's Farm, forded Terrell Creek, and moved well out on a narrow road passing a large stubblefield on the southern end of Sharp's Farm.[6]

Carr, from his vantage point, had been able to watch the Rebel cavalry scatter under Sigel's bombardment. Now, he watched as his commander led his troops into the area where the Confederates had been camped. As he watched, he spotted Chilton's battalion, now reinforced by whatever "strays" the major could gather, in line of battle and moving toward Sigel. Carr ordered a messenger to ride at a gallop to warn his commander, while he remounted his troops and set off behind the courier.

Sigel had also spotted this new threat, which he wildly overestimated as twenty-five hundred men instead of the actual strength of not more than one thousand. He halted his column and sent for the guns that he had left behind. As soon as the artillery arrived, he ordered his command into line of battle to the left of the road that they had been following. When they were in position—the infantry on the left, the artillery on the right, and the cavalry on the far right between the artillery and Wilson's Creek—the artillery opened fire. Despite the heavy fire, the Rebel cavalrymen attempted to maintain their formation in preparation for a charge. The effort was too much, though. In the face of the heavy artillery fusillade, they gave way to superior force. According to Sigel, they retreated ". . . in disorder toward the north and into the woods." They had gone, all right, but their leaders had not given up easily. Carr noted the retreat occurred ". . . though their officers raved and stormed and tore their hair in trying to make their men advance."[7]

With the cavalry threat eliminated and his entire force recombined, Sigel moved his troops back into column and ordered them forward. They moved on past the stubblefield, along Sharp's cornfield, passing through a bunch of cattle near Sharp's house. Just beyond it, they marched up a knoll and through a lot that had been used as a slaughter site by McCulloch's troops. There in front of them was the Wire Road—the only avenue of escape for the Confederate forces, should Lyon prevail.

As they marched, Sigel's troops had picked up about one hundred retreating Rebels. After interrogating them, Sigel called a meeting of his officers to consider the intelligence they had developed. The consensus was that Lyon was winning the fight. Therefore, Sigel reasoned, the proper thing for them to do would be to deploy in this area near the crest of the rise where the Wire Road climbed out of the valley after crossing Wilson's Creek. Operating from the advantage of the high ground offered by the plateau, they could easily observe what was happening and move to sweep up the defeated Rebels as Lyon drove them back. With this in mind, he positioned Carr on the far left, then Salomon just left of the road, Albert just to its right, and Farrand on the far right between Albert and Wilson's Creek. The artillery was left just slightly to the rear, a bit higher up on the slaughter pen knoll.

As soon as the artillery was unlimbered, it opened a sporadic fire on the Confederate line. The cannoneers split their attention between Burbridge and Col. Thomas H. Rosser. Burbridge's troops had been making good progress against the Union line before this bombardment struck them and forced them to pull back. Rosser, who had been informed of Sigel's advance, had formed his force and a battalion of Weightman's brigade along the slope behind the Rebel line on the southern face of Bloody Hill. His visibility, more than anything else, drew the attention of the artillery. It had little effect, however, amounting mostly to aggravation. Because his job was to block Sigel and the latter was not moving, Rosser held fast, ignoring the occasional rounds that came his way.[8]

Once in line, Sigel's troops took advantage of the respite they were enjoying, while waiting for the "defeated" Rebels. In groups, the "Dutch" infantrymen wandered away from their assigned positions to explore the recently abandoned cavalry camp. Although their commander would later deny it, they made the most of their opportunity, eating the food and picking up personal belongings, arms, or equipment that caught their eye. Much of what they found and did not need, nor want, they destroyed. Some of the wagons were set on fire, adding their smoke to those already burning as a result of artillery fire from Totten, Du Bois, and their own guns. Dr. Melcher, whose experience was not unique, confessed that ". . . I with my orderly, Frank Ackoff, 5th Missouri, went into the abandoned Arkansas camp where I found a good breakfast of coffee, biscuit, and fried green corn."[9]

After about thirty minutes, the sound of combat on Bloody Hill began to subside. Fearful that he would fire into the troops of a victorious Lyon, Sigel ordered his artillery to cease fire. Here and there, through the smoke in front of them, they could see Confederates moving, undoubtedly in retreat. Finally, all sounds of combat faded, except for an occasional few stray shots.

After sending McIntosh forward toward Ray's cornfield, McCulloch satisfied himself that Pearce's men were where he wanted them and headed down the creek to check on Sigel. As he surveyed the area, he noted the Confederate cavalry reforming and watched as Sigel moved his force forward and halted. Believing that Pearce and the cavalry could hold the advancing Union force if it moved again, he turned back to ascertain the status of the attack he had ordered back upstream.

He found a portion of that force, chased out of Ray's fields by Du Bois' artillery, in the process of collecting itself under cover of the timber lining the east bank of the creek. McIntosh quickly joined him, informing the Texan that, although the Confederates had fallen back, the federal threat on the east bank of Wilson's Creek had been dissipated. That mission accomplished, McCulloch was free to give his full attention to Sigel.

Upon being informed that their services were needed in the valley, Hyams expressed concern about Hébert's absence. To put him at ease, McCulloch permitted him to dispatch a messenger to find his missing commander, but told him that they could not wait. McIntosh was instructed to stay with McCulloch and leave the 2nd Arkansas under Embry's command. Hyams was then ordered to take the lead with the 3rd Louisiana, and Embry to follow with the 2nd Arkansas.

Dispositions made, McCulloch waved the men forward, shouting to them, "Come, my brave lads, I have a battery for you to charge, and the day is ours!"[10]

The command briskly headed downstream until it reached the ford, where McCulloch halted it. For a few minutes, the troops stood watching as he surveyed the field in front of him through his field glasses. Apparently satisfied with what he saw, he lowered the glasses and sent word to Pearce to support him with Reid's artillery when he attacked. Then, with a wave of his hand to his troops, he quietly said, "Come on."[11]

They crossed Wilson's Creek and made their way around the foot of Bloody Hill where Rosser's troops, positioned to block Sigel, were added to the force. Halting again, McCulloch told Bledsoe's Battery to move across Sigel's line of march, unlimber, and provide artillery cover when he attacked the federal force. Again, the command started forward through the smoke from guns and burning wagons blanketing the valley, adding scattered troops from various units as they marched.[12]

Ahead, the waiting Yankees spotted them through the undulating smoke. In those days, gray and blue had not been decided upon as the opposing colors, and some units on both sides were dressed in gray uniforms that looked much alike. Confused by the color of the uniforms, and having already convinced themselves that Lyon had routed the Rebels, they mistook the gray-clad Louisianans for the similarly clad 1st Iowa. Dr. Melcher, anxious to confirm the identity of the approaching troops, moved forward a few paces in an attempt to get a better view. Because they were coming from the direction where he had last heard Lyon's guns, and their style of marching looked familiar, he returned and told Sigel that he believed they were the 1st Iowa. From other points, skirmishers who had been out in front confirmed the doctor's opinion.

Concerned that their men might fire on friendly troops, the federal infantry and cavalry commanders told them not to fire. Sigel gave these same instructions to the artillery. All then watched intently as the gray-clad force came steadily on through the smoke. No colors were visible by which they could confirm the identity of these faceless men who were moving with the swinging stride reminiscent of the Iowa troopers of marching fame.

Melcher was now becoming uneasy. Something about these silent gray-clad men marching steadily toward them made him anxious. Eager to establish their identity and fearful that they would be fired on, even if these troops were friendly, he suggested to Sigel that he better show his colors.

Sigel turned and ordered, "Color-bearer, advance with your colors, and wave them—wave them three times."

Just as the color-bearer began to wave the flag, Farrand and an orderly rode across the front of the formation, carrying two Rebel guidons they had picked up in the Arkansas camp. The sight of these captured flags brought some mild cheers, but increased the concern that the friendlies in front might fire on them. There was no response from the advancing troops.[13]

The oncoming infantry was now only about forty yards away and still had not been positively identified. Sigel, undoubtedly beginning to realize that something must be terribly wrong, ordered a Corporal Tod forward to make a positive identification. As the corporal hurried over the crest of the rise, McCulloch halted his men and shouted to him, "Whose forces are those?"

Tod answered, "Sigel's."

"Whose did you say?" McCulloch asked.

"Union. Sigel's," came the response as Tod, who, suddenly realizing these were not "friendlies," started to lift his weapon.

Quick as a flash, Cpl. Henry Gentles, standing behind McCulloch, whipped up his rifle and dropped Tod in his tracks.

Without turning a hair, McCulloch turned, looked at Gentles, and calmly said, "That was a good shot."[14]

The Texan then said to Capt. John P. Vigilini, who was in the lead with his company of Pelican Rifles, "Captain, take your company up and give them hell."

On top of the hill, the realization that he was in trouble exploded on Sigel. Frantically, he gave the order to fire, but it was too late.[15]

As his troops tried to shake off their shock and comply, across the creek, Pearce, who had seen the Union colors wave in the slight breeze, ordered Reid to fire. In seconds, a cloud of grapeshot descended on the Yankees, splattering into the fences and trees. West of the creek, Bledsoe joined in, Old Sacramento adding her "bell" tones to the bass chorus of artillery fire. Although this salvo did little damage, Melcher reported that the startled federals ". . . hunted cover like a flock of young partridges, suddenly disturbed."

Because they believed that the Confederates had no grape, although Reid was well supplied, courtesy of the Little Rock Arsenal, and this was clearly grapeshot, the artillery barrage only increased the confusion of Sigel's force. The Yankees now thought that they had come under friendly fire, undoubtedly caused by Farrand's flaunting the Rebel guidons. As they scrambled frantically for cover, voices were heard shouting in English and German, "They are firing against us! It is Totten's battery."

Sigel and Salomon had no illusions. They knew that they were under Confederate attack. Frantically, they tried to regroup their terrified men. Sigel was reported to have threatened, bullied, and coaxed, while Salomon cursed them in German, French, and English. Neither had much luck, as the demoralized troops were thinking only of safety.[16]

Below them, in response to McCulloch's instructions, Vigilini ordered his troops forward; with a whoop, they charged up the hill toward the confused federals. At the crest, the captain halted them and, accompanied by Sergeant Tunnard, hurried forward to survey his front. To his astonishment, he found himself looking down the muzzle of two cannons less than twenty paces in front of him. Startled, he shouted for the gunners to identify themselves.

Tunnard did not need a response. He told his captain, "Look at their Dutch faces!"

Instantly, the two Rebels threw themselves over the edge of the hill. A heartbeat later, the guns sent two rounds through the suddenly vacant space as their gunners yanked the lanyards. Vigilini, surprised to be alive, shouted, "Fire."

His men rushed up the hill, loosed a volley, and charged the federal gun positions with bayonets. The Union gun crews were not disposed to debate the issue. They took to their heels, hunting for a place of safety.[17]

As the Pelican Rifles charged, on their left, Lt. William A. Lacey, leading the Shreveport Rangers of Caddo Parish, jumped on top of a log, swung his sword forward, and shouted, "Come on Caddo!" His yelling troops took off at a run, pouring over the hilltop and charging directly into the face of the remaining artillery. The gun crew members, who had not been shot down, followed the example being set on their right and departed.

The Louisianans left the captured weapons as they were and rushed after the retreating Yankees. After a short distance, they came to a fence and took shelter behind it, continuing to fire at the fleeing enemy. Suddenly, artillery fire crashed down around them—killing one man and wounding another. Reid, unable to keep track of friend or foe in the dust, smoke, and confusion, was firing on them. Hurriedly, word was sent back to the artillery to cease fire.[18]

Close behind the Louisianans, on their right, McRae's men poured over the top and blasted away at the fleeing Union men. Trying to block the only avenue of escape remaining to any Yankees who had not already fled the hill, the Arkansans halted in a position that gave them a commanding view of the road leading away. They had been in position only a few minutes, when McRae spotted a large group moving down the road. In response to his challenge, the men gave a thunderous cheer for the South. Accepting that as friendly identification, he let most of the group pass before realizing that he had been tricked. He immediately ordered his men to open fire, but it did little good. Disgusted, he re-formed his unit and moved back to join McCulloch at the captured artillery.

Rosser's force and Brown's dismounted regiment soon joined the victorious group gathering on top of the hill. Then Major Tunnard, minus two companies that had gone with Hébert to support Price, brought up the remainder of the 3rd Louisiana. McCulloch, aware that he and his force were needed at Bloody Hill, was content to leave pursuit to the cavalry units that were already chasing the Yankees. While some of the Louisiana troops were moving three of the captured cannons down the hill and presenting the fourth to the Arkansas gunners, McCulloch prepared his force to move to Bloody Hill in support of Price. As they left, he told the 3rd Louisiana, "You have beaten the enemy's right and left wings, only their center is left, and with all our forces concentrated upon that, we will soon make short work of it."[19]

Across the creek, Pearce had watched the Confederates roll over Sigel but did not realize that he had been completely routed. Before moving his command to Bloody Hill, he decided to take precautions against Sigel's returning to surprise them, which he did by ordering Rector to take his 4th Arkansas and portions of the 5th Arkansas and assume a blocking position. Rector took this force to his left and deployed it near the spot where Sigel had first fired on the Rebels.[20]

As the Confederate infantry moved back off the hill, Lt. Emile Thomas, Sigel's only officer who had the grit to do so, got his men stopped and started to reorganize them. After a considerable struggle, he managed to settle them down and get them into formation. No sooner had he done so than a Rebel cavalry "battalion," hastily formed by the companies of captains Charles B. Alexander, Charles L. Crews, and Thomas E. Staples, charged in and assumed a position across the road, separating him from Sigel. As the two commands eyed each other as warily as strange dogs, Melcher reported that they heard ". . . a terrible rattle of musketry, and a great hubbub and confusion in the direction of Sigel's command. . . ."

At that, despite Thomas's best efforts, the re-formed federals took off down the road toward the sound and, incidentally, the cavalry. Inexplicably, the cavalry apparently thought Thomas's troops were charging them. Without the slightest effort at resistance, they wheeled and galloped out of the road to safety. Unmolested, the federals raced past to rejoin their command.[21]

Behind them, the confused cavalry regained its composure and, under the command of Staples, who was the senior captain, charged off past Salomon's portion of the retreating federals. A considerable distance down the Wire Road, a Confederate wagon train's poor timing had brought it up behind Sigel just as he was attacked. Fearing the loss of the train, the improvised cavalry battalion was hurrying to insert itself between it and Salomon. Once far past him, they established a line across the Wire Road, blocking any Union retreat that might come that far while the wagon train rumbled off to safety.[22]

Carr, who had been positioned in the woods to Sigel's left, had hardly been involved in the fight. Unable to see what was happening, he held his position as stray "bullets, shot, and shell" flew among the trees causing his troops some apprehension. In fact, these were so frequent, he said, "At that time many were in doubt if it were not our own troops firing upon us."

That doubt was cleared up shortly, however, when a staff officer from Sigel brought orders for him to retreat. He did so promptly, bringing with him one of the two Union cannon that had not been captured. Their retreat was largely uneventful, except for one slashing attack by a group concealed on a brushy hillside. Carr's men wheeled into line and easily repelled the attack, but lost the cannon when a wheel horse was killed. Without further incident, he reached Moody's Spring and joined Sigel, who had split off from Salomon.[23]

Salomon continued his retreat down the Telegraph Road, capturing a Dr. Smith, who belonged to Rains's command, and several wagons carrying mostly medical supplies. Dr. Melcher, who was with Salomon, immediately pressed him to release the captured physician. After some discussion, Salomon did so, thus enabling both physicians to proceed toward the battle area.

Continuing his retreat, Salomon came upon the gun Carr had abandoned. Unwilling to leave it behind, he ordered Capt. Samuel A. Flagg to have it pulled by his troops and their prisoners. They did so, progressing slowly, until they managed to acquire some horses. The command, followed by the artillery piece, plodded on a bit farther; they then turned off the Wire Road, before encountering the Rebel cavalry blocking it, and headed in a northeasterly direction. Soon, the team pulling the artillery gave out, and the cannon was abandoned. After going a bit farther, they hit the Little York Road and trudged back to Springfield.[24]

Farrand, who had been in the field but had been unable to contribute much to the fight, suddenly found himself all alone. As soon as he discovered his plight, he immediately ordered a retreat toward the south. Hurrying along, not entirely sure of what had happened

Map 5. The Battle of Wilson's Creek, 0800-1000

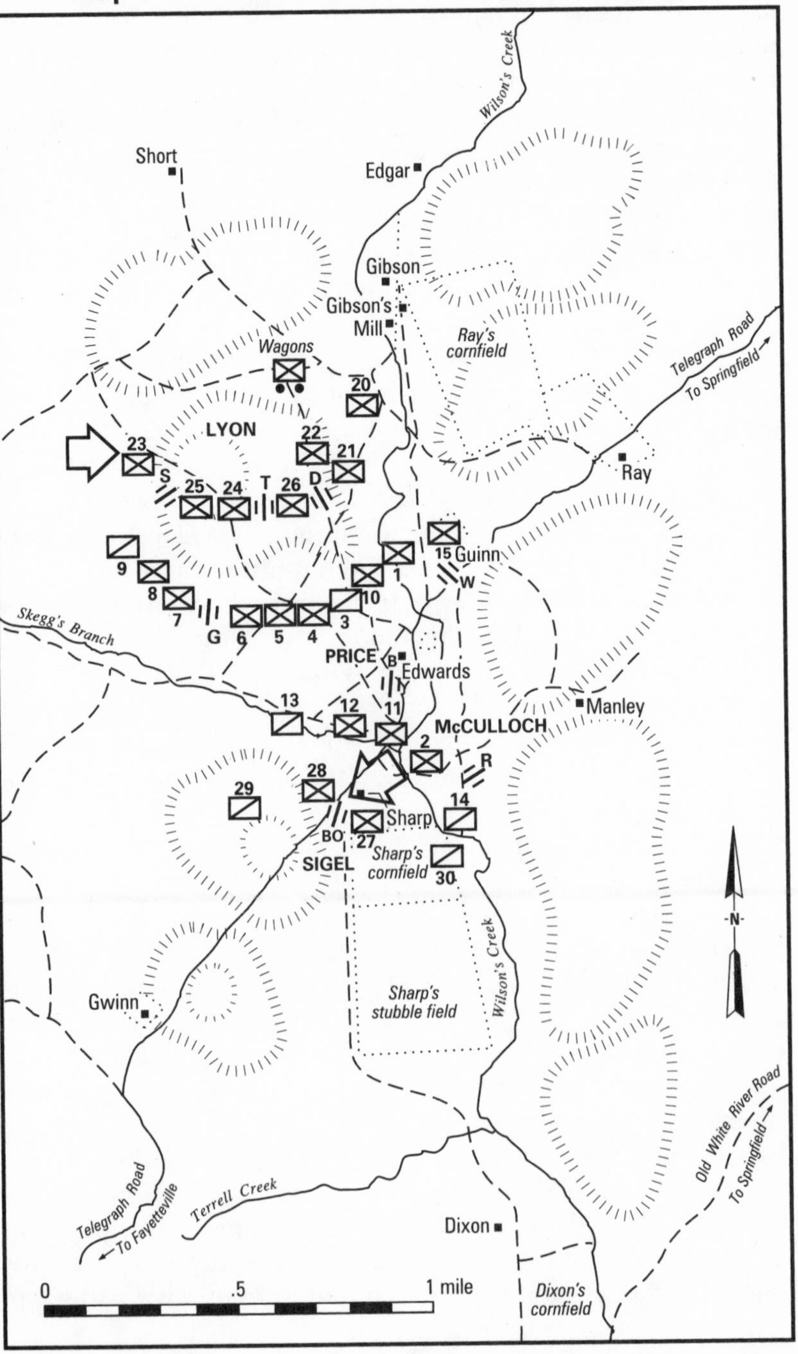

Chronology

- Price holds Lyon and begins to extend the Confederate line to the west.
- McCulloch routs Sigel.
- Greer's cavalry unsuccessfully attacks Lyon's flank and rear.
- Both sides pause to regroup.
- McCulloch realigns his forces to support Price.

Confederate Forces

W	Woodruff		7	1st Arkansas Mounted Rifles
R	Reid		8	McBride
B	Bledsoe		9	1st Arkansas Cavalry
G	Guibor		10	Foster
1	2d Arkansas Mounted Rifles		11	4th Missouri State Guard
2	3d Louisiana Infantry		13	1st Missouri State Guard
3	Cawthorn		12	Greer
4	Weightman		14	Brown
5	Slack		15	1st Missouri
6	Clark			

Federal Forces

T	Totten		24	1st Iowa
D	Du Bois		25	2d Kansas
S	Sokalski		26	Steele
BO	Backoff		27	3d Missouri
20	Plummer		28	5th Missouri
21	Osterhaus		29	Carr
22	1st Missouri		30	Farrand
23	1st Kansas			

Not shown:

Many stragglers in and around the Confederate camps.

Company D, 1st U.S. Cavalry, and Home Guards deployed near the wagons.

Legend

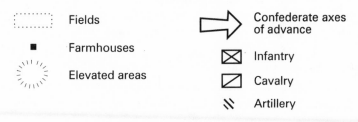

Fields	Confederate axes of advance
Farmhouses	Infantry
Elevated areas	Cavalry
	Artillery

but aware that there was a general retreat, he bumped into L.A.D. Crenshaw who had scouted for Sigel. Farrand sorely needed a scout, but Crenshaw was apparently hesitant to render additional service. Farrand, however, was not inclined to negotiate. He took the reluctant scout forcibly under his control, and after spending considerable time rounding up as many "strays" as he could, the lieutenant ordered the uncooperative guide to take them to Springfield.

Crenshaw's chosen route was to head toward Little York Road. En route, they found the much abandoned artillery piece left by Salomon. Farrand, determined not to lose the weapon, managed to secure some horses and resumed his march. A bit later, he came upon a caisson full of ammunition. Again, he determined to take this equipment with him, found some horses, and added it to his train. After a few more miles, he was informed that the team pulling the cannon was exhausted. Farrand was not about to give up this weapon. He had the ammunition and caisson destroyed, moved that team to the cannon, added a team of mules requisitioned from a nearby farm, and started toward his destination.[25]

Back at Moody's Spring, Sigel had decided that the Little York Road offered too much opportunity for them to be cut off. Instead, he decided to proceed down the Wire Road, until they found a suitable road toward the left that would lead them back to Springfield. Consequently, he ordered his group, consisting of a portion of Albert's regiment and Carr's cavalry, to move south. Carr was ordered ". . . to remain in advance, keep his flankers out, and report what might occur in front."

While all of this was happening, Lt. Col. James P. Major, unable to use his cavalry effectively on Bloody Hill, heard that Sigel was in full retreat with four hundred men. This appeared to offer an ideal target of opportunity for his cavalry. Taking his Windsor Guards and two companies of Texas cavalry—Capt. Hinche P. Mabry's Dead-Shot Rangers and Capt. Jonathan Russell's Cypress Guards—he dashed off Yankee hunting. Once across Terrell Creek, he added Staples's "battalion" to his force and headed for the ford over the James River. This was the route that the retreating Sigel would have to follow in his search for a better path of escape than that chosen by Salomon.[26]

Carr had gone about a mile and a half when he spotted Major's force a quarter of a mile ahead filing out onto the Wire Road. He immediately rushed this information back to Sigel, who ordered him to take the first road to the left. Carr happened to be at such a road, so he immediately took it. Feeling the pressure of the cavalry ahead of him, he maintained a fairly brisk pace. Shortly, word came up from Sigel to ". . . march slowly, so the infantry could keep up."

Carr, in his concern for what the enemy cavalry in front of him would do, responded that they needed to hurry because the enemy would try to cut them off at the James River. Further, he told his commander, a bit impatiently, the troops and artillery piece ought to be able to move as fast as his horses when they were held to an ordinary walk. Sigel agreed and the command continued to move at what Carr thought was his commander's pace.

At the ford, the captain was surprised and disturbed to find that Sigel was nowhere in sight. Worse, he did not appear by the time the cavalrymen finished watering their horses. The Rebels had appeared, however, and it was clear to Carr that he would shortly be under attack. Without further delay, he led his troops away from the river and the approaching Rebel horsemen. Carr later said, "To use a Westernism, there was no time for fooling then, and as I had waited long enough on the slow-motioned infantry to water my horses, and they were not yet in sight, I lit out for a place of safety . . . and after waiting . . . [there] another while for Sigel, I went on to Springfield. I was sorry to leave Sigel behind . . . [but] it would have done no good for my company to have remained and been cut to pieces. . . ."[27]

When Sigel arrived at the James River ford, Major was waiting for him. Without preamble, he waved his horsemen forward. They struck the already demoralized Germans like a thunderstorm. Bullets began kicking up splashes as horses and men churned up the water, which quickly started turning red from the casualties that dropped into it. The terrified Union soldiers ran, and the cavalry went after them. When the smoke cleared, sixty-four of Sigel's men lay dead, one hundred forty-seven were prisoners, and the Rebels had his last cannon. As icing on the cake, Staples was waving the 3rd Missouri's colors, which he would later present to Price.

The end of this sudden clash did not mean rest for the Yankees, however. Major's men fanned out across the country hunting them down in twos and threes. The hunt was merciless for those who did not come quietly. At Nowlan's Mill, the Rebels found four of their quarry hiding up against the mill dam. When ordered out, the Yankees refused to move. Wasting no time in persuasion, the Rebels blasted them with buckshot and moved on. Of the hard-bitten cavalrymen, Henry Clay Neville said, "The daring riders who had done service for years on the Indian frontier now did deadly execution with their carbines and big revolvers."

Sigel was neither dead nor captured. Wrapped in an old blue blanket and wearing a slouch hat, he and an orderly hid with their horses in a cornfield on the east bank of the James, while the Rebels searched for them. Crouched low in the corn, a death grip on their mounts' reins, they waited apprehensively, seeking a chance to run. Finally, it came. They swung to horse and galloped off, with the Rebels only seconds behind them. After a hard race of about six miles, the Confederates, probably unaware that it was Sigel, abandoned the chase. The thoroughly whipped and routed Yankee commander finally clattered into Springfield at half past four that afternoon—twenty-two hours after his departure—and went to bed![28]

Much of Sigel's force had retreated along the flanks of Lyon's command while the battle was still in progress, but it apparently never occurred to any of them to reinforce their leader. Instead, he was left to his own devices, completely ignorant of what had happened to the other arm of his command. The reinforcements could have been used, too. For, throughout the morning, while Sigel's men scurried around seeking Springfield and safety, the little Home Guards captain at that location had dutifully ridden up each half hour to announce, "Colonel Boyd! Sir! The cannings is still a-firin'."[29]

Sigel's rout, abject flight, and abandonment of his leader led to the composition of a nasty little verse in a song that was sung around Confederate campfires afterward:

> Old Sigel fought some on that day,
> But lost his army in the fray;
> Then off to Springfield he did run,
> With two Dutch guards, and nary a gun.[30]

CHAPTER XVII

"And Glad to See Him Go"

While Sigel and McCulloch were fighting, both Union and Rebel forces on Bloody Hill were regrouping in preparation for the next phase of the battle. Lyon, dismounted as a result of the loss of his horse, was taking advantage of the lull in combat to retire to a quieter position and, perhaps, try to sort out what had happened and what could be expected. Limping from his leg wound, his scraggly beard matted with blood from the other one on the side of his head, drawn and pale, and dressed in his old captain's uniform, he was the image of despondency. Seemingly dazed, he waved off his staff's attempts to get him a new mount and proceeded to a sheltered area to sit down.

Here, Schofield found him, slightly hunched over, as a member of his staff applied temporary field dressings to his wounds. Looking up at his chief of staff, Lyon said, rather abjectly, "I fear the day is lost."

Hoping to jar his leader out of his obvious despondency, Schofield replied, "No, General, let us try it again."[1]

Even this little encouragement seemed to enliven the general a bit. His features became animated and his eyes brightened as he stood up.

Sturgis, who was nearby, now came over and instructed one of his orderlies to give his horse to the general. Lyon refused, saying, "I do not need a horse."[2]

He then sent Sturgis and Schofield to rally some of the units that had fallen back from the fierce encounter that had just ended. Apparently enheartened by his brief exchange with Schofield, or perhaps because the shock of his wounds was wearing off, he now decided that he had a chance to win the contest. Without further delay, he returned to the front, determined to lead personally whatever effort was demanded. No longer in a frame of mind to remain dismounted, he allowed himself to be assisted onto the horse that Sturgis had left standing by for his use. As he mounted and turned toward the front, his staff pleaded with him not to expose himself so dangerously. His response to their pleas was "I am but doing my duty."[3]

As he moved up, he passed Totten and stopped from a moment. "He was wounded, he told me, in the leg," Totten said, "and I observed blood trickling from his head. I offered him some brandy, of which I had a small supply in my canteen, but he declined and rode slowly to the right and front."[4]

Sweeney had also expressed concern about the general's wounds. His worry had been dismissed with a curt "It is nothing."[5]

As Lyon neared the crest of the hill, he noticed a line of the enemy almost directly in front of him. As he watched, a group of horsemen pushed through the line and paused to reconnoiter the front. He immediately recognized Price and Emmett MacDonald, who had refused his parole following the Camp Jackson affair and was easily recognizable by his long hair, which he had sworn not to cut until the Confederacy was victorious. This sight instantly restored Lyon's full fighting spirit. Seeing an opportunity to confront Price one-on-one, Lyon moved forward, ordering his staff to "draw pistols and follow."

One of the general's aides, Lt. William Wherry, immediately objected and pointed out to his commander the folly of placing himself in such a position with a large enemy contingent just ahead of him. Instead, he suggested that Lyon bring up more troops. Accepting this, Lyon dispatched Wherry to order up the 2nd Kansas and, at the same time, ordered Totten to move some of the artillery to support the 1st Kansas on the right.[6]

Lieutenant Colonel Blair, who had unknowingly passed Wherry as the latter rushed to the rear, arrived under orders from Mitchell to request that Lyon commit the 2nd Kansas. Blair hastily reminded Lyon that the 2nd Kansas was not engaged and asked him to move the unit forward. Unaware that Wherry and Blair had failed to connect, Lyon apparently thought that the latter was asking for confirmation of his order. "That is right, sir," Lyon said, waving him back toward the rear. "Order the 2nd Kansas to the front."[7]

Down the hill, the Rebels, reinforced by the men McCulloch had brought from his encounter with Sigel, had regrouped. From right to left, their line now consisted of: the 1st MSG, 2nd Arkansas Mounted Rifles, Foster, Cawthorn, Weightman, Slack, Clark, Guibor's Battery, 1st Arkansas Mounted Rifles, McBride, and 1st Arkansas Cavalry. The 3rd, 4th, and 5th Arkansas Infantry, 3rd Texas Cavalry, and 3rd Louisiana remained in reserve.

The Union had also used this respite to regroup. Their line, left to right, now consisted of: Osterhaus, 1st Missouri, Du Bois's Battery, Steele, Totten's Battery, 1st Iowa, 2nd Kansas, Sokalski's Section, and 1st Kansas. Plummer's troops were to the rear of Osterhaus.

At the foot of Bloody Hill, the Rebels now prepared for another assault on the stubborn Union force in their front. The attack was initiated by a thrust on the federal right aimed toward Sokalski's artillery that had just been moved into position by Totten. The Arkansans, who were leading the assault, were carrying both the Union and Confederate colors. Unaware of Sigel's fate, and uncertain about the identity of the advancing troops, Sokalski held his fire. Then, without warning, the approaching troops suddenly fired a volley. As if this were the signal, violent fighting erupted all down the line.[8]

Lyon responded by ordering his force forward. Responding to him, some of the Iowans, coming up behind a staff officer, shouted, "We have no leader. Give us a leader."

Lyon, blood dripping from his heel, looked about and saw Sweeney. He waved him toward the Iowa troops, saying, "Sweeney, lead those troops forward and we will make one more charge."[9]

Cheers coming from the rear marked the movement of the 2nd Kansas as they hurried up. Responding to their enthusiasm, Lyon joined Mitchell when they arrived. Then, waving his hat, he shouted to the men, "Come on, my brave boys, I will lead you. Forward!"

As the cheering regiment poured over the crest of the hill, a cloud of small-arms fire poured from the bushes and engulfed them. Mitchell pitched from his saddle, critically wounded. Beside him, Lyon jerked erect, pulled his horse to a halt, and started trying to dismount. His orderly, Pvt. Albert Lehman, dashed to the injured man and helped him to the ground. Barely conscious and struggling for breath, the tough little Yankee lasted only long enough to gasp, "Lehman, I am killed."[10]

In minutes, Lehman was joined by Lt. Gustavus Schreyer, who took charge. Calling a couple of his men, the little group picked up Lyon's body and headed for the rear. As soon as they reached shelter, they placed the body under a tree. Wherry, who had now joined them, was concerned about the impact of Lyon's death on the troops. Hoping to conceal it from them, he covered Lyon's face with a coat, told Lehman to stop his loud wailing, and took off to find Schofield, who arrived shortly along with Surgeon Cornyn. After the surgeon completed a brief examination, Schofield sought out Sturgis to inform him that he was now commander of the army.[11]

The 2nd Kansas, which had been momentarily repulsed, surged forward again behind Blair, who was determined not to disgrace either his fallen commander or his state. With gun muzzles almost touching, they fought it out with the hated Missourians, doggedly forcing them back down the hill. As the Rebels reluctantly gave ground under the scalding fire, their commander, Weightman, fell with a wound that would kill him before three more hours could pass.

Over on the far right, the hard-pressed Deitzler, in an attempt to gain the initiative, sortied forward in strength. Charging through a sheet of musket fire, his Kansans were able to press the Missourians back almost to their camp; then Deitzler fell—critically wounded. Seeing more Rebels coming up, the injured commander, in an attempt to avoid being trapped, shouted for his men to retreat.

Capt. Powell Clayton, leading Company E of the 1st Kansas, did not hear the order and continued to press forward. Suddenly, he found himself alone but confronted by an advancing unit that he thought belonged to Sigel. He immediately started to align his company on the new unit. But before his men had completed the movement, Clayton discovered that he was about to join the enemy. He had recognized the new unit's commander as an old foe from Kansas, Col. James J. Clarkson, the former proslave postmaster of Leavenworth.

The trapped Yankee, hoping to bluff it out, ordered his company to march away from the newly arrived organization that, unknowingly, had trapped him. Clayton's troops had gone only a few paces when Clarkson's adjutant raced forward and ordered them to halt. They did so, about-facing to confront the enemy force. The adjutant then asked, "What troops are these?"

"I belong to the 1st Kansas Regiment," Clayton told him. "Who are you?"

"I am adjutant of the 5th Missouri Volunteers," the officer answered.

"What, Confederate or United States?" Clayton wanted to know.

"Confederate," was the response.

Clayton whipped out his pistol, aimed it at the officer, and commanded, "Then dismount, God damn you! You're my prisoner!"

Stunned, the officer complied.

"Now," Clayton told him, "order your men not to fire, or you're a dead man."

Placing the adjutant between himself and the federal unit, Clayton and his men started moving away slowly. Now, the adjutant regained his wits and ordered his troops to fire. As soon as he shouted the order, Clayton shot him, and a sergeant bayoneted him. Shouting for his men to run for their lives, the captain led the way as they raced for the hilltop amid a swarm of Rebel bullets. They made it, regrouped, and turned back to the battle.[12]

All across the hillside, shrouded by a cloud of gunsmoke and sweltering under a blazing sun, men fought desperately. The Confederates, sometimes in three ranks—one prone, one kneeling, and one standing—poured a galling fire into the Union ranks. The federals were returning as good as they got, many of them also dropping to the prone position as they fired blindly through the smoke at the men massed in front of them. Over both sides, artillery shells whistled as canister and grape tore gaping holes in the lines of their opponents. Peter Lane of Texas described the scene, saying ". . . vast sheets of the deadly musket and mini-balls came pouring through our ranks tearing the grass and bushes, throwing the dust and gravel in our faces, crippling our comrades, and killing our friends. The fearful and terrific storm of death was raging around. . . . Here amid this horrible scene we still maintained the deadly and unequal contest, murdering and being murdered."[13]

On the other side, Ware reported, ". . . how long it lasted I do not know. It might have been an hour, it seemed like a week; it was probably twenty minutes. Every man was shooting as fast . . . as he could, and yelling as loud as his breath would permit. . . . The other side were yelling, and if any orders were given nobody heard them.

Every man assumed the responsibility of shooting as much as he could."[14]

Du Bois observed a Rebel attack moving up a gully that curved its way down the south slope of Bloody Hill and adjusted his fire to concentrate on them. He was unable to judge accurately the effect of his fire because of the heavy undergrowth but felt he forced a deviation in the thrust of the Confederate attack. Du Bois' action caused Guibor to divert his attention to silencing that battery, lessening his support of the infantry attack. The Yankee responded to his threat by zeroing in on him. After a brisk exchange of artillery fire, the Missouri guns were partially silenced. The federal guns and what remained of the Rebel capability went back to supporting the infantry.

One of the problems that had faced the Union force from the start—and would continue to bedevil it throughout the battle—was lack of knowledge regarding Sigel's location. That missing information, and the general confusion caused by lack of standardized uniforms, resulted in federal units often waiting in doubt until Rebel units had closed on them and opened fire. Du Bois summed it up for all of them when he later said, "During the entire engagement, I was so embarrassed by my ignorance of General [Colonel] Sigel's position, that on several occasions I did not fire upon their troops until they had formed within a few hundred yards of our line."[15]

The battle continued to seesaw, as first one side would gain a few yards and then be driven back to lose a few. After about half an hour of this, the Confederates realized that they were not going to take the hill on this attempt. Slowly, they started trying to fall back and disengage. To help them, McCulloch ordered Greer to take his cavalry, backed up by De Rosey Carroll's 1st Arkansas, break the Union line, and overrun the artillery.

The 3rd Texas had been formed on the federal right since moving up after Sigel's opening bombardment. Huddled in the trees, the horsemen had waited somewhat apprehensively as bullets frequently flew through the timber near them. Each time one of these death messengers whispered by, the men would duck in anticipation of being struck. A Captain Chisholm noticed this reaction and decided a brief lesson on military decorum was in order. The next time the men ducked, he said, "Boys, you mustn't dodge."

Just then, a cannonball came rushing through like a steam engine and Chisholm reflexively dropped low in his saddle. Straightening up somewhat abashedly, he added, "Except when the big ones come."[16]

Up in front, Greer, upon receiving McCulloch's order, stood up in his stirrups, waved his saber, and shouted, "Draw your pistols, men, and charge!"

The noise of the battle and the thick timber combined to keep a large part of the unit from hearing the command. Those nearest him responded by sinking spurs to their mounts and, "with a shout for Texas," plunged forward while the others followed raggedly, almost like a long freight train taking up the slack as it gets into motion. The charge was further fragmented by the heavy growth through which the cavalrymen were forced to push their mounts. Nonetheless, their appearance was a shock to the blue infantry, which had not anticipated facing a cavalry charge.

Although some broke and ran, most stood their ground, fired at the approaching horsemen, and then stepped aside into the underbrush to fire again into their flanks as they galloped by. Farther back, infantry with more time fired, fixed bayonets, and waited to take the charge. Totten saw them coming and ordered his guns to swing right to meet them. The cannoneers did so promptly. Totten's men then waited until the cavalry was within forty yards of the guns and blew them away.

The big guns fired with a crash and sent a cloud of canister into the charging horsemen. Saddles suddenly were empty, as the Union shot raked men from their horses or dropped their mounts from under them. In seconds, the cavalry charge dissolved into a rout, as those who survived the cannonade hurriedly sought shelter. The day's only cavalry action ended as suddenly as it had begun. Later, Totten disdainfully said of it: "This was the only demonstration made by their cavalry and it was so effete and ineffectual in its force and character as to deserve only the appellation of child's play. Their cavalry is utterly worthless on the battlefield."[17]

The cavalry had succeeded, however, in enabling the infantry to disengage and move back down to the base of Bloody Hill. Once again, by mutual consent, silence settled over the smoke-covered hill, except for the agonized screams, moans, and pleas of the wounded who covered the ground, often lying in rows or piled in heaps. So great was their number that Du Bois later said he had had to make a lane through the dead and wounded before he could move his guns.[18]

As the smoke slowly lifted, the 1st Iowa called in Rebel riders, who had been shot down but were able to walk, and made them prisoners. During this process, they noticed a flag lying on the ground about

Map 6. The Battle of Wilson's Creek, 1000-1130

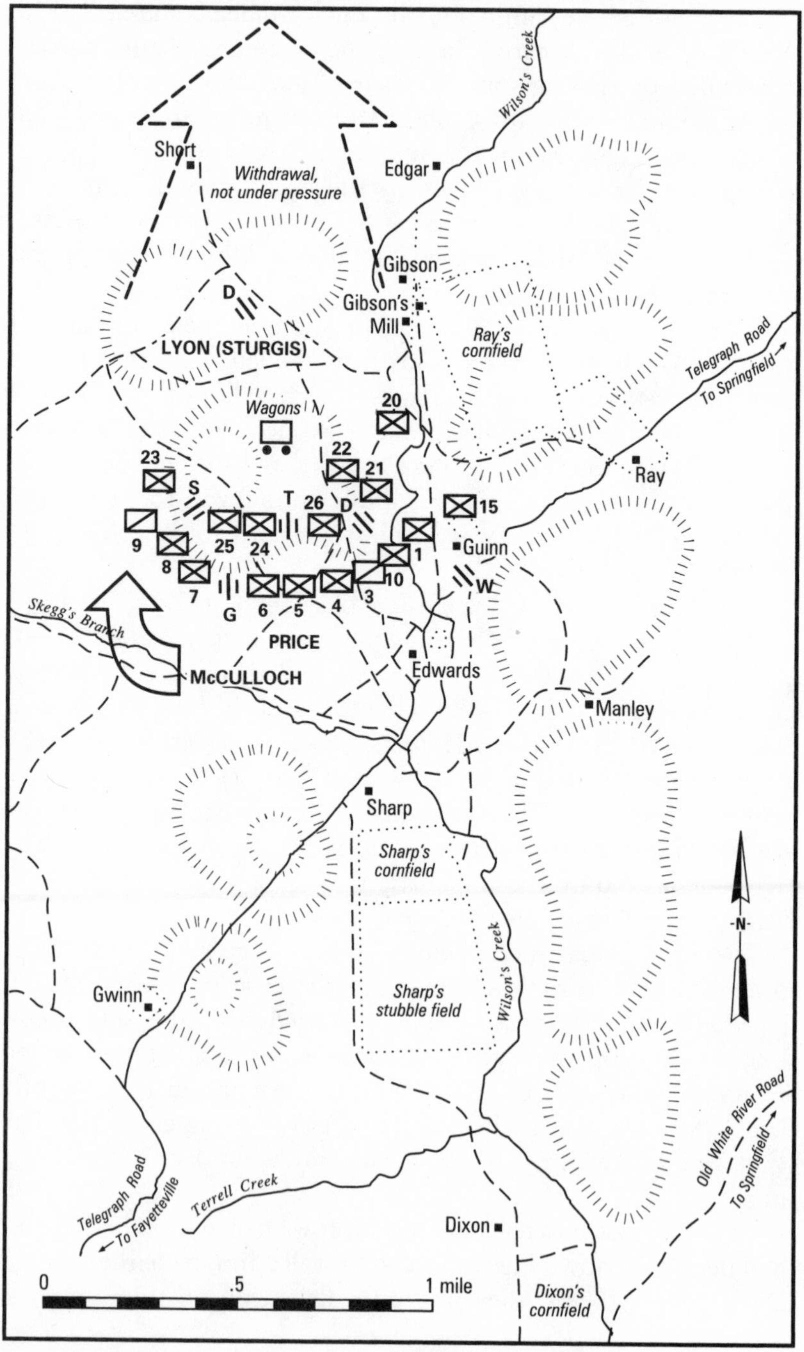

Short

*Withdrawal,
not under pressure*

Edgar

Wilson's Creek

Gibson

Gibson's
Mill

D

LYON (STURGIS)

*Ray's
cornfield*

Telegraph Road
To Springfield

Wagons

20

23

22

21

S

T   26   D

15

Ray

9   25   24

1

Guinn

8

10

W

7   G   6   5   4   3

Skegg's Branch

PRICE

McCULLOCH

Edwards

Manley

Sharp

*Sharp's
cornfield*

Gwinn

*Sharp's
stubble field*

Wilson's Creek

-N-

Telegraph Road
To Fayetteville

Terrell Creek

Dixon

Old White River Road
To Springfield

0   .5   1 mile

*Dixon's
cornfield*

Chronology

- Lyon dies leading the Federal attack.
- McCulloch comes to Price's aid, and they attack the Federals together.
- Sturgis, now in command, decides to withdraw.
- The Confederates are too tired and disorganized to pursue the Federals.

Confederate Forces

W	Woodruff	5	Slack
R	Reid	6	Clark
B	Bledsoe	7	1st Arkansas Mounted Rifles
G	Guibor	8	McBride
1	2d Arkansas Mounted Rifles	9	1st Arkansas Cavalry
3	Cawthorn	10	Foster
4	Weightman	15	1st Missouri State Guard

Federal Forces

T	Totten	22	1st Missouri
D	Du Bois	23	1st Kansas
S	Sokalski	24	1st Iowa
20	Plummer	25	2d Kansas
21	Osterhaus	26	Steele

Legend

Fields		Confederate axis of advance	
Farmhouses		Federal withdrawl	
Elevated areas		Infantry	
Artillery		Cavalry	

one hundred fifty yards in front of them. After a few minutes, a lone horseman emerged from the undergrowth riding slowly toward them. Thinking that he intended to surrender, several of the troops shouted, "Don't shoot!"

When the rider got within about twenty yards of the flag, he suddenly sank spurs to his mount and dashed for it. With one fluid motion the rider leaned low, swept up the fallen flag, and raced for safety waving the "Lone Star banner" over his head. Ware said, ". . . we didn't shoot the horseman because we liked his display of nerve." War was a new experience. As time passed, the opposing sides lost their appreciation for displays of "nerve."[19]

While the Texas rider was making his escape, a riderless horse came trotting slowly through the area he had just vacated. As the horse started to pass a bush, a wounded man in a bloodstained white shirt rose painfully from the ground and stopped it. The Iowans watched as the injured trooper slowly pulled himself into the saddle and headed for the Confederate lines. Again, the troops shouted, "Don't shoot," as they watched him ride away.[20]

On top of the hill, Wherry was still concerned about word of Lyon's death reaching the troops. He had had the general's body wrapped in a blanket to reduce the chance of it being identified. Now, it was concealed in a wagon, the driver given strict orders that it was not to be uncovered or removed. The effort was wasted. Such information was impossible to conceal from the troops, and word was already spreading. Hoping to minimize the impact on the army, officers were now sent to the various units with orders to try to bolster the troops' spirit. Ware reported that a big Regular Army cavalry officer spoke to them. The officer, he said, ". . . shouted and swore in a manner that was attractive even on the battlefield, and wound up with a great big oath and the expression, 'Life ain't long enough for them to lick us in.'"[21]

Meanwhile, Sturgis called the principal commanders to a meeting to decide upon their course of action. The overriding question before them was, "Where is Sigel?" If he were engaged in the Confederate rear, there remained the possibility of victory. If not, then retreat seemed the sensible decision. It was true that they had been able to hold off the Rebels, but they had been unable to advance. Lyon was dead. Sweeney, Deitzler, and Andrews were wounded—the last two critically and perhaps fatally. There seemed little prospect of victory without Sigel's support.[22]

Down below them, McCulloch and Price were preparing for another assault. Hébert and his 3rd Louisiana were ordered to swing wide in an attempt to outflank the Union force. A large part of Pearce's Arkansas troops had not yet been committed on Bloody Hill, and McCulloch now ordered them forward. Pearce told McIntosh to take charge of the 5th Arkansas and Reid's Battery and started for the front accompanied by Gratiot and the 3rd Arkansas. They forded Wilson's Creek and proceeded along the Confederate rear until they met Price, who told them that he wanted them on his left flank and led them toward the desired position. Although they were in cannon range of the federals during their entire movement, they received no fire, because the Yankees were uncertain of their identity and thought that they were probably Sigel's men.

Once he had pointed out their place to them, "Old Pap" told the fresh Arkansas troops, "You will soon be in a pretty hot place. . . . Keep as cool as the inside of a cucumber and give them thunder."

He then turned to Gratiot, who had served under him in the Mexican War, and said, "That's your position, Colonel; take it and hold it whatever you do. I will see that you are not too hard-pressed. Don't yield an inch."[23]

Earlier, as the Arkansans had left their position and moved toward Wilson's Creek, a staff officer, whom Sturgis had left forward to observe, came rushing up to the Union commander's meeting shouting, "Yonder comes Sigel! Yonder comes Sigel!"

Sturgis immediately went forward and watched through field glasses as the Arkansans forded the creek, crossed the Rebel rear, and went into position. His observation left him reasonably certain that the staff officer had been correct. He noted the soldiers ". . . wore a dress much resembling that of Sigel's brigade, and carried the American flag."

Once fully deployed, the new troops began a steady march forward up the sloping hillside. As they came on, the Yankees watched, frozen in place at the thought of joining the other element of the command. Then, from skirmishers out in front came the cry, "They are Rebels!"[24]

The "friendlies" now opened up, and all along the line, the Confederates again began an assault on Bloody Hill that Sturgis would call "the fiercest and most bloody engagement of the day." In response, Totten's cannon spewed a deluge of canister, and the Kansas troops laid down a sheet of small-arms fire. Gratiot's men, now supported by McIntosh and the 5th Arkansas, and perhaps remembering "Pap's" instructions, refused to break under the barrage. They simply dropped to the ground and returned fire as effectively as they could. Their stubbornness would cost them almost twenty percent of their strength in casualties.[25]

Like a rising tide, the Rebel army once again swelled up the hill. Behind them, Price was everywhere as he had been all day—encouraging, cajoling, directing. Several times earlier, musket fire had ripped through his clothing. Now, one struck him in the side, causing a painful wound. Although a bit unsettled by the injury, Price still maintained a sense of humor. Turning to his aide, he said, "That isn't fair. If I were as skinny as Lyon, that fellow would have missed me entirely."[26]

There was little room for humor on that hill that day, however. It was now as hot as the hinges of hell, for the breeze had died away. From the ground to high in the air, a dirty cloud of gunsmoke clogged the atmosphere, and the summer day trembled with the roar of guns, the wail of ricochets, and the terrible screams of those wounded and dying in what amounted to mutual, unbridled murder. Virtually muzzle to muzzle, the combatants blazed away at one another, loading and firing as fast as human hands could move. For perhaps twenty minutes, they stood like that as ". . . some of the best blood in the land was being spilled as recklessly as if it were ditch water."[27]

For the first time that day, the Union line held and never bent nor wavered. On the Union right, where the Arkansans were trying to breach his line, Blair had told his troops to "lay down and fire from that position," while canister whistled over them into their opponents. He later said, "The fire upon us was terrific, but not a man under my command broke ranks or left his place."[28]

That was true all along the line. At last, it proved to be too much for the attacking Rebels. They abruptly broke off and headed down the hill. The battle ended "as quick as a clap of thunder ceases." It was half past eleven in the morning.[29]

Just as the Rebels were breaking off, Sturgis received word that his troops were running out of ammunition. They had been engaged since daylight without food and with little water, and they were exhausted. Still, there was no sign of Sigel and, ominously, there had been reports of his ammunition being fired at the federal troops. Without Sigel's force and with his own low on ammunition, Sturgis believed that he faced annihilation. Determined not to lose this army that he had inherited, he gave the order to retreat.

The order was not well received by many of the commanders. Blair bemoaned the order saying he "was humiliated beyond expression." Granger rushed up to protest and suggested that they just fall back a short distance, regroup, and wait for word from Sigel. Sturgis, reflecting the importance of Granger's influence on him, agreed to take the plea under advisement for the moment. Then, from the side, a Sergeant Fraelich rode up on a lathered horse. Sigel's organization, he told Sturgis, was in full retreat, completely routed, and Sigel himself had been either killed or captured. That sealed it. Sturgis ordered retreat to Springfield.[30]

Granger could not believe his ears. He was convinced that they were on the verge of victory. Once again, he protested the order, pointing out that they had successfully met every Rebel challenge and that, even now, their opponents were in retreat.

Sturgis heard him out, then said, "I order you to leave the field."

"But they have burned their trains," Granger pointed out.

"I order you to leave the field!" Sturgis snapped.

The discipline of the old army told, and Granger nodded obediently.[31]

The army was already moving off at a normal pace and in good order. As they moved, Steele suddenly spotted an advancing Rebel force on the flank. It was Hébert, who had been told to try to outflank the Union line at the beginning of the last assault, just arriving. Granger quickly rounded up some troops to support Steele and drove the Louisianan off. The retreat now proceeded unmolested.[32]

Unaware of what was happening above them, McCulloch and Price were preparing for another assault. Like the federals, they had suffered serious damage to their senior commanders. Generals Price, Slack, and Clark, and colonels Weightman and Ben Brown had all been wounded—the latter two mortally. Still, they formed up the men and sent them up the hill again. This time neither canister, grape, nor small-arms fire met them—only silence. When they topped the hill and looked in front of them, they saw the federals retiring. Immediately, a loud cheer resounded down the line.

Over in the Ray House, where he lay suffering, Weightman asked, "What is it?"

"We have whipped them. They are gone," someone told him.

"Thank God!" he said, and died.[33]

On the crest of Bloody Hill, the senior Confederate commanders stood, field glasses in hand, and watched the retreating Union troops.

As they faded in the distance, Pearce probably spoke for the entire Rebel army when he said, "[We] *were glad to see him go.*"[34]

Back in Springfield, the doughty little Home Guards captain, carrying his lath like a field marshal's baton, once more rode up and reported. "Colonel Boyd! Sir! The cannings is ceased a-firin'!"[35]

CHAPTER XVIII

"A Mean Fowt Fight"

Sturgis marched his weary army about two miles from the battle site and halted it near some springs. For the first time since before daylight, the troops had a chance to eat a bite of whatever rations they had with them and to replenish their water supply. As they gathered around the cool water, battle weary and grimy with powder, smoke, and sweat, they slowly unwound from the tenseness battle had placed in them. So, too, must they have talked and wondered why they had fought so hard, only to retreat with Bloody Hill still in their possession.

After a time, orders came for them to resume their march. They climbed wearily to their feet and headed back toward the Little York Road they had come down the previous night. When they reached it, they spotted Farrand coming in, his mixed team pulling the rescued cannon Sigel had lost to the Rebels. He and the motley crew he had collected en route were given a rousing cheer as they joined the remainder of the army. Then, the entire force moved slowly down the road to Springfield, arriving at about five o'clock that afternoon.[1]

In Springfield, Sturgis learned that Sigel had escaped and was in town. He immediately sent Schofield to obtain information concerning Sigel's command and to inform the colonel that Sturgis had scheduled a meeting of the officers at Lyon's old headquarters.

Schofield was also instructed to inform Sigel that, because he was the senior surviving officer, Sturgis was prepared to relinquish command to him. Once Schofield had briefed Sigel, the former agreed to assume command and left the meeting as scheduled.

Sigel presided when the surviving officers who were able to participate gathered in the headquarters. Their mutual assessment was that, in all likelihood, McCulloch would attack the city the next morning. In any event, it would be foolhardy to assume otherwise. They also agreed that they lacked the strength to withstand a determined assault. Therefore, they must retreat to Rolla. And time was of the essence. Sigel gave the order of march and dismissed the meeting—ordering the officers to be ready to depart at two o'clock the next morning.[2]

Schofield was up early to ensure that all necessary preparations had been made and that the command was ready to start. He also made provisions for the wounded who could not be transported, and detailed four surgeons to care for them. One by one he went to each camp for a final check, finding each standing by in readiness. Then he went to Sigel's camp. "At 1:30 o'clock, I went to Colonel Sigel's camp," he said, "and found his wagons not loaded, his men apparently making preparations to cook their breakfast, and no preparations to march. I could find no officer to execute my commands nor any one to pay the slightest heed to what I said.

"I rode at once to Colonel Sigel's quarters, arriving there at 2 o'clock, and found him asleep in bed," he continued. "I aroused him, told him the hour for marching had arrived and that all were ready except his brigade. I urged upon him the importance of marching at once if at all. He said, 'Yes, I will move at once.' I started the train immediately, and sent the Iowa regiment ahead, directing it to halt about a mile from town. In this condition the column was delayed more than two hours while waiting for Colonel Sigel's brigade, so that the rear guard could not leave town till about 6 o'clock."[3]

This sorry state of affairs turned out to be the norm, not an anomaly. For two days, this inept management of the retreat continued. Repeatedly, troops stood idly, swearing in the hot sun while Sigel's brigade held things at a standstill to prepare a meal or to get leisurely under way. Typically, morning departure was delayed for breakfast, then a long halt was made at midday for lunch, and, finally, Sigel's brigade would stop early to prepare supper. The result was that units near the end of the column arrived at the campsite long after dark. Frequently, many companies were unable to find rations, as they scattered through the rough hilly country to camp, so many men went for twenty-four hours with nothing to eat. These problems were brought to the attention of the commander, but he remained impervious to suggestions for improving the conditions of the march.

On the morning of the third day, the column waited for three hours while Sigel's men butchered a beef and had breakfast. This incident broke the camel's back. The officers, other than those from Sigel's unit, besieged Sturgis with requests that he stop the nonsense that was going on by resuming command of the army. With the situation approaching mutiny, the major agreed to do so, and went to find Sigel. Once he found him, Sturgis informed him that he intended to resume command on the basis that ". . . Sigel, although mustered into the United States service, had no commission from any competent authority."

Sigel immediately protested this action. He soon withdrew that protest, however, when he discovered that most of the officer corps supported Sturgis. Salomon was not among them, however, so he proposed instead that the matter be put to a vote of the officers present.

Sturgis told him that he would not do that, noting that, if he did, the vote might go to Sigel. "Then," he told Salomon, "some of you might refuse to obey my orders, and I should be under the necessity of shooting you."[4]

That ended any expressed interest in elections. With Sturgis in command, the retreat promptly got under way and proceeded in an orderly fashion to Rolla without further incident. The Union's great sweep to subdue southwestern Missouri was over—a failure in the eyes of the South; a victory in the eyes of the North. The sweep was indeed a failure if one considers only that the Union left the field to the Rebels. It was a victory, however, if one looks at the larger picture—Missouri certainly would not leave the Union in the near term nor, in all likelihood, would it ever secede.

As for the doughty little general who had led them, they had inadvertently left his body lying on the battlefield. The wagon in which his body had been placed was pressed into service as an ambulance. As it was about to leave for Springfield carrying wounded, a sergeant ordered Lyon's body removed and placed under a nearby tree, saying, "There will be an ambulance here in a minute for it." No ambulance came.

As the body lay there unattended, some of the Union wounded gathered about their fallen leader. In about an hour, this gathering attracted the attention of a group of Arkansans who, when they discovered who it was, hurriedly sent word back to McCulloch. The body was then loaded on a wagon to be taken to McCulloch's headquarters. Before this could be done, however, an order arrived to turn the body over to Dr. Melcher, who had returned to the battlefield with Rains's surgeon. Lyon's remains were then taken to Price's headquarters where, after Price and some of his officers had viewed them, they were turned over to Dr. Melcher.[5]

Approximately halfway to Springfield, Sturgis was advised that the general's body had been left behind. He immediately dispatched a detail commanded by Lt. Charles W. Canfield, under a flag of truce, to see whether he could obtain McCulloch's permission to retrieve the body. McCulloch readily granted the request, saying ". . . he wished he had a thousand other dead Yankee bodies to send off." By then, however, the general's remains were well on their way to Springfield.

Melcher, escorted by Rains and some of his cavalry, had taken the body to the Ray House. There, in the front room with Rains as a witness, the doctor examined the body and had it cleaned. It was then wrapped in a counterpane, loaded on an ambulance, and taken to Springfield, accompanied by an escort of Rebel volunteers.

Upon arrival in the city, Lyon's body was taken to his old headquarters, and Sturgis was notified of its return. In consultation with his officers, Sturgis decided to remove the body to Rolla with the army, if at all possible. Dr. E. C. Franklin was contacted and asked to embalm the body, or preserve it by some other means. Dr. Franklin soon discovered that the nature of Lyon's injuries made it impossible to preserve the remains and personally advised Sturgis of his findings. In response to his report, Franklin was given ". . . verbal orders to attend to the disposal of the body in the best possible manner."

At this point, the remains were claimed by Mrs. Mary Phelps, wife of Congressman (Colonel) John S. Phelps, to have it prepared for burial. Once again, the Union army marched away in retreat, leaving the mortal remains of its late commander behind.

Because the body could not be embalmed, Mrs. Phelps had it hermetically sealed in a zinc-encased coffin and placed in a milk cellar at her farm, pending instructions for its final disposition. The Rebels soon discovered its location, and many went to the farm in an effort to view it, which led to considerable unpleasantness. There were some who threatened to take it and drag it behind a horse like Hector had been dragged at Troy or to "cut the damned heart out" to be shown as a relic. One officer of Parson's division went so far as to say callously to Mrs. Phelps, "There is quite a contrast betwixt the resting place of old Lyon's body and his soul, isn't there, Madame? The one is in the ice house; the other in hell!"

Mrs. Phelps pleaded with Price for help in preventing the desecration of the remains of his late adversary. He responded by providing a burial detail that interred it in her rose garden. About a week later, Lyon's cousin, Danford Knowlton, and his brother-in-law, John B. Hasler, arrived to escort the body East for final interment. Under their direction, it was disinterred, placed in a three-hundred-pound lead coffin, and started on its journey to its final resting place.[6]

In the interim, Lyon, the first Civil War general to die on the battlefield, had become a national hero. After his body lay in state for two days at Frémont's headquarters, the train carrying his remains made its way slowly across the flag- and crepe-draped country. It was besieged at every small town and village by those who wished to express their grief and place flowers on the coffin. In Cincinnati, Philadelphia, New York, and Hartford, it was removed from the train and lay in state, as thousands passed to view the casket containing the country's newest hero. Finally, on September 5, after a massive funeral and long procession, the coffin was lowered into the earth in a small cemetery in Phoenixville, Connecticut—a short distance from where Lyon had sprung from New England's rocks. A few months later, he was voted the Thanks of Congress, one of only fifteen individuals so honored during the Civil War.[7]

And what of the senior commander who had left Nathaniel Lyon out on the end of the string to die? Frémont, whom Lincoln is alleged to have once described as ". . . the damnedest scoundrel that ever lived, but in the infinite mercy of Providence . . . also the damnedest fool," remained firmly ensconced in his palatial headquarters in St. Louis.[8] Although the ultimate responsibility for his actions clearly lay with Lyon, he deserved better than he got from his commander. Frémont's belated, halfhearted actions to provide long-needed support and reinforcements were far less than his subordinate had every right to expect. Further, Frémont, who possessed overall responsibility for that theater of the war, had an obligation to weigh carefully the actions of his subordinate. And, if he were in danger of overstepping his authority or capability, he had a duty to stop him. Frémont failed miserably in both regards.

"The Pathfinder" was a dreamer, content to isolate himself behind his own Praetorian guard, seemingly ignorant of, and disinterested in, the real world that was his responsibility. His reception of Schofield after Wilson's Creek clearly demonstrates how little he appreciated either what had occurred or his role in it.

When Schofield arrived back in St. Louis, he found that Frank Blair had returned from the congressional session. The congressman asked Schofield to accompany him to see Frémont. Schofield noted that the headquarters was surrounded by guards with all ingress apparently blocked. Blair knew the secret "word or sign," however, and they were immediately ushered into the general's office, which occupied a suite that stretched from the front to the rear of the building. Schofield describes what happened: "The general received me cordially, but, to my great surprise, no questions were asked, nor any mention made, of the bloody field from which I had just come, where Lyon had been killed, and his army, after a desperate battle, compelled to retreat. I was led at once to a large table on which maps were spread out, from which the general proceeded to explain at length the plans of the great campaign for which he was then preparing. . . . I listened attentively for . . . more than an hour. . . . [then] the explanation . . . ended [and] Colonel Blair and I took our leave. . . ."

As they walked down the street, Blair broke a long silence to ask, "Well, what do you think of him?"

Schofield, who shared the disdain in which most of the army held the Pathfinder, said of this question, "I replied, in words rather too strong to repeat in print, to the effect that my opinion as to his wisdom was the same as it always had been."

Blair responded, "I have been suspecting that for some time."[9]

There was now an instant hue and cry, led by the Blair family, for Frémont's head. He found himself pilloried for his failure to support his subordinate, as well as for the state of affairs in Missouri. Desperate to recover, he now began marshaling forces to retake the portion of the state that had been lost and to regain his position. As a part of his overall effort, he even issued his own "emancipation proclamation" and refused to withdraw it when requested to do so by the president. The commander in chief took the only course left to him. He sacked the Pathfinder.[10]

As for Lyon's subordinate, Sigel, he lived up to the prophecy Steele had made. At Carthage, Wilson's Creek, and during the retreat, he demonstrated that his ability to command was questionable at best and that he was probably "not to be trusted with a separate command." This conclusion is confirmed by the word of many of the senior officers who served under or with him during that time. Still, he went on to wear the two stars of a major general, probably largely owing to his ability to attract the support of the German-American community. In any event, he served out his time in the army still showing an "odd combination of ineptitude and ability," with emphasis on the former.[11]

One must also question Sturgis's decision to retreat. Although his concern about the loss of Sigel's force is understandable, the fact remains that his army had firmly withstood the best the Rebels had been able to give. Further, he had been privy, before the start of the engagement, to intelligence that told him the Rebels were also short of ammunition, which meant that they were probably no better off than his own force. Finally, most of his subordinate commanders were opposed to leaving the field—chief among them Granger upon whom he had relied in the past. The possibility of his losing does not seem to offset the possibility that he could have won the engagement.

At Wilson's Creek, Confederate response to the Union retreat was tentative at best, which led to another confrontation between Price and McCulloch. Initially, the Confederates were not certain that the federal troops had really thrown in the towel. Cautiously, they prepared themselves for another attack, but skirmishers probing ahead soon sent back word that the Union army was in full retreat. As soon as Price acquired this bit of intelligence, he demanded that McCulloch immediately launch a full-scale pursuit and capitalize on this golden opportunity to destroy their exhausted and retreating foe. To Price's dismay, McCulloch, who initially appeared to agree, waffled, then flatly refused. He gave as his reasons the lack of ammunition and the exhausted condition of the troops after a morning's combat. Price countered that their enemy was in no better condition in either category and, if necessary, they could crush him with sword and bayonet. McCulloch remained unmoved. A furious Price exercised his prerogative to resume independent command, but then, for reasons of his own, did nothing.

Apparently, during all the discussion of ammunition shortages and fatigue, little consideration was given to the fact that plenty of cavalry was available that had done little service that day. A shortage of ammunition notwithstanding, it represented a highly mobile force that, properly employed, had the capability to deliver a devastating blow to an army strung out in retreat. Yet McCulloch chose not to employ it, other than a bit in pursuit of Sigel, which amounted to no more than a follow-up to the pursuit Major had initiated at the beginning of Sigel's retreat. Greer and Carroll were sent after Sigel's command, while the remainder of the army was ordered back to camp. McCulloch later said that he had ordered the army to be ready to march that night, but, if he had, nothing came of it.

The cavalry force that he dispatched advanced only a short distance before it met Major's command coming in with prisoners and a captured artillery piece. This suggested to Greer that a further attempt at pursuit of Sigel would probably be fruitless. Therefore, he limited his activity to crossing the James River, reconnoitering the Delaware Road toward Springfield for a short distance, and returning to camp. The termination of Greer's small effort completed Confederate attempts to follow up on their questionable "victory" at Wilson's Creek.[12]

More than just a shortage of ammunition and troop fatigue influenced McCulloch's decision not to pursue Sturgis, however. Actually, he still had no confidence in the Missourians, for he trusted neither the troops nor their leaders. True, they had fought that day with unquestioned determination and valor, but the Texan still questioned their capability. Moreover, he remained uneasy about leading his men into Missouri, because he was uncertain that he had the full support of the Confederacy in such an endeavor. Given the Confederacy's response to his desire for a combined campaign with Rebel forces in Missouri, its commitment appeared to him to be about as certain as Frémont's support of Lyon.

Considering all of this, one must still question the Southern failure to follow up when the Union left the field of battle. A determined pursuit, capitalizing on their overwhelming advantage in cavalry, would have given them an opportunity to have destroyed the Union army at an apparently acceptable level of risk. Had that occurred, the long-term picture in Missouri might well have been different. Their failure to pursue virtually eliminated any chance, if indeed there had been one, to reverse the flow of military and political fortune in Missouri. And, in retrospect, one must say for very poor reasons.

The night passed uneventfully; no federal attack materialized. Early the next morning, McCulloch ordered Lt. Col. Walter P. Lane of the 3rd Texas Cavalry to take a force to Springfield and "see what the enemy was doing." Lane arrived about eleven o'clock that morning and, because he expected to find a large Union force, entered the outskirts very cautiously. As the Texans slowly moved along, Lane spotted a Rebel soldier nonchalantly carrying his gun on his shoulder and eating from a large chunk of bread as he walked along.

"Who the devil are you and what are you doing here?" Lane wanted to know.

"[I'm] one of you-uns, and belong to General Price's company," the man told him. He then went on to explain that he had gotten "mighty hungry" on duty the night before and decided to ". . . drop into town and see what them Federals was up to, and get something to eat."

Satisfied that a threat no longer existed in Springfield, Lane promptly secured the town, raising the 3rd Texas Cavalry's flag over the Green County courthouse. He then sent the all clear back to McCulloch. The Texan moved the remainder of his force to the city and put them in camp around it. The remainder of the wounded were also moved to town, and all available buildings were converted into hospitals, where "almost every woman in Springfield, of either side, who could stand the sight of mangled soldiers" went to work tending for them. All federal supplies and equipment were confiscated for the use of the Rebels. Prisoners were either exchanged or released, with McCulloch saying ". . . he had rather fight than feed them."[13]

The day after arriving in Springfield, McCulloch issued a conciliatory proclamation to the people of Missouri. In it he said, "I do not come among you to make war upon any of your people, whether Union or otherwise; the Union people will be protected in their rights and property. . . . Prisoners of the Union army, who have been arrested by the army, will be released and allowed to return to their friends. Missouri must be allowed to choose her own destiny. . . . the time has now arrived for the people of the State to act. You can no longer procrastinate. Missouri must now take her position, be it North or South."

The Texan could not make it stick, however. He tried to keep his men out of any questionable activity by issuing a "victory" order which concluded, ". . . the general hopes that the laurels you have gained will not be tarnished by a single outrage. The private property of citizens of either party must be respected. Soldiers who fought as well as you did . . . cannot rob or plunder." It was ignored by many. There were arrests of Union sympathizers, property was confiscated, and individuals were harmed. In the end, much of the population had little good to think or say about the army that had "liberated" them, causing McCulloch to say, "We had as well been in Boston as far as the friendly feelings of the inhabitants are concerned."[14]

Perhaps a Union prisoner stated the feelings of the Missourians in that locality best of all. Hearing a group of the 3rd Louisiana singing "Dixie," he said, "Ah, well! I only wish you had stayed in Dixie."[15]

Price, on the other hand, was by no means conciliatory. He, too, issued a proclamation in which he promised to protect ". . . every peaceable citizen . . . if he has not taken an active part in the cruel warfare, which has been waged against the good people of this State, by the ruthless enemies whom we have just defeated." He then ended the proclamation by warning ". . . all evil disposed persons, who may support the usurpations of any one claiming to be provisional or temporary Governor of Missouri, or who shall in any other way give aid or comfort to the enemy, that they will be held as enemies, and treated accordingly."[16]

So, between the two commanders, it ended much as it had begun. One neither liked, trusted, nor agreed with the other. When Price urged that they continue their joint efforts and press forward with retaking the state, McCulloch declined. He had all he wanted of "Pap" Price and Missouri for the time being. He took Pearce with him and headed back to Arkansas. As for Price, he was determined to go it alone. He gathered his force and started north on a short campaign that resulted in the capture of Lexington, but the effort soon petered out. For both of them, just down the road lay Pea Ridge— where the Texan would die and the Missourian would see the last faint hope that his state would fall to the South virtually disappear.

Worst of all, the battle just ended had really not finally settled anything nor, for that matter, probably been necessary. There was no compelling reason for Lyon to have engaged in it. Springfield had no special strategic value and, although the loss of southwestern Missouri was not particularly desirable to the Union, neither was it particularly important. Lyon had achieved the major strategic goal of the Union when he captured Jefferson City and Boonville, and with them control of the Missouri River. By doing so, he cut the state in two, acquired control of all major transportation routes in Missouri between the East and West, effectively made it impossible for the elected officials of the state to govern, and isolated those in the northern part of the state who were Southern sympathizers. The Union only had to hold that line, and Missouri was saved. The remainder of the state could be cleaned up at her leisure.

There simply was no compelling reason for Lyon to attack a force that outnumbered him two to one. Retreat to either Rolla or Fort Leavenworth was clearly open to him. He had little intelligence to support his expressed concern about being attacked. Virtually all of his officers believed that retreat was the proper course of action; Schofield advocated it to the point of insubordination—confident, he said, that the verdict of history would support him. Furthermore, there was little to assure Lyon that the risk he was taking in attacking was not a far greater threat to the safety of his army.

To have run, however, would not have been in character for Nathaniel Lyon. He had come to impose his will, which could not be accomplished by retreating. To the grizzled little Yankee, this was a crusade, worth any risk to prove the righteousness of his cause. Those who defied his government, especially for the purpose of enslaving others, must be punished, and Lyon considered himself the instrument of their punishment. Therefore, he went to battle with an improbable plan that required him to violate the most basic military principles by splitting his small force to attack a superior one. But, in the end, it was a close thing. Although Lyon's army left the field, it was clearly not defeated, and many of its officers believed that they would have won if they had only stood their ground.

Sadly, the battle accomplished little where its major purpose was concerned. It truly had little impact on either side insofar as the larger war was concerned, unlike Lyon's overall campaign, which was clearly an important strategic victory for the Union. It did, however, have major impact on the region in that it would increase, rather than settle, the "bad blood" that existed along the broad area of the Kansas-Missouri border. Many of its participants discovered that they did not like "organized" war, so they sought to satisfy their destructive inclinations in guerrilla warfare and, later, outlawry. For years to come, Missouri, Arkansas, and Kansas would be marked by lone blackened chimneys where homes had once stood, as their people suffered and died at the hands of the likes of Quantrill, Lane, Anderson, Jennison, and Montgomery. Col. John M. Palmer was right on the mark when he remarked, "The truth is that the battle of Wilson's Creek was a folly . . . ."[17]

For a battle that solved so little, it was singularly ferocious and costly. Until then, it was the second largest battle ever fought on the North American continent and there had never been a fiercer one. Poorly trained men—most of whom had never seen combat; some mesmerized by anticipated glory—faced one another on the side of a blackjack-covered Ozark hill that hot August day and met a grim reality. There was neither glory, nor justice, nor solutions in battle—only death, suffering, and destruction. They learned that too late, however, and there was nothing for them to do but tough it out as long as they could. So, they marched up and down the hill, stood in lines, and slaughtered one another for five hours. Ultimately, there was no victor; not much was proved other than that volunteer soldiers could stand and fight and kill and die just as well as the professionals. It also gave a nation reason to think. The supposedly nice, quick, clean, and easy war was only a fantasy. The battle along Wilson's Creek was a preview of the coming horror, which left a legacy that lingers in the nation more than a century later.

When the toll was tallied, there were thirteen hundred seventeen Union casualties—258 killed, 873 wounded, and 186 missing or captured. The Confederates suffered 1,230 casualties—279 dead and 951 wounded. In terms of the number of troops engaged, it would be one of the bloodiest battles of a long and bloody war. Of it, Snead said, "Never before—considering the number engaged—had so bloody a battle been fought upon American soil; seldom has a bloodier one been fought on any modern field."[18]

As Col. Hardy A. Kemp put it, "It was a soldier's battle, and it was fought that way." Down in the dirt and rocks and brush they went at it nose to nose and gave all that could be given. A Rebel officer probably summed it up best when he said, "It was a mean fowt fight."[19]

A visitor to the battlefield, about two weeks after the battle ended, described what he saw: "Dead horses, old clothes, broken wagons, canteens and haversacks, were strewn over the field. . . . Oak trees a foot in diameter were cut in two by the cannon balls. More corpses were found here [Bloody Hill] than elsewhere on the field. Here Lyon fell. Here the last of the battle was fought. Evidently many of the wounded had crawled into the shade of the trees and died there, while others died in the ranks as they fell. The whole scene was a mournful picture of war's desolation." He also said of it, "The hill is now called, by the citizens living thereabout, 'Bloody Hill'"—and so it is today.[20]

Appendix A

NORTHERN ORDER OF BATTLE AT WILSON'S CREEK[1]

Union Army (5,600)[2]
Brig. Gen. Nathaniel Lyon

1st Brigade (884), Maj. Samuel D. Sturgis
  1st U.S. Infantry, Capt. Joseph B. Plummer (4 cos., 300 men)
  2nd Missouri Infantry Battalion, Maj. Peter J. Osterhaus (150)
  Company I, 2nd Kansas Mounted Infantry and Company D, 1st U.S. Cavalry (350)
  Company F, 2nd U.S. Artillery, Capt. James Totten (6 guns, 84 men)

2nd Brigade (1,200), Col. Franz Sigel
  3rd Missouri Infantry, Lt. Col. Anselm Albert, and 5th Missouri Infantry, Col. Charles E. Salomon (990)
  Company I, 1st U.S. Cavalry, Capt. Eugene A. Carr (65)
  Company C, 2nd U.S. Dragoons, 2nd Lt. Charles E. Farrand (60)
  Backoff's Battery, lieutenants Edward Schuetzenbach and Frederick Shaefer (6 guns, 85 men)

3rd Brigade (1,116), Lt. Col. George Andrews
  1st Missouri Infantry, Lt. Col. George L. Andrews (775)
  2nd U.S. Infantry, Capt. Frederick Steele (4 cos., 275 men)
  Du Bois's Battery, 2nd Lt. John V. Du Bois (4 guns, 66 men)

4th Brigade (2,400), Col. George W. Deitzler
  1st Kansas Infantry, Col. George W. Deitzler (800)
  2nd Kansas Infantry, Lt. Col. Charles W. Blair (600)
  1st Iowa Infantry, Col. John F. Bates (800)
  Home Guards, Capt. Clark Wright (200)

Courtesy U.S. Army Command and General Staff College

Appendix B

SOUTHERN ORDER OF BATTLE AT WILSON'S CREEK[1]

Confederate Army (10,175)[2]
Brig. Gen. Ben McCulloch

Pearce's Brigade (2,234), Brig. Gen. N. B. Pearce
  1st Arkansas Cavalry, Col. De Rosey Carroll (350)
  Carroll's Cavalry, Capt. Charles A. Carroll (40)
  3rd Arkansas Infantry, Col. John R. Gratiot (500)
  4th Arkansas Infantry, Col. J. D. Walker (550)
  5th Arkansas Infantry, Col. Tom P. Dockery (650)
  Woodruff's Battery, Capt. W. E. Woodruff, Jr. (4 guns, 71 men)
  Reid's Battery, Capt. J. G. Reid (4 guns, 73 men)

McCulloch's Brigade (2,720), Brig. Gen. Ben McCulloch
  3rd Louisiana Infantry, Col. Louis Hébert (700)
  Arkansas Infantry, Lt. Col. Dandridge McRae (220)
  1st Arkansas Mounted Rifles, Col. T. J. Churchill (600)
  2nd Arkansas Mounted Rifles, Col. James McIntosh (400)
  South Kansas-Texas Mounted Regiment (3rd Texas Cavalry), Col. Elkanah Greer (800)

Missouri State Guard (5,221)
Maj. Gen. Sterling Price

2nd Division (2,526), Brig. Gen. James S. Rains

Infantry Brigade (1,250), Col. Richard H. Weightman
  1st Missouri State Guard Infantry
  2nd Missouri State Guard Infantry
  3rd Missouri State Guard Infantry
  4th Missouri State Guard Infantry

Cavalry Brigade (1,210), Col. James Cawthorn
  Peyton's Cavalry
  McCowan's Cavalry
  Hunter's Cavalry

Bledsoe's Battery (3 guns, 66 men), Capt. Hiram Bledsoe

3rd Division (573), Brig. Gen. Charles Clark
  Burbridge's Infantry, Col. John Q. Burbridge (273)
  Major's Cavalry, Lt. Col. James P. Major (300)

4th Division (934), Brig. Gen. William Y. Slack
  Hughes Infantry, Col. John T. Hughes and Thornton's Infantry,
    Maj. C. C. Thornton (650)
  Rives' Cavalry, Col. Benjamin A. Rives (234)

6th Division (601), Brig. Gen. Monroe M. Parsons
  Kelly's Infantry, Col. Joseph M. Kelly (195)
  Brown's Cavalry, Col. Ben Brown (406)
  Guibor's Battery, Capt. Henry Guibor (4 guns, 61 men)

7th Division (645), Brig. Gen. James H. McBride
  Wingo's Infantry, Col. Edmund T. Wingo (300)
  Foster's Infantry, Col. Robert A. Foster (305)
  Campbell's Cavalry, Capt. Campbell (40)

Courtesy U.S. Army Command and General Staff College

Notes

CHAPTER 1: A WOLF BY THE EARS

1. Milton D. Rafferty, *Historical Atlas of Missouri*, 25.
2. August K. Klapp, *The Ray House*, 1–3.
3. Mark M. Boatner III, *The Civil War Dictionary*, 556–557.
4. Sen. Robert C. Byrd. *The Senate: 1797–1989*, CD-ROM, *U. S. History on CD-ROM*.
5. Ibid.
6. Robert Leckie, *None Died in Vain*, 31.
7. Ibid., 26.
8. Patricia L. Faust, ed., *Historical Times Illustrated Encyclopedia of the Civil War*, 725.
9. Ibid., 408.
10. Bryd, *The Senate*.
11. James M. McPherson, *Battle Cry of Freedom*, 88.
12. Bryd, *The Senate*.
13. Ibid.
14. Ibid.
15. McPherson, *Battle Cry*, 122–123.
16. Kenneth Lauren Burns, *The Civil War*, video.

CHAPTER 2: A LOT LIKE WAR

1. Stephen Z. Starr, *Jennison's Jayhawkers*, 5.
2. Jay Monaghan, *Civil War on the Western Border*, 5.
3. Ibid., 5–12.
4. Starr, *Jennison's*, 7–8.
5. Monaghan, *Civil War*, 20.
6. Ibid., 28–29.
7. Alice Nichols, *Bleeding Kansas*, 42–43.
8. Monaghan, *Civil War*, 34.

9. Nichols, *Bleeding Kansas*, 49–54.

10. Starr, *Jennison's*, 10.

11. "John Brown's War," *Civil War Journal*, video.

12. Nichols, *Bleeding Kansas*, 62–63.

13. Monaghan, *Civil War*, 34–44.

14. Ibid., 46–48.

15. Christopher Phillips, *Damned Yankee*, 82.

16. Monaghan, *Civil War*, 50–52.

17. Ibid., 56–58.

18. Stephen B. Oates, *To Purge This Land with Blood*, 130–135.

19. Monaghan, *Civil War*, 63.

20. Oates, *To Purge this Land*, 155.

21. Monaghan, *Civil War*, 64.

22. Nichols, *Bleeding Kansas*, 128–129.

23. Monaghan, *Civil War*, 71–78.

24. Ibid., 79.

25. Ibid., 80–82.

26. Nichols, *Bleeding Kansas*, 142–143.

27. Ibid., 150–156.

28. Monaghan, *Civil War*, 88–89.

29. Ibid., 94–95.

30. Nichols, *Bleeding Kansas*, 190–199.

31. Leckie, *None Died in Vain*, 62.

32. Monaghan, *Civil War*, 99–101.

33. Ibid., 101–104.

34. Leckie, *None Died in Vain*, 61.

35. Oates, *To Purge This Land*, 254; Monaghan, *Civil War,* 103–104.

36. Monaghan, *Civil War*, 104–105.

37. Oates, *To Purge This Land*, 261.

38. Ibid., 261–263.

39. Monaghan, *Civil War*, 111–113.

40. Ibid., 113–116.

41. Burke Davis, *They Called Him Stonewall*, 7.

CHAPTER 3: "A HELL OF A FIX"

1. Elmo Ingenthron, *Borderland Rebellion*, 30–33; Edward Conrad Smith, *The Borderland in the Civil War*, 30–32.

2. Hans Christian Adamson, *Rebellion in Missouri: 1861*, 72.

3. Robert E. Shalhope, *Sterling Price*, 108.

4. William E. Parrish, *Turbulent Partnership: Missouri and the Union*, 4–5.

5. Ibid., 5.

6. Rachel Sherman Thorndike, ed., *The Sherman Letters*, 85.

7. Smith, *The Borderland*, 78.

8. Robert Leckie, *The Wars of America*, Vol. 1, 400.

9. William S. McFeely, *Grant*, 82.

10. John McElroy, *The Struggle for Missouri*, 19.

11. James M. McPherson, *Battle Cry of Freedom*, 290.

12. Parrish, *Turbulent Partnership*, 6–7.

13. McElroy, *The Struggle*, 29–30.

14. Ibid., 33.

15. Robert Leckie, *None Died in Vain*, 127.

16. McElroy, *The Struggle*, 35–36.

17. Ibid., 30–33.

18. Capt. Richard Scott Price, *Nathaniel Lyon: Harbinger from Kansas*, 1.

19. Parrish, *Turbulent Partnership*, 16.

20. Christopher Phillips, *Damned Yankee*, 68–69.

21. McElroy, *The Struggle*, 28.

22. Ibid., 44–45.

23. Parrish, *Turbulent Partnership*, 12.

24. Shelby Foote, *The Civil War*, Vol. 1, 535.

25. *War of the Rebellion Official Records of the Union and Confederate Armies*, Series I, Vol. 1 (*OR, 1*) 656, 658.

26. Ibid., 658–659.

27. Adamson, *Rebellion*, 28.

28. *OR*, 1, 661.

29. Ibid., 653.

30. Ibid., 661, 663.

31. Parrish, *Turbulent Partnership*, 6–8; Basil W. Duke, *Reminiscences of General Basil W. Duke, CSA*, 42.

32. Gen. William T. Sherman, *Memoirs of General William T. Sherman*, 171.

CHAPTER 4: "THE SECESSIONISTS ARE EUCHRED"

1. Eugene F. Ware, *The Lyon Campaign in Missouri*, xv; Elmo Ingenthron, *Borderland Rebellion*, 37.

2. Robert Leckie, *None Died in Vain*, 146–147; Christopher Phillips, *Damned Yankee*, 156.

3. John McElroy, *The Struggle for Missouri*, 50.

4. Bruce Catton, *The Coming Fury*, 371.

5. *War of the Rebellion Official Records of the Union and Confederate Armies*, Series I, Vol. 1 (*OR, 1*), 666–667.

6. Ibid., 667.

7. Hans Christian Adamson, *Rebellion in Missouri: 1861*, 26–27.

8. Ibid., 27; Edward Conrad Smith, *The Borderland in the Civil War*, 227.

9. Col. Hardy A. Kemp, *About Nathaniel Lyon*, 65.

10. Ibid., 65; *OR*, 1, 668.

11. Kemp, *About Nathaniel Lyon*, 63.

12. Frank Moore, ed., *The Rebellion Record*, Vol. 2, 447.

13. *OR*, 1, 649.

14. Ibid., 669.

15. Adamson, *Rebellion in Missouri*, 16.

16. Ibid., 28.

17. Ibid., 28–29.

18. Ibid., 29–31.

19. *OR*, 1, 670.

20. L. U. Reavis, *The Life and Military Services of Gen. William Selby Harney*, 354.

21. *OR*, 1, 688.

22. Moore, *The Rebellion*, 147–148; Adamson, *Rebellion in Missouri*, 35–36; Phillips, *Damned Yankee*, 166–167; Allan Nevins, *The War for the Union*, Vol. 1, 123.

23. *OR*, 1, 675–676.

24. Ibid., 675.

25. Ibid., 652.

26. Ibid., 679–680.

27. Ibid., 690.

28. Robert E. Shalhope, *Sterling Price*, 156–157.

29. Catton, *The Coming Fury*, 372–373.

30. Phillips, *Damned Yankee*, 177.

CHAPTER 5: "SWEENEY, THEY SURRENDER"

1. Hans Christian Adamson, *Rebellion in Missouri: 1861*, 40.

2. Ibid.

3. Jay Monaghan, *Civil War on the Western Border 1854–1865*, 130.

4. Tamora is a type of marble.

5. Christopher Phillips, *Damned Yankee*, 181.

6. Ibid., 182.

7. Authorities differ over whether Lyon actually visited Camp Jackson in disguise. It seems to me that such an escapade fits Lyon's impetuous nature and, therefore, I have elected to include it.

8. Adamson, *Rebellion*, 41–50; John McElroy, *The Struggle for Missouri*, 58–59.

9. Phillips, *Damned Yankee*, 184–185.

10. Adamson, *Rebellion*, 51–53.

11. William E. Parrish, *Turbulent Partnership*, 23.

12. Phillips, *Damned Yankee*, 185–187.

13. *War of Rebellion Official Records of the Confederate and Union Armies*, Series I, Vol. 3, (*OR*, 3), 5–6.

14. Phillips, *Damned Yankee*, 187.

15. Ibid., 187–188; Adamson, *Rebellion*, 58–59.

16. Ibid., 60.

17. McElroy, *The Struggle*, 62–63.

18. Phillips, *Damned Yankee*, 189.

19. McElroy, *The Struggle*, 63.

20. Phillips, *Damned Yankee*, 189.

21. Ibid., 189–190; Adamson, *Rebellion*, 60–62.

22. Adamson, *Rebellion*, 62–63.

23. Phillips, *Damned Yankee*, 191–192.

24. Gen. William T. Sherman, *Memoirs of General William T. Sherman*, 173–174.

25. Phillips, *Damned Yankee*, 192.

26. Col. Hardy A. Kemp, *About Nathaniel Lyon*, 73–74.

27. *OR*, 3, 7–9.

28. Parrish, *Turbulent Partnership*, 24.

29. Ibid.; Kemp, *About Nathaniel Lyon*, 73.

30. Adamson, *Rebellion*, 70.

31. Ibid., 74–75; Wiley Britton, *The Civil War on the Border*, 14–16; Frank Moore, *The Rebellion Record*, Vol. 1, 242.

32. Monaghan, *Civil War*, 133.

33. Britton, *The Civil War on the Border*, 12; Edward Conrad Smith, *The Borderland in the Civil War*, 238–239.

34. *OR*, 3, 9.

35. Phillips, *Damned Yankee*, 195–197; Adamson, *Rebellion*, 80–81; McElroy, *The Struggle*, 66–67.

CHAPTER 6: "THIS MEANS WAR"

1. Robert E. Shalhope, *Sterling Price*, 158–159.

2. Ibid., 39–40, 66–67; Steven E. Woodworth, *Jefferson Davis and His Generals*, 148–151.

3. Ibid., 158–159.

4. Col. Hardy A. Kemp, *About Nathaniel Lyon*, 83–85.

5. Ibid., 90.

6. Hans Christian Adamson, *Rebellion in Missouri: 1861*, 84–86.

7. Kemp, *About Nathaniel Lyon*, 90.

8. *War of the Rebellion Official Records of the Union and Confederate Armies*, Series I, Vol. 3 (*OR*, 3), 369–372.

9. Ibid., 373–374.

10. Christoper Phillips, *Damned Yankee*, 192, 204.

11. *OR*, 3, 374–375.

12. William E. Parrish, *Turbulent Partnership*, 29.

13. *OR*, 3, 375–376.

14. Ibid., 376.

15. Ibid., 377.

16. L. U. Reavis, *The Life and Military Services of Gen. William Selby Harney*, 373.

17. Adamson, *Rebellion*, 93.

18. Reavis, *The Life*, 381.

19. *OR*, 3, 381.

20. Ibid., 383.

21. Kemp, *About Nathaniel Lyon*, 81–83; OR, 3, 384.

22. OR, 3, 382.

23. Kemp, *About Nathaniel Lyon*, 87–88; Adamson, *Rebellion*, 105–106.

24. Adamson, *Rebellion*, 107–108.

25. Phillips, *Damned Yankee*, 212–214; Robert Leckie, *None Died in Vain*, 177.

26. John McElroy, *The Struggle for Missouri*, 96–97.

CHAPTER 7: THE BOONVILLE RACES

1. Albert Castel, *General Sterling Price and the Civil War in the West*; John McElroy, *The Struggle for Missouri*; Jay Monaghan, *Civil War on the Western Border: 1854–1865*, 135.

2. Frank Moore, *The Rebellion Record*, Vol. 1, 363–364.

3. Col. Hardy A. Kemp, *About Nathaniel Lyon*, 91, 104; Wiley Britton, *The Civil War on the Border*, 38–39; Hans Christian Adamson, *Rebellion in Missouri: 1861*, 115–116.

4. *War of the Rebellion Official Records of the Union and Confederate Armies*, Series I, Vol. 3 (OR, 3), 384.

5. Adamson, *Rebellion*, 116, 119–120; Christopher Phillips, *Damned Yankee*, 216–217.

6. McElroy, *The Struggle*, 103; Phillips, *Damned Yankee*, 217.

7. Phillips, *Damned Yankee*, 217–218.

8. Adamson, *Rebellion*, 125.

9. Phillips, *Damned Yankee*, 218.

10. Castel, *General Sterling Price*, 25–26.

11. Lyn McDaniel, ed. *Bicentennial Boonslick History*, 87; Castel, *General Sterling Price*, 26; Phillips, *Damned Yankee*, 218–219.

12. Adamson, *Rebellion*, 125–126; Moore, *The Rebellion*, 408.

13. Adamson, *Rebellion*, 126–127; Moore, *The Rebellion*, 408–409; OR, 3, 12–13.

14. Moore, 409–411; OR, 3, 14.

15. Phillips, *Damned Yankee*, 223–225.

16. Ralph R. Rea, *Sterling Price: The Lee of the West*, 35.

17. Phillips, *Damned Yankee*, 221; Kemp, *About Nathaniel Lyon*, 106.

CHAPTER 8: CLASH AT COLE CAMP

1. Frank Moore, *Rebellion Record*, Vol. 1, 412; William L. Shea and Earl J. Hess, *Pea Ridge*, 1.

2. Eugene Ware, *The Lyon Campaign*, 119, 355–377; Christopher Phillips, *Damned Yankee*, 235.

3. *War of the Rebellion Official Records of the Union and Confederate Armies*, Series I, Vol. 3 (OR, 3), 575, 579–580.

4. Thomas W. Cutrer, *Ben McCulloch and the Frontier Military Tradition*, 6.

5. *War of the Rebellion Official Records of the Union and Confederate Armies*, Series I, Vol. 3 (OR, 3), 594–595.

6. Albert Castel, *General Sterling Price and the Civil War in the West*, 30–31.

7. Lt. Col. Robert L. Owens, *Der Maibaum*, 12.

8. Lt. Col. Robert L. Owens, *Cole Camp Courier*, 2.

9. Ibid.; Leonard Brauer and Evelyn Goosen, eds., *Here We Speak Low German*, 183.

10. Brauer and Goosen, eds., *Here We Speak*, 182–184.

11. Owens, *Cole Camp Courier*, 3.

12. Brauer and Goosen, eds., *Here We Speak*, 182.

13. Owens, *Cole Camp Courier*, 3.

14. Brauer and Goosen, eds., *Here We Speak*, 186–188; Wiley Britton, *The Civil War on the Border*, 44–45.

15. Brauer and Goosen, eds., *Here We Speak*, 188; Owens, *Cole Camp Courier*, 3.

16. Owens, *Cole Camp Courier*, 3–4; Owens, *Der Maibaum*, 13; Brauer and Goosen, eds., *Here We Speak*, 290–292; John McElroy, *The Struggle for Missouri*, 111. Casualty numbers are only approximate, as no adequate and fully trustworthy records of casualties exist.

17. Brauer and Goosen, eds., *Here We Speak*, 188–189; Owens, *Cole Camp Courier*, 4.

18. Hans Christian Adamson, *Rebellion in Missouri: 1861*, 135–136.

19. Eugene Ware, *The Lyon Campaign*, 127–128.

CHAPTER 9: THE "FOX" CHASE

1. Christopher Phillips, *Damned Yankee*, 225–227.

2. Eugene Ware, *The Lyon Campaign*, 130; Phillips, *Damned Yankee*, 225.

3. Ware, *The Lyon Campaign*, 151–152, 154–155.

4. Ibid., 132–133, 137–138.

5. *War of the Rebellion Official Records of the Union and Confederate Armies*, Series I, Vol. 3 (OR, 3), 599.

6. Thomas W. Cutrer, *Ben McCulloch and the Frontier Military Tradition*, 209.

7. *OR*, 3, 600.

8. W. H. Tunnard, *The History of the Third Regiment Louisiana Infantry*, 42.

9. Hans Christian Adamson, *Rebellion in Missouri: 1861*, 135–136.

10. Patrica A. Faust, ed., *Historical Times Illustrated Encyclopedia of the Civil War*, 688.

11. Frank Moore, *The Rebellion Record*, Vol. 2, 271.

12. Faust, *Historical Times*, 86–87; Ware, *The Lyon Campaign*, 151–152.

13. Ware, *The Lyon Campaign*, 157, 295.

14. Phillips, *Damned Yankee*, 227–228; OR, 3, 390.

15. Allan Nevins, *Frémont*, 475–477.

16. Phillips, *Damned Yankee*, 226–227.

17. Tunnard, *The History*, 40.

18. Phillips, *Damned Yankee*, 230.

19. Cutrer, *Ben McCulloch*, 209–210.

20. Adamson, *Rebellion*, 136; *Battles and Leaders of the Civil War*, Vol. 1, 268.
21. Ibid., 137–138, 140.
22. *OR*, 3, 388; Ware, 152.

CHAPTER 10: WAR CALLS ON CARTHAGE

1. Eugene F. Ware, *The Lyon Campaign*, 162–165.
2. *War of the Rebellion Official Records of the Union and Confederate Armies*, Series I, Vol. 3 (*OR*, 3), 16–17.
3. Frank Moore, *The Rebellion Record*, Vol. 2, 275.
4. Wiley Britton, *The Civil War on the Border*, 64; John McElroy, *The Struggle for Missouri*, 122.
5. Hans Christian Adamson, *Rebellion in Missouri: 1861*, 144–145.
6. Ibid., 145–146.
7. Ware, 165–170.
8. Col. Hardy A. Kemp, *About Nathaniel Lyon*, 97–98.
9. *OR*, 3, 38–40; Elmo Ingenthron, *Borderland Rebellion*, 49.
10. *OR*, 3, 607.
11. Adamson, *Rebellion*, 146.
12. Steve Cottrell, *The Battle of Carthage and Carthage in the Civil War*, 8–12.
13. Adamson, *Rebellion*, 147.
14. *OR*, 3, 17, 20–21.
15. Cottrell, *Carthage*, 7–8, 12; Jay Monaghan, *Civil War on the Western Border: 1854–1865*, 154–156.
16. Britton, *The Civil War*, 56–57; Monaghan, *Civil War*, 154; Phillip W. Steele and Steve Cottrell, *Civil War in the Ozarks*, 18–20.
17. Cottrell, *Carthage*, 14; *OR*, 3, 18, 23.
18. Cottrell, *Carthage*, 15–17; *OR*, 3, 35–36.
19. Ibid., 17–18; *OR*, 3, 18.
20. Cottrell, *Carthage*, 19.
21. *OR*, 3, 32–33; Cottrell, *Carthage*, 2–3.
22. Cottrell, *Carthage*, 20, 23.
23. Ibid., 25–26.
24. Robert E. Shalhope, *Sterling Price*, 171; Thomas W. Cutrer, *Ben McCulloch and the Frontier Military Tradition*, 214.

CHAPTER 11: SORTIE TO FORSYTH

1. Col. Hardy Kemp, *About Nathaniel Lyon*, 100.
2. Eugene F. Ware, *The Lyon Campaign*, 171–172.
3. Christopher Phillips, *Damned Yankee*, 228.
4. Ware, *The Lyon Campaign*, 183–186; Hans Christian Adamson, *Rebellion in Missouri: 1861*, 158–159.
5. Jay Monaghan, *Civil War on the Western Border 1854–1865*, 148.
6. Ware, *The Lyon Campaign*, 192–195.

7. Edwin C. Bearss, *The Battle of Wilson's Creek*, 1.

8. *War of the Rebellion Official Records of the Union and Confederate Armies*, Series I, Vol. 3 (*OR*, 3), 394.

9. Ibid.

10. Carl Sandburg, *Abraham Lincoln: The War Years*, Vol. 1, 227.

11. *OR*, 3, 397.

12. Ibid., 397–398.

13. Robert Underwood Johnson and Clarence Clough Buel, eds., *Battles and Leaders of the Civil War*, Vol. I, 269–270; Albert Castel, *General Sterling Price and the Civil War in the West*, 28–30.

14. Elmo Ingenthron, *Borderland Rebellion*, 57–60; Robert E. Shalhope, *Sterling Price*, 172; Hans Christian Adamson, *Rebellion in Missouri: 1861*, 182–183.

15. Jay Monaghan, *Civil War*, 157.

16. Castel, *General Sterling Price* 34–35; Thomas W. Cutrer, *Ben McCulloch and the Frontier Military Tradition*, 216–217.

17. Cutrer, *Ben McCulloch*, 220.

18. Ibid., 220–221; Adamson, *Rebellion*, 184.

19. Ingenthron, *Borderland Rebellion*, 62.

20. Ware, *The Lyon Campaign*, 230–233; Daniel Matson, *Life Experiences of Daniel Matson*, 30.

21. Ware, *The Lyon Campaign*, 235–236.

22. Kemp, *About Nathaniel Lyon*, 112; *OR*, 3, 44.

23. Ware, *The Lyon Campaign*, 237; *OR*, 3, 44.

24. Ingenthron, *Borderland Rebellion*, 65–67.

25. Ibid., 67–69; Frank Moore, *The Rebellion Record*, Vol. 2, 438–439.

26. Moore, *The Rebellion Record*, 439.

27. Ingenthron, *Borderland Rebellion*, 69; Ware, *The Lyon Campaign*, 240.

28. *OR*, 3, 44–45; Ingenthron, *Borderland Rebellion*, 71–72.

29. Ware, *The Lyon Campaign*, 244–245.

30. Kemp, *About Nathaniel Lyon*, 112.

CHAPTER 12: "A WORSE ENEMY TO ME"

1. Pamela Herr, *Jessie Benton Frémont*, 323.

2. Shelby Foote, *The Civil War*, Vol. 1, 90, 168; Eugene F. Ware, *The Lyon Campaign*, 248.

3. Foote, *The Civil War*, 90.

4. John McElroy, *The Struggle for Missouri*, 124–125.

5. Christopher Phillips, *Damned Yankee*, 236–237.

6. Herr, *Jessie Benton Frémont*, 325.

7. Robert Underwood Johnson and Clarence Clough Buel, eds., *Battles and Leaders of the Civil War*, Vol. 1, 280.

8. Ibid.; *War of the Rebellion Official Records of the Union and Confederate Armies*, Series I, Vol. 3 (*OR*, 3), 416–417.

9. Maj. George E. Knapp, *The Wilson's Creek Staff Ride and Battlefield Tour*, 27.

10. Phillips, *Damned Yankee*, 238.

11. Hans Christian Adamson, *Rebellion in Missouri: 1861*, 179–180.

12. Allan Nevins, *Frémont: Pathmarker of the West*, 481.

13. *OR*, 3, 407; Edwin C. Bearss, *The Battle of Wilson's Creek*, 9.

14. *OR*, 3, 408.

15. Ware, *The Lyon Campaign*, 252–252, 254–256.

16. Adamson, *Rebellion in Missouri*, 172.

17. Bearss, *The Battle of Wilson's Creek*, 12–14.

18. *Battles and Leaders*, 281; Bruce Catton, *Terrible Swift Sword*, 13–15.

19. Phillips, *Damned Yankee*, 237.

20. Ware, *The Lyon Campaign*, 259; Adamson, *Rebellion in Missouri*, 186. The "snake doctor" referred to is a dragonfly.

21. Bearss, *The Battle of Wilson's Creek*, 19–20.

22. Johnson and Buel, eds., *Battles and Leaders*, Vol. 1, 270–271.

23. Bearss, *The Battle of Wilson's Creek*, 20–21; *OR*, 3, 745.

24. Victor M. Rose, *The Life and Services of Gen. Ben McCulloch*, 135.

25. *OR*, 3, 622–623.

26. Ibid., 102–103; Bearss, *The Battle of Wilson's Creek,* 21–22.

27. Bearss, *The Battle of Wilson's Creek,* 22; Lt. Col. Wesley Thurman Leeper, *Rebels Valiant*, 34.

CHAPTER 13: RAINS'S SCARE

1. Leo E. Huff, and Allen Weatherly, *130th Anniversary Reenactment, The Battle of Wilson's Creek*, 4.

2. Return I. Holcombe and W. S. Adams, *An Account of the Battle of Wilson's Creek or Oak Hills*, 11–12.

3. Jay Monaghan, *Civil War on the Western Border: 1854–1861*, 161; Christopher Phillips, *Damned Yankee*, 240.

4. Edwin C. Bearss, *The Battle of Wilson's Creek*, 23; *War of the Rebellion Official Records of the Union and Confederate Armies*, Series 1, Vol. 3 (*OR*, 3), 99.

5. *OR*, 3, 745.

6. Ibid., 47.

7. Ibid., 49.

8. Ibid., 50: Phillips, *Damned Yankee*, 241.

9. *OR*, 3, 51; E. R. Hagemann, *Fighting Rebels and Redskins*, 128.

10. *OR*, 3, 51.

11. Ibid., 49, 51; Bearss, *The Battle of Wilson's Creek*, 24–25.

12. *OR*, 3, 49–50; Wiley Britton, *The Civil War on the Border*, 80–81.

13. *OR*, 3, 51–51; W. E. Woodruff, *With the Light Guns*, 36–37.

14. W. H. Tunnard, *A History of the Third Regiment Louisiana Infantry*, 65; Thomas W. Cutrer, *Ben McCulloch and the Frontier Military Tradition*, 224.

15. *OR*, 3, 745; Bearss, *The Battle of Wilson's Creek*, 26–27; Hans Christian Adamson, *Rebellion in Missouri: 1861*, 189.

16. William E. Parrish, *Turbulent Partnership: Missouri and the Union*, 50–51; Frank Moore *The Rebellion Record*, Vol. 2, 472–473, 479–481.

17. Huff and Weatherly, *130th Anniversary*, 5; Robert Underwood Johnson and Clarence Clough Buel, eds., *Battles and Leaders of the Civil War*, Vol. 1, 289.

18. Daniel Matson, *Life Experiences of Daniel Matson*, 63.

19. *OR*, 3, 47–48; Phillips, *Damned Yankee*, 241–242.

20. Phillips, *Damned Yankee*, 242–243; Bearss, *The Battle of Wilson's Creek*, 29–30.

21. Bearss, *The Battle of Wilson's Creek*, 31; *OR*, 3, 745.

22. *OR*, 3, 745.

23. Albert Castel, *General Sterling Price and the Civil War in the West*, 39; Shelby Foote, *The Civil War*, Vol. 1, 92.

24. Douglas Hale, *The Third Texas Cavalry in the Civil War*, 57–58.

25. Tunnard, *A History of the Third Regiment*, 65.

26. Adamson, *The Battle of Wilson's Creek*, 193–194.

27. Ibid., 197.

28. Eugene F. Ware, *The Lyon Campaign*, 291–292.

29. Ibid., 292–293.

30. Phillips, *Damned Yankee*, 244.

CHAPTER 14: "WE'LL SABER HELL OUT OF THEM"

1. Leo E. Huff and Allen Weatherly, *130th Anniversary Reenactment, The Battle of Wilson's Creek*, 5; Douglas Hale, *The Third Texas Cavalry in the Civil War*, 59.

2. Hans Christian Adamson, *Rebellion in Missouri: 1861*, 194; *War of the Rebellion Official Records of the Union and Confederate Armies*, Series I, Vol. 3 (*OR*, 3); 745.

3. Edwin C. Bearss, *The Battle of Wilson's Creek*, 37–38.

4. Ibid., 38; Thomas W. Cutrer, *Ben McCulloch and the Frontier Military Tradition*, 227–228.

5. Adamson, *Rebellion*, 205; Albert Castel, *General Sterling Price and the Civil War in the West*, 39–40.

6. Bearss, *The Battle of Wilson's Creek*, 38; Castel, *General Sterling Price*, 40.

7. Robert Underwood Johnson and Clarence Clough Buel, eds., *Battles and Leaders of the Civil War*, Vol. 1, 299.

8. Bearss, *The Battle of Wilson's Creek*, 39.

9. W. E. Woodruff, *With the Light Guns in '61–'65*, 38–39; W. H. Tunnard, *The History of the Third Regiment Louisiana Infantry*, 50; Return I. Holcombe and W. S. Adams, *An Account of the Battle of Wilson's Creek or Oak Hills*, 52.

10. Christopher Phillips, *Damned Yankee*, 244–245.

11. Bearss, *The Battle of Wilson's Creek*, 42.

12. Phillips, *Damned Yankee*, 245; Lt. Gen. John M. Schofield, *Forty-Six Years in the Army*, 39.

13. Bearss, *The Battle of Wilson's Creek*, 42; Holcombe and Adams, *An Account*, 20.

14. Ashbel Woodward, M.D., *Life of General Nathaniel Lyon*, 302–303.

15. Holcombe and Adams, *An Account*, 21–22; Phillips, *Damned Yankee*, 246–247; Bearss, *The Battle of Wilson's Creek*, 46; Adamson, *Rebellion*, 198–199; Allan Nevins, *The War for the Union*, Vol. 1, 315.

16. Bearss, *The Battle of Wilson's Creek*, 46–47; Adamson, *Rebellion*, 199–200.

17. Phillips, *Damned Yankee*, 247; Capt. Richard Scott Price, *Nathaniel Lyon, Harbinger from Kansas*, 40.

18. Eugene F. Ware, *The Lyon Campaign*; Jay Monaghan, *Civil War on the Western Border: 1854–1865*, 164.

19. Bearss, *The Battle of Wilson's Creek*, 47–49; Col. Hardy A., Kemp, *About Nathaniel Lyon*, 134–135.

20. Phillips, *Damned Yankee*, 250.

21. Schofield, *Forty-Six Years*, 42.

22. Price, *Nathaniel Lyon*, 41.

23. Kemp, *About Nathaniel Lyon*, 129; Schofield, *Forty-Six Years*, 39–43.

24. Ware, *The Lyon Campaign*, 314; Phillips, *Damned Yankee*, 250; There is considerable disagreement among authorities regarding the dates of meetings preceding the actual movement of the troops on August 9 and when certain comments relevant to this movement were made. I have constructed what I believe to be a logical and reasonable sequence of these events, all of which can be supported or inferred from one or more of the authorities.

25. Holcombe and Adams, *An Account*, 23, 27; Bearss, *The Battle of Wilson's Creek*, 45.

26. Ware, *The Lyon Campaign*, 310–311.

27. Bearss, *The Battle of Wilson's Creek*, 51–55; Maj. George E. Knapp, *The Wilson's Creek Staff Ride and Battlefield Tour*, 85.

28. Bearss, *The Battle of Wilson's Creek*, 51–51; Ware, *The Lyon Campaign*, 314–315.

29. Phillips, *Damned Yankee*, 3, 252.

30. Kenneth Elkins, *Bloody Hill Walking Tour*, 12.

CHAPTER 15: "THE CANNINGS IS A-FIRIN'!"

1. Hans Christian Adamson, *Rebellion in Missouri: 1861*, 225; George E. Knapp, *The Wilson's Creek Staff Ride and Battlefield Tour*, 35–37.

2. Adamson, *Rebellion*, 224.

3. Bearss, *The Battle of Wilson's Creek*, 65.

4. Adamson, *Rebellion*, 224–225.

5. Bearss, *The Battle of Wilson's Creek*, 57–58.

6. Ibid., 58–59.

7. Ibid., 55; *War of the Rebellion Official Records of the Union and Confederate Armies*, Series I, Vol. 3 (OR, 3), 86.

8. Jay Monaghan, *Civil War on the Western Border: 1854–1865*, 171; Return I. Holcombe and W. S. Adams, *An Account of the Battle of Wilson's Creek or Oak Hills*, 53.

9. Bearss, *The Battle of Wilson's Creek*, 62; Holcombe and Adams, *An Account*, 53.

10. Knapp, *The Wilson's Creek*, 36–37; Robert Underwood Johnson and Clarence Clough Buel, eds., *Battles and Leaders of the Civil War*, Vol. 1, 299–300.

11. Bearss, *The Battle of Wilson's Creek*, 80; Kenneth Elkins, *Bloody Hill Walking Tour*, 3; Eugene F. Ware, *The Lyon Campaign*, 317–318.

12. August K. Klapp, *The Ray House*, 11.

13. Monaghan, *Civil War*, 171.

14. Thomas W. Cutrer, *Ben McCulloch and the Frontier Military Tradition*, 230–231; Douglas Hale, *The Third Texas Cavalry in the Civil War*, 61.

15. Elkins, *Bloody Hill*, 8; Bearss, *The Battle of Wilson's Creek*, 60–61, 63–65.

16. W. H. Tunnard, *The History of the Third Regiment Louisiana Infantry*, 50–51.

17. Bearss, *The Battle of Wilson's Creek*, 76–77; Cutrer, *Ben McCulloch*, 232.

18. Knapp, *The Wilson's Creek*, 39; Bearss, *The Battle of Wilson's Creek*, 84–85; OR, 3, 72.

19. Tunnard, *The History*, 66.

20. Ibid.

21. Ibid., 67.

22. Leo E. Huff and Allen Weatherly, *130th Anniversary Reenactment, The Battle of Wilson's Creek*, 8.

23. Bearss, *The Battle of Wilson's Creek*, 84–85; Tunnard, *The History*, 51–52; Huff and Weatherly, *The Battle of Wilson's Creek*, 8; John K. Hulston, *West Point and Wilson's Creek*, 16.

24. Bearss, *The Battle of Wilson's Creek*, 85–86; OR, 3, 72, 80, 111, 113.

25. Bearss, *The Battle of Wilson's Creek*, 78–84; OR, 3, 66, 74.

26. Wiley Britton, *The Civil War on the Border*, 93.

27. Bearss, *The Battle of Wilson's Creek*, 79, 84, 113.

28. OR, 3, 77.

29. Albert Castel, *General Sterling Price and the Civil War in the West*, 43, 45.

30. Ware, *The Lyon Campaign*, 318–320.

31. Holcombe and Adams, *An Account*, 67.

CHAPTER 16: "TWO DUTCH GUARDS, AND NARY A GUN"

1. Return I. Holcombe and W. S. Adams, *An Account of the Battle of Wilson's Creek or Oak Hills*, 46.

2. *War of the Rebellion Official Records of the Union and Confederate Armies*, Series I, Vol. 3 (OR, 3), 89.

3. Douglas Hale, *The Third Texas Cavalry in the Civil War*, 61–62.

4. Ibid., 65.

5. Edwin C. Bearss, *The Battle of Wilson's Creek*, 67–69.

6. Robert Underwood Johnson and Clarence Clough Buel, eds., *Battles and Leaders of the Civil War*, Vol. 1, 304; Bearss, *The Battle of Wilson's Creek*, 69–70.

7. *OR*, 3, 87, 89; Johnson and Buel, *Battles and Leaders*, 304.

8. Ibid., 87, 89, 91; Bearss, *The Battle of Wilson's Creek*, 71–72.

9. Holcombe and Adams, *An Account*, 46; Hale, *Third Texas Cavalry*, 64; Jay Monaghan, *Civil War on the Western Border: 1854–1865*, 177.

10. *OR*, 3, 111, 115; Bearss, *The Battle of Wilson's Creek*, 86–87; W. H. Tunnard, *The History of the Third Regiment Louisiana Infantry*, 52.

11. *OR*, 3, 120–121; Tunnard, *The History*, 52.

12. *OR*, 3, 128; Bearss, *The Battle of Wilson's Creek*, 87.

13. Holcombe and Adams, *An Account*, 41–42, 46–47.

14. Johnson and Buel, *Battles and Leaders*, 305; Tunnard, *The History*, 53.

15. *OR*, 3, 117; Johnson and Buel, *Battles and Leaders*, 305.

16. Holcombe and Adams, *An Account*, 47; Bearss, *The Battle of Wilson's Creek*, 89–90; Johnson and Buel, *Battles and Leaders*, Vol. 1, 301.

17. *OR*, 3, 117.

18. Ibid., 115–118.

19. Ibid.; Bearss, *The Battle of Wilson's Creek*, 91–92; Thomas W. Cutrer, *Ben McCulloch and the Frontier Military Tradition*, 236.

20. *OR*, 3, 121.

21. Bearss, *The Battle of Wilson's Creek*, 92–93; Holcombe and Adams, *An Account*, 48.

22. Bearss, *The Battle of Wilson's Creek*, 93.

23. *OR*, 3, 89–90.

24. Bearss, *The Battle of Wilson's Creek*, 93.

25. *OR*, 3, 91–92.

26. Bearss, *The Battle of Wilson's Creek*, 95, 97.

27. *OR*, 3, 90; Holcombe and Adams, *An Account*, 49–50.

28. Hale, *Third Texas Cavalry*, 65, 68; Bearss, *The Battle of Wilson's Creek*, 97–98; Cutrer, *Ben McCulloch*, 236.

29. Holcombe and Adams, *An Account*, 68.

30. Ibid., 44.

CHAPTER 17: "AND GLAD TO SEE HIM GO"

1. Lt. Gen. John M. Schofield, *Forty-Six Years in the Army*, 44; Christopher Phillips, *Damned Yankee*, 254.

2. Phillips, *Damned Yankee*, 254; *War of the Rebellion Official Records of the Union and Confederate Armies*, Series I, Vol. 3 (*OR*, 3), 67.

3. Phillips, *Damned Yankee*, 255.

4. *OR*, 3, 74.

5. John McElroy, *The Struggle for Missouri*, 144.

6. Robert Underwood Johnson and Clarence Clough Buel, eds., *Battles and Leaders of the Civil War*, Vol. 1, 295.

7. OR, 3, 84; Bearss, *The Battle of Wilson's Creek*, 115.

8. Maj. George E. Knapp, *The Wilson's Creek Staff Ride and Battlefield Tour*, 61, 66–67.

9. Return I. Holcombe and W. S. Adams, *An Account of the Battle of Wilson's Creek or Oak Hills*, 36.

10. Johnson and Buel, *Battles and Leaders*, 295; Bearss, *The Battle of Wilson's Creek*, 115–116.

11. Johnson and Buel, *Battles and Leaders*, 295–296.

12. Bearss, *The Battle of Wilson's Creek*, 107–108.

13. Leo E. Huff and Allen Weatherly, *130th Anniversary Reenactment: The Battle of Wilson's Creek*, 9; Col. Hardy A. Kemp, *About Nathaniel Lyon*, 146.

14. Huff and Weatherly, *130th Anniversary*, 9.

15. OR, 3, 80.

16. D. J. Cater, *As It Was*, 99.

17. Douglas Hale, *The Third Texas Cavalry in the Civil War*, 66–67; Kenneth Elkins, *Bloody Hill Walking Tour*, 10.

18. Hale, *Third Texas Cavalry*, 65; Hans Christian Adamson, *Rebellion in Missouri: 1861*, 254.

19. Eugene F. Ware, *The Lyon Campaign*, 323.

20. Ibid., 323–324.

21. Johnson and Buel, *Battles and Leaders*, 296; Ware, *The Lyon Campaign*, 324–325.

22. OR, 62, 67–68; Holcombe and Adams, *An Account*, 37.

23. Bearss, *The Battle of Wilson's Creek*, 124–127.

24. Ibid., 122–123, 156.

25. Ibid., 127–128, OR, 3, 68.

26. Albert Castel, *General Sterling Price and the Civil War in the West*, 45.

27. Elkins, *Bloody Hill*, 4.

28. OR, 62, 84–85.

29. Elkins, *Bloody Hill*, 11.

30. OR, 3, 68–69; Bearss, *The Battle of Wilson's Creek*, 130–134.

31. Adamson, *Rebellion*, 259; Kemp, *About Nathaniel Lyon*, 150.

32. OR, 3, 79.

33. Bearss, *The Battle of Wilson's Creek*, 134–135.

34. Johnson and Buel, *Battles and Leaders*, Vol. 1, 303.

35. Holcombe and Adams, *An Account*, 68.

CHAPTER 18: "A MEAN FOWT FIGHT"

1. Robert Underwood Johnson and Clarence Clough Buel, eds., *Battles and Leaders of the Civil War*, Vol. 1, 297; *War of the Rebellion Official Records of the Union and Confederate Armies*, Series I, Vol. 3 (OR, 3), 63, 69.

2. OR, 3, 63, 95.

3. Hans Christian Adamson, *Rebellion in Missouri: 1861*, 273.

4. Ibid., 273–275; Lt. Gen. John M. Schofield, *Forty-Six Years in the Army*, 47–48.

5. Return I. Holcombe and W. S. Adams, *An Account of the Battle of Wilson's Creek or Oak Hills*, 98.

6. Ibid., 99–103; August K. Klapp, *The Ray House*, 14–15.

7. Christopher Phillips, *Damned Yankee*, 260–261; Mark M. Boatner III, *The Civil War Dictionary*, 834.

8. Geoffrey C. Ward, Ken Burns, and Ric Burns, *The Civil War: An Illustrated History*, 74.

9. Schofield, *Forty-Six Years* 48–49.

10. Carl Sandburg, *Storm Over the Land*, 68; Shelby Foote, *The Civil War*, Vol. 1, 95–99.

11. *OR*, 3, 93–98.

12. Adamson, *Rebellion* 268–271; Albert Castel, *General Sterling Price and the Civil War in the West*, 45–46; Edwin C. Bearss, *The Battle of Wilson's Creek*, 135–136; Thomas W. Cutrer, *Ben McCulloch and the Frontier Military Tradition*, 237–241.

13. Cutrer, *Ben McCulloch*, 245–246.

14. *OR*, 3, 109, 672; John McElroy, *The Struggle for Missouri*, 161.

15. W. H. Tunnard, *The History of the Third Regiment Louisiana Infantry*, 63.

16. Frank Moore, *The Rebellion Record*, Vol. 2, 541.

17. Allan Nevins, *The War for the Union*, Vol. 1, 316.

18. Johnson and Buel, eds., *Battles and Leaders*, 296; George E. Knapp, *The Wilson's Creek Staff Ride and Battlefield Tour*, 13, 19, 69.

19. Col. Hardy A. Kemp, *About Nathaniel Lyon*, 151.

20. Victor M. Rose, *The Life and Services of Gen. Ben McCulloch*, 178.

APPENDIX A

1. Maj. George E. Knapp, *The Wilson's Creek Staff Ride and Battlefield Tour*, 86.

2. All numbers inside parentheses indicate unit strengths.

APPENDIX B

1. Maj. George E. Knapp, *The Wilson's Creek Staff Ride and Battlefield Tour*, 87–88.

2. All numbers inside parentheses indicate unit strengths.

Bibliography

ARTICLES, PAMPHLETS, AND SHORT ACCOUNTS

A State Divided: Missouri and the Civil War. Jefferson City: Missouri Department of Natural Resources, undated.

Bradbury, John F., Jr., and Richard W. Hatcher, III. "Civil War in the Ozarks: An Introduction and Chronology." *Ozarks Watch*, Vol. V (Spring-Summer 1991), pp. 4–6.

Carthage Missouri: Site of the First Full-Scale Land Battle of the Civil War. Carthage: Carthage Chamber of Commerce, undated.

Collins, Jeanette Rea. "Wilson's Creek: The Impact on Civilians." *130th Anniversary Reenactment, The Battle of Wilson's Creek*, Springfield, Mo.: Wilson's Creek National Battlefield Foundation, 1991, pp. 21–22.

Cottrell, Steve. *Battle of Carthage.* Carthage: Carthage Chamber of Commerce, undated.

———. *Battle of Carthage: Markers on Civil War Road.* Carthage: Carthage Chamber of Commerce, 1993.

———. *The Battle of Carthage and Carthage in the Civil War.* Carthage: Carthage Chamber of Commerce, 1990.

Crumpler, Hugh. "Yankee Avenger: Gen. Nathaniel Lyon, Union Commander at the Battle of Wilson's Creek." *Ozarks Watch*, Vol. 1 (Spring-Summer 1991), pp. 47–51.

"Death of General Lyon." *Frank Leslie's Illustrated Newspaper*, August 24, 1861.

Elkins, Kenneth. *Bloody Hill Walking Tour.* Wilson's Creek National Battlefield, 1993.

"Great Battle at Wilson's Creek, Missouri." *Frank Leslie's Illustrated Newspaper*, August 24, 1861.

Huff, Leo E., and Allen Weatherly. "The Battle of Wilson's Creek and the Struggle in Missouri During 1861." *130th Anniversary Reenactment,*

The Battle of Wilson's Creek, Springfield, Mo.: Wilson's Creek National Battlefield Foundation, 1991, pp. 1–14.

Huff, Leo E. "Guerrillas, Jayhawkers, and Bushwhackers in Northern Arkansas During the Civil War." *Ozarks Watch*, Vol. 1 (Spring-Summer 1991), pp. 52–57.

Hulston, John K. *West Point & Wilson's Creek*, Republic, Mo.: Western Printing Company, 1991.

Kelso, Margaret Gilmore. "A Memory Story, Part II: Bushwhackers and Wilson's Creek." *Ozarks Watch*, Vol. 1 (Spring-Summer 1991), pp. 7–9.

Klapp, August K. *The Ray House.* Wilson's Creek National Battlefield Foundation, undated.

McDaniel, Lyn, ed. "Col. J. B. Barnes' History of the First Battle of Boonville." *Bicentennial Boonslick History*, Boonslick Historical Society, Boonville, Mo., undated.

———. "Slavery Issue Brings Missouri to a Boil." *Bicentennial Boonslick History*, Boonslick Historical Society, Boonville, Mo., undated.

McDonough, James L., "John McAllister Schofield," *Civil War Times Illustrated*, Vol. XIII, (August 1974). pp. 10–17.

Owens, Robert L. "The Battle of Cole Camp." *The Cole Camp Courier*, Cole Camp, Mo.: June 1991, pp. 11–13.

———. "The Battle of Cole Camp." *Der Maibaum*, Herman, Mo: Deutschheim Association, Spring 1994.

"Ozark's Civil War Timeline." *130th Anniversary Reenactment, The Battle of Wilson's Creek*, Springfield, Mo.: Wilson's Creek National Battlefield Foundation, 1991, pp. 16–17.

Piston, William Garrett. "More Than Bullets: The Social Impact of Guerrilla War in the Ozarks." *Ozarks Watch*, Vol. 1 (Spring-Summer 1991), pp. 10–13.

Rowan, Steven. "A Near Lynching of Seven Confederate Prisoners, 1861." *Der Maibaum*, Herman, Mo.: Deutschheim Association, Spring 1994, pp. 5–7, excerpt from Bernstein, Heinrich, *Funfundsiebzig Jahre in der alten und neuen Welt*, Leipzig, 1881.

Sharp, James R. "Confederate Military Leaders at Wilson's Creek." *130th Anniversary Reenactment, The Battle of Wilson's Creek*, Springfield, Mo.: Wilson's Creek National Battlefield Foundation, 1991, pp. 26–27.

———. "Union Military Leaders at Wilson's Creek." *130th Anniversary Reenactment, The Battle of Wilson's Creek*, Springfield, Mo.: Wilson's Creek National Battlefield Foundation, 1991, pp. 28–29.

Sweeney, Thomas, M.D. "Civil War Medicine" *130th Anniversary Reenactment, The Battle of Wilson's Creek*, Springfield, Mo.: Wilson's Creek National Battlefield Foundation, 1991, p. 20.

———. "Medicine in the Bloodiest War." *Ozarks Watch*, Vol. 1 (Spring-Summer 1991), pp. 43–46.

"The Cole Camp Massacre, June 1861." *Der Maibaum*, Herman, Mo.: Deutschheim Association, Spring 1994, p. 7.

Wilson's Creek National Battlefield, Missouri. National Park Service, U.S. Department of the Interior, undated.

"Wilson's Creek Vignettes." *130th Anniversary Reenactment, The Battle of Wilson's Creek.* Springfield, Mo.: Wilson's Creek National Battlefield Foundation, 1991, pp. 18–19.

MAPS

Battlefields of the Civil War. Washington: National Geographic Society, 1974.

Civil War and the Ozarks. Springfield: Southwest Missouri State University and *Ozarks Watch* magazine, undated.

Kansas/Missouri. Heathrow, Fla.: American Automobile Association, 1993.

Tour Historic Carthage. Carthage: Carthage Chamber of Commerce, 1993.

Western States and Provinces. Heathrow, FL: American Automobile Association, 1993.

Wilson's Creek National Battlefield, Missouri. Civil War Battlefield Series, Aurora, Co.: Trailhead Graphics, 1994.

FILM/VIDEO

Burns, Kenneth Lauren. *The Civil War.* Washington, D.C.: Florentine Films and WETA-TV, 1989.

Hillman, Sam, and Darryl F. Zanuck. *The Return of Frank James.* Hollywood: 20th Century, Fox, 1940.

"John Brown's War," *Civil War Journal.* Hearst, ABC, NBC, Greystone Communications, Inc., 1993.

Johnson, Nunally, and Darryl F. Zanuck. *Jesse James,* Hollywood: 20th Century–Fox, 1939.

BOOKS

ABA Standing Committee on Lawyers in the Armed Forces. *Lawyers in Uniform.* Washington, D.C.: ABA Press, 1974.

Adamson, Hans Christian. *Rebellion in Missouri: 1861 Nathaniel Lyon and His Army of the West.* New York: Chilton Company, 1961.

An English Combatant. *Battlefields of the South.* New York: John Bradburn, 1864.

Anderson, Ephraim McD. *Memoirs: Historical and Personal; including the Campaigns of the First Missouri Confederate Brigade.* St. Louis: Times Printing Company, 1868.

Angle, Paul M. *A Pictorial History of the Civil War Years.* Garden City: Doubleday & Company, Inc., 1967.

———. *The American Reader.* New York: Rand McNally & Company, 1958.

Angus, Fern. *Down the Wire Road in the Missouri Ozarks*. Cassville, Mo.: Litho Printers, 1993.

Basler, Roy P., ed. *The Collected Works of Abraham Lincoln*. Vol. 4. New Brunswick, N.J.: Rutgers University Press, 1953.

Barron, Samuel B. *The Lone Star Defenders: A Chronicle of the Third Texas Cavalry, Ross' Brigade*. New York, 1908.

Barry, James P. *Bloody Kansas, 1854–65*. New York: Franklin Watts, Inc., 1972.

Bearss, Edwin C. *The Battle of Wilson's Creek*. Cassville, Mo.: Litho Printers and Bindery, 1992.

Bernays, Thekla. *Augustus Charles Bernays: A Memoir*. St. Louis: C. V. Mosby Company, 1912.

Bevier, R. S. *History of the First and Second Missouri Confederate Brigades, 1861–1865*. St. Louis: Bryan, Brand & Company, 1879.

Boatner, Mark M., III. *The Civil War Dictionary*. New York: Vintage Books, 1987.

Boyer, Richard O. *The Legend of John Brown: A Biography and a History*. New York: Alfred A. Knopf, 1973.

Brauer, Leonard, and Evelyn Goosen, eds. *Hier Snackt Wi Platdeutsch (Here We Speak Low German)*. Cole Camp, Mo.: City of Cole Camp, 1989.

Britton, Wiley. *The Civil War on the Border*. Vol. 1. New York: G. P. Putnam's Sons, 1899.

Brownlee, Richard S. *Gray Ghosts of the Confederacy: Guerrilla Warfare in the West 1861–1865*. Baton Rouge: Louisiana State University Press, 1958.

Byrd, Sen. Robert C. *The Senate: 1798–1989, U.S. History on CD ROM*. Parsippany: Bureau Development, Inc., 1991.

Castel, Albert. *General Sterling Price and the Civil War in the West*. Baton Rouge: Louisiana State University Press, 1968.

Cater, D. J. *As It Was*. Privately published, 1981.

Catton, Bruce. *Grant Moves South*. Boston: Little, Brown and Company, 1960.

———. *Terrible Swift Sword*. Garden City: Doubleday & Company, Inc., 1963.

———. *The American Heritage Picture History of the Civil War*. New York: American Heritage/Bonanza Books, 1960.

———. *The Coming Fury*. Garden City: Doubleday & Company, Inc., 1961.

———. *This Hallowed Ground*. Garden City: Doubleday & Company, Inc., 1956.

Collier, Capt. Calvin L., USAF. *They'll Do To Tie To: The Story of the Third Regiment, Arkansas Infantry, CSA*. Little Rock: Pioneer Press, 1959.

Commager, Henry Steele, ed. *The Blue and the Gray*. New York: The Fairfax Press, 1982.

Cutrer, Thomas W. *Ben McCulloch and the Frontier Military Tradition.* Chapel Hill: The University of North Carolina Press, 1993.

Davis, Burke. *They Called Him Stonewall: A Life of Lt. General T. J. Jackson, CSA.* New York: Wings Books, 1988.

Davis, Maj. George B., USA, Leslie J. Perry, Joseph W. Kirkley, and Capt. Calvin Cowles, USA. *The Official Military Atlas of the Civil War.* New York: Arno Press/Crown Publishers, Inc., 1978.

Drew, Col. Dennis M., USAF, and Donald M. Snow, Ph.D. *The Eagle's Talons, 1988, U. S. History on CD ROM,* Parsipanny: Bureau Development Inc., 1991.

Duke, Basil W. *Reminiscences of General Basil Duke, CSA.* Garden City: Doubleday, Page & Company, 1911.

Dyer, Robert L. *Jesse James and the Civil War in Missouri.* Columbia: University of Missouri Press, 1994.

Eaton, Clement. *Jefferson Davis.* New York: The Free Press, 1977.

Eddy, T. M., D.D., *The Patriotism of Illinois.* Vol. 1. Chicago: Clarke & Co., Publishers, 1865.

Edwards, John N. *Shelby and His Men.* Cincinnati: Miami Printing and Publishing Co., Print, 1867.

Eisenchiml, Otto, and Ralph Newman. *The American Iliad.* New York: The Bobbs-Merrill Company, 1947.

Faust, Patricia L., ed. *Historical Times Illustrated Encyclopedia of the Civil War.* New York: Harper and Row, Publishers, 1986.

Fellman, Michael. *Inside War: The Guerrilla Conflict in Missouri During the American Civil War.* New York: Oxford University Press, 1989.

Foote, Shelby. *The Civil War.* Vol. 1. New York: Random House, 1958.

Gallaway, B. P., ed. *Texas: The Dark Corner of the Confederacy.* Lincoln: University of Nebraska Press, 1994.

Garrison, Webb. *A Treasury of Civil War Tales.* Nashville: Rutledge Hill Press, 1988.

Gragg, Rod. *The Civil War Quiz and Fact Book.* New York: Harper & Row, Publishers, 1985.

Grant, U. S. *Personal Memoirs of U.S. Grant.* New York: Konecky & Konecky, 1990.

Greene, A. Wilson, and Gary W. Gallagher. *National Geographic Guide to the Civil War National Battlefield Parks.* Washington, D.C.: National Geographic Society, 1992.

Hagemann, E. R., ed. *Fighting Rebels and Redskins: Experiences in Army Life of Colonel George B. Sanford, 1861–1862.* Norman: University of Oklahoma Press, 1969.

Hale, Douglas. *The Third Texas Cavalry in the Civil War.* Norman: University of Oklahoma Press, 1993.

Hammock, Capt. John C., USN. *With Honor Untarnished: The Story of the First Arkansas Infantry Regiment, Confederate States Army.* Little Rock: Pioneer Press, 1961.

Herr, Pamela. *Jessie Benton Frémont*. New York: Franklin Watts, 1987.

Hesseltine, William B. *Lincoln and the War Governors*. New York: Alfred A. Knopf, 1948.

Holcombe, Return I., and W. S. Adams. *An Account of the Battle of Wilson's Creek or Oak Hill*. Independent Printing, Inc., 1985.

Hudleston, F. J. *Warriors in Undress*. Boston: Little, Brown, and Company, 1926.

Hutton, Paul Andrew, ed. *Soldiers West: Biographies from the Military Frontier*. Lincoln: University of Nebraska Press, 1987.

Immigration and Naturalization Service. *United States History 1600–1987, U. S. History on CD ROM*, Parsippany: Bureau Development, Inc., 1991.

Ingenthron, Elmo. *Borderland Rebellion*. Branson, Mo.: The Ozark Mountaineer, 1980.

Johnson, Robert Underwood, and Clarence Clough Buel, eds. *Battles and Leaders of the Civil War*. Secaucus, N.J.: Castle, 1991.

Jordan, Robert Paul. *The Civil War*. Washington, D.C.: National Geographic Society, 1969.

Kemp, Col. Hardy A., AUS. *About Nathaniel Lyon, Brigadier General, United States Army Volunteers, and Wilson's Creek*. Published by the author, 1978.

Kerby, Robert L. *Kirby Smith's Confederacy*. Tuscaloosa: The University of Alabama Press, 1972.

Ketchum, Richard M., ed. *The American Heritage Pictorial History of the Civil War*. New York: American Heritage/Bonanza Books, 1960.

Knapp, Maj. George E., USA. *The Wilson's Creek Staff Ride and Battlefield Tour*. Ft. Leavenworth, Kans.: U.S. Army Command and General Staff College, 1993.

Leckie, Robert. *None Died in Vain: The Saga of the American Civil War*. New York: HarperCollins Publishers, 1990.

———. *The Wars of America*. Vol. 1. New York: Harper & Row, Publishers, 1968.

Leeper, Lt. Col. Wesley Thurman, USAFR. *Rebels Valiant: Second Arkansas Mounted Rifles*. Little Rock: Pioneer Press, 1964.

Lewis, Lloyd. *Sherman: Fighting Prophet*. New York: Harcourt, Brace, and Company, 1932, reprinted by Konecky & Konecky.

Long, E. B. *The Civil War Day by Day: An Almanac 1861–1865*. New York: Da Capo Press, Inc., 1971.

Lossing, Benson J. *Our Country*. Vols. 5 & 6, 1905, *U.S. History on CD ROM*, Parsippany: Bureau Development, Inc., 1991.

McElroy, John. *The Struggle for Missouri*. Washington D.C.: The National Tribune Company, 1913.

McFeely, William S. *Grant*. New York: W. W. Norton & Company, 1981.

McPherson, James M. *Battle Cry of Freedom: The Civil War Era*. New York: Oxford University Press, 1988.

Matlof, Maurice, ed. *American Military History*. CMH Pub 30–1, U.S. Army, 1985, *U.S. History on CD ROM*, Parsipanny: Bureau Development, Inc., 1991.

Mattes, Merrill J. *Scotts Bluff*, Handbook 28, National Park Service, 1983, *U.S. History on CD ROM*, Parsippany: Bureau Development, Inc., 1991.

Matson, Daniel. *Life Experiences of Daniel Matson*. Fowler, Colo.: Tribune Printing, 1924.

Meredith, Roy. *Mr. Lincoln's Contemporaries: An Album of Portraits by Matthew Brady*. New York: Charles Scribner's Sons, 1951.

Miers, Earl Schenk. *The General Who Marched to Hell: Sherman and the Southern Campaign*. New York: Dorset Press, 1990.

Miller, Francis Trevelyan. *The Photographic History of the Civil War: The Opening Battles*. Vol. 1. New York: Thomas Yoseloff, 1957.

Moehring, Eugene P., and Arleen Keylin, eds. *The Civil War Extra: From the Pages of* The Charleston Mercury *and* The New York Times. New York: Arno Press, 1975.

Monaghan, Jay. *Civil War on the Western Border: 1854–1865*. Boston: Little, Brown and Company, 1955.

Moore, Frank, ed. *The Rebellion Record*. Vols. 1 & 2. New York: Arno Press, 1977.

National Park Service. *John Brown's Raid*. 1984, *U.S. History on CD ROM*, Parsippany: Bureau Development, Inc., 1991.

Nevins, Allan. *Frémont: Pathmarker of the West*. New York: Longmans, Green and Co., 1955.

———. *The War for the Union*. Vol. 1. New York: Charles Scribner's Sons, 1959.

Nichols, Alice. *Bleeding Kansas*. New York: Oxford University Press, 1954.

Oates, Stephen B. *Confederate Cavalry West of the River*. Austin: University of Texas Press, 1961.

———. *To Purge This Land With Blood: A Biography of John Brown*. New York: Harper & Row, Publishers, 1970.

Parrish, William E. *Turbulent Partnership: Missouri and the Union, 1861–1865*. Columbia: University of Missouri Press, 1963.

Phillips, Christopher. *Damned Yankee: The Life of General Nathaniel Lyon*. Columbia: University of Missouri Press, 1990.

Phillips, William. *The Conquest of Kansas by Missouri and Her Allies*. Boston: Phillips, Sampson and Company, 1856.

Pollard, Edward A. *The Lost Cause*. New York: E. B. Treat & Company, Publishers, 1867.

Pratt, Fletcher. *A Short History of the Civil War*. New York: Pocket Books, Inc., 1951.

Price, Capt. Richard Scott, USA. *Nathaniel Lyon: Harbinger from Kansas*. Springfield, Mo.: The Wilson's Creek National Battlefield Foundation, 1990.

Pride, Capt. W. F., USA. *The History of Fort Riley*. Fort Riley, Kans.: Privately printed, 1926.

Rafferty, Milton D. *Historical Atlas of Missouri*. Norman: University of Oklahoma Press, 1981.

Rea, Ralph R. *Sterling Price: The Lee of the West*. Little Rock: Pioneer Press-Publisher, 1959.

Reavis, L. U. *The Life and Military Services of Gen. William Selby Harney*. St. Louis: Bryan, Brand & Co., Publishers, 1878.

Rose, Victor M. *The Life and Services of Gen. Ben McCulloch*. Austin: The Steck Company, 1958.

Sandburg, Carl. *Abraham Lincoln: The War Years*. Vol. 1. New York: Harcourt, Brace and Company, 1939.

———. *Storm Over the Land*. New York: Harcourt, Brace and Company, 1942.

Schofield, Lt. Gen. John M., USA. *Forty-Six Years in the Army*. New York: The Century Company, 1897.

Shalhope, Robert E. *Sterling Price: Portrait of a Southerner*. Columbia: University of Missouri Press, 1971.

Shea, William L. and Earl J. Hess. *Pea Ridge: Civil War Campaign in the West*. Chapel Hill: The University of North Carolina Press, 1992.

Sheridan, Gen. Phillip, USA. *Civil War Memoirs*. New York: Bantam Books, 1991.

Sherman, Gen. William T., USA. *Memoirs of General William T. Sherman*. Vol. 1. New York: D. Appleton and Company, 1876.

Sifakis, Stewart. *Who Was Who in the Union*. New York: Facts on File, 1988.

———. *Who Was Who in the Confederacy*. New York: Facts on File, 1988.

Smith, Edward Conrad. *The Borderland in the Civil War*. Freeport: Books for Libraries Press, 1969.

Smith, Page. *Trial by Fire*. New York: McGraw-Hill Book Company, 1982.

Starr, Stephen Z. *Jennison's Jayhawkers: A Civil War Cavalry Regiment and Its Commander*. Baton Rouge: Louisiana State University Press, 1973.

Steele, Phillip W., and Steve Cottrell. *Civil War in the Ozarks*. Gretna, La: Pelican Publishing Company, 1993.

Stepp, John W. and I. William Hill, eds. *Mirror of War: The Washington Star Reports the Civil War*. Englewood Cliffs: Prentice-Hall, Inc., 1961.

Strode, Hudson. *Jefferson Davis: Confederate President*. New York: Harcourt, Brace and Company, 1959.

Thomas, Benjamin Platt. *Abraham Lincoln*. New York: Alfred A. Knopf, 1952.

Thorndike, Rachel Sherman. *The Sherman Letters: Correspondence between General and Senator Sherman from 1827 to 1891*. New York: AMS Press, Inc., 1971.

Tunnard, W. H. *A Southern Record: The History of the Third Regiment Louisiana Infantry.* Dayton, Ohio: Morningside Bookshop, 1970.

Utley, Robert M. *Frontiersmen in Blue: The United States Army and the Indian, 1848–1865.* New York: Macmillan Publishing Co., Inc., 1967.

Ward, Geoffrey C., with Ken Burns and Ric Burns. *The Civil War: An Illustrated History.* New York: Alfred A. Knopf, Inc., 1990.

Ware, E. F. *The Lyon Campaign in Missouri.* Iowa City: Press of The Camp Pope Bookshop, 1991.

Warner, Ezra J. *Generals in Gray.* Baton Rouge: Louisiana State University Press, 1959.

War of the Rebellion Official Records of the Union and Confederate Armies. Series I, Vols. 1 and 3, and Series 3, Vol. 1. Washington: Government Printing Office, 1880–1901.

Williams, T. Harry. *Lincoln and His Generals.* New York: Alfred A. Knopf, 1952.

Wood, William. *Captains of the Civil War.* New Haven: Yale University Press, 1921.

Woodruff, W. E. *With the Light Guns in '61–'65.* Little Rock: Central Printing Company, 1903.

Woodward, Ashbel, M. D. *Life of General Nathaniel Lyon.* Hartford: Case, Lockwood & Co., 1862.

Woodworth, Steven E. *Jefferson Davis and His Generals: The Failure of Confederate Command in the West.* Lawrence: University of Kansas Press, 1990.

INDEX

ABOUT THE AUTHOR

WILLIAM RILEY BROOKSHER, a retired U.S. Air Force brigadier general, grew up in Arkansas not far from Wilson's Creek. He is coauthor of *Glory at a Gallop: Tales of the Confederate Cavalry* and a frequent contributor to *Civil War Times Illustrated*, *Military History*, and *Military Review*. He lives in Richland, Washington.